Wild Ways

Wild Ways

A field guide to the behaviour of Southern African mammals

Peter Apps

Illustrations by
Penny Meakin

SOUTHERN
BOOK PUBLISHERS

To the field workers:
with sympathy, envy and admiration

ISBN 1 86812 373 1

First edition, first impression 1992
First edition, second impression 1992
First edition, third impression 1994
First edition, fourth impression 1995

Published by
Southern Book Publishers (Pty) Ltd
PO Box 3103, Halfway House, 1685

Cover design by William Steyn
Illustrations by Penny Meakin
Set in 10 on 12 point Palatino
by Book Productions, Pretoria
Printed and bound by National Book Printers,
Drukkery Street, Goodwood, Western Cape

CONTENTS

PREFACE

This book is aimed mainly at amateur naturalists – visitors to National Parks and other conservation areas, hunters, hikers, farmers and others who take their leisure or make a living in the places where southern Africa's mammals are still to be seen. I hope at the same time that it will be useful, at least as a starting point, to those who are professionally involved with wildlife but who are not specialists in the study of animal behaviour – especially film makers, journalists, authors and tour guides who have the privilege and responsibility of bringing to the general public an appreciation of the richness and complexity of our natural heritage. For the specialist, who knows where to find it and how to use it, the scientific literature will provide more detail and greater depth than could ever be compressed into a book like this one.

The 1983 publication of Reay Smithers' authoritative *The Mammals of the Southern African Subregion* has been followed by the appearance of a variety of very good field guides to the identification, distribution and general biology of southern Africa's mammals. This guide is intended to complement the others by providing more detail on behaviour for readers interested in not only what species an animal belongs to but also what it is doing, and why.

The extent of our knowledge about the behaviour of southern African mammals is variable in the extreme. For some species no more is known than some of the things they eat and whether they are active by day or by night. About other species whole books could be, and have been, written. In deciding what to squeeze into the limited space of a field guide I took into account the abundance, distribution and habits of the various species and included only those whose behaviour an amateur had some chance of actually observing. Consequently many of the bats and rodents, and nearly all of the marine mammals have been left out.

The taxonomic arrangement, and common and scientific names, follow the updated edition of Reay Smithers' *Land Mammals of Southern Africa – A Field Guide* (1992, Southern Books) except that some marine mammals have been included. To make cross-referencing easier I have given the 'Smithers number' from *The Mammals of the Southern African Subregion* (1983, University of Pretoria).

To save undue repetition, behavioural features that occur in all members of a taxonomic group who have most of their behaviour in common are presented at the beginning of the appropriate section.

For most mammals what they do rather than why they do it is as far as our knowledge goes. Establishing the reasons for behaviour needs more detailed study than the great majority of species have received. It is for this reason that most of the following chapters are descriptions of what southern African mammals do, where, when and how often they do it, and who they do it with, rather than why they do it.

I have not always been able to draw on work done in southern Africa – sometimes the only available information has been obtained north of the Zambezi. In such cases I have had to assume that the behaviour and its causes are cosmopolitan.

Some professional biologists may rebuke me for telling 'just-so' stories. I can only answer that some of the stories might just be so, and that there is not nearly enough space in this book to go into the issues involved.

To keep within the size of a field guide I have had to summarise, simplify and skip certain things. Some peoples' favourite animals and pet theories have had to be neglected, and the pictures of behaviour have had to be painted with a rather broad brush. For readers who would like more detail I have included a list of further reading.

When using this book you should keep in mind that at any time animals can do something that the theories do not predict. That, of course, is one of the reasons why ethology is so exciting!

ACKNOWLEDGEMENTS

Because I have no other way of thanking them all, I hope that the researchers in ethology whose results I have drawn on will accept this expression of my gratitude for them making their results accessible by writing and talking about them.

I should especially like to thank Dr David Macdonald, Anette Knight and Brigitte Wenhold for letting me use results on suricates, ground squirrels and yellow mongooses respectively that they had not published at the time.

Southern Book Publishers' editors Rita van Dyk and Louise Grantham managed to get most things out of me more or less on time, and the production team did a fast and efficient conversion of manuscript to book.

Penny Meakin's detailed and accurate drawings are better than my sketches and photographs deserved.

PART 1

ETHOLOGY: THE SCIENCE OF ANIMAL BEHAVIOUR

INTRODUCTION

Ethology is the science of animal behaviour, and behaviour is what an animal does, from a mouse nibbling a seed to a lion pride pulling down a buffalo bull, from a dominant male baboon's stern glance at a subordinate to the dramatic clash between fighting musth elephants. In addition to the questions of what an animal does, when, where, how and how often, and with whom, ethology asks and tries to answer the question, 'Why?'

There are four aspects to the question of why an animal behaves in a particular way at a particular time. First, the question of causation: what stimulus from the environment and change within the animal triggers a particular behaviour? Second, the question of development: is the behaviour innate or did the animal learn how to do it? Third, the question of function: what is the behaviour for? In other words how does it contribute to the animal's survival and reproductive success? Fourth, the question of evolution: what ancestral behaviours gave rise to what we see today, and what evolutionary course did they follow to their present form?

These four aspects are all related. A hungry, hunting leopard stalks when it sees an unsuspecting buck (causation); stalking enables it to get within striking range (function) and the leopard's knowledge of its prey's habits and the terrain of its home range allows it to make best use of the available cover (development). Stalking is a typical hunting tactic for cats who hunt alone where there is good cover, and who cannot run fast over long distances (evolution). A wild dog's motivation for hunting depends as much on its pack's behaviour as on its own hunger, and when prey is sighted the dogs approach openly because stalking on a short-grass plain would be useless. Wild dogs' hunting techniques are an extreme specialisation evolved from those of a canine ancestor that hunted in packs by running down large prey in open country.

To qualify as scientific our answers to the question of why an animal behaves in a certain way have to be logical and have to relate to what goes on in the real world. If the explanations we come up with do not match what really happens, we can be sure that no matter how elegant, persuasive, all-encompassing and fervently held our ideas are, they are somehow wrong. Ethology, like all sciences, progresses by discarding faulty explanations and replacing them with ones that fit the world more closely.

Occam's razor: do not use a complicated explanation if a simple one suffices, applies as well to ethology as to other branches of science. Another guiding principle in the interpretation of behaviour is Lloyd-Morgan's canon: never explain an animal's behaviour as the outcome of a higher capacity or power of mind if it can be satisfactorily explained by a lower one.

Although Occam and Lloyd-Morgan seem to be saying the same thing there are times when using the simplest explanation according to Occam's razor goes against Lloyd-Morgan's canon by invoking a higher capacity of mind. For example, learning is a higher capacity of mind than genetic programming, but to try to account for the patterns of social interaction within a baboon troop in terms of genetics would demand an explanation of dreadful and incomprehensible complexity.

Because an animal's behaviour impinges on all the rest of its biology and because such diverse techniques are needed to research it, the boundaries between scientific disciplines have blurred and broken down. Specialists have had to

3

become generalists, and then become experts in new fields. Although ethological questions should, in the end, be answered in the field, an ethologist interested in how mammals communicate by smell may suffer the misfortune of spending nearly all his time in a chemistry laboratory.

There is no such thing as typical mammal behaviour because the typical mammal is a mythical beast. At a finer level there is no such creature as *the* lion or *the* hippopotamus; a single specimen that can stand for a whole species. The usage is still common in scientific, medical, veterinary and even some popular writing but it is a relic of the days when it was thought that all animals of a species varied within such narrow limits that to study one was to obtain results relevant to all. Such a presumption is less valid for behaviour than for any other aspect of biology because behaviour varies more, both from one animal to another and within individual animals, than any other feature.

Despite, or more likely because of, a fertilizing dose of lively controversy, the modelling of the evolution of behaviour (the function and evolution questions considered at the beginning of this chapter) has been one of the most fruitful corners of the ethological field over the past 30 years. The evolution of behaviour requires more subtle modelling than simple population dynamics and genetics because behaviour can be culturally inherited, and while a leopard cannot change its spots it can very easily change its habits. The basis of evolutionary ethology is that, all else being equal, we should expect to see animals behaving in ways that increase the number of offspring that they can rear to independence with a good chance of reaching maturity and producing offspring of their own. This expectation is fulfilled often enough to survive the exceptions. A corollary of this is that we would be surprised to see an animal doing something 'for the good of the species', because one that did so instead of looking to its own interests would not do as well against natural selection as one who took the 'selfish' course. The true coin in behavioural evolution is reproductive success and genetic fitness but, for practical reasons, researchers in the field often draw up accounts in terms of number of successful matings, harem sizes, time spent in various activities, injuries, loss in weight, etc, which are more accessible to measurement.

For instance we might find that large carnivores who hunt in groups have a higher success rate than those who operate alone. If we compare the diets of solitary leopards and social lions we find that lions are more successful than leopards at preying on large herbivores; leopards have about a 5 per cent success rate while lions score 15 to 30 per cent – a difference that might be accounted for by the lions' co-operative hunting techniques. This suggests that group hunting is a way to solve some of the problems of tackling large, dangerous prey, and that being able to hunt such prey is a reason why lions live in prides. Corroborating evidence comes from other comparisons between species; comparing lions with leopards, and spotted hyaenas with brown hyaenas gives the same answer – group hunting is more effective.

On the other hand it could be that the differences in hunting success are due to something other than teamwork. Lions are bigger than leopards, and spotted hyaenas are bigger than brown hyaenas, even when hunting alone members of the larger species might be more successful with large prey. There might also be some species for which we can make no comparisons – for instance there is no solitary equivalent of a hunting dog.

Stronger evidence than is provided by comparisons between species comes from comparing the performance of solitary and grouped animals of the same species, because differences in body size, speed, colouring and so on then fall away. More persuasive still are the variations in success that a particular individual experiences when it joins a group rather than operating alone. For example spotted hyaenas in the Ngorongoro Crater hunt for small, defenceless Thompson's gazelle fawns in pairs, which is five times as effective as hunting alone, but they join up into groups of up to 27 when in pursuit of zebra, which are larger, faster and much more dangerous.

Some of the most illuminating insights into the functions of behaviour have come from studies like these on populations of animals of a single species making their livings in different areas, where they must respond to different challenges of climate, food availability, predators and disease.

Behaviour affects every aspect of an animal's life, and interpretations of behaviour vary according to the aspect from which it is considered. The need to flee from predators has moulded antelope into the sleek athletes we see today, but running is insignificant from the point of view of how much energy blue wildebeest use because it only takes up 0,6 per cent of their time – but then saving energy is not very important to a wildebeest with a lion in its slipstream!

As a rule mammals are more difficult subjects than, say, birds when it comes to studying their behaviour. Most birds are diurnal, whereas most mammals are active at night. Birds communicate by sound and visual signals that are obvious to human observers, while mammals communicate by ultrasound and infrasound which humans cannot hear, and by scent which humans can barely smell. Birds live alone, in pairs, in small, simple groups or in structureless flocks; mammal groups are often bound by complex and subtle ties of kinship and division of labour.

Ethology is essentially about wild animals in the wild, and the wild is diminishing day by day. Everywhere migrations are constrained by fences and by human settlement of traditional game areas. Only in the largest of conservation areas can the interactions among the large carnivores and herbivores still be studied. As well as tenaciously conserving what is left, we must take what opportunities remain for ethological work in disappearing natural systems. A laboratory scientist can build new laboratories, but once ethology's subject matter is gone it is gone forever.

Animals never do nothing. A gemsbok standing motionless in the shade of a Kalahari camel-thorn is using a behavioural way of regulating its body temperature. A small rodent sleeping in its burrow is as surely avoiding predators as the antelope that raises its head from grazing every few seconds to check for approaching danger. Of course some types of behaviour are more exciting to watch than others, no-one can deny the dramatic impact of a lion kill, or a fight between two sable bulls.

Besides ethology the other major scientific approach to animal behaviour is animal psychology. Classically, psychologists, when they study animals, are hoping to learn about humans. The boundary between the two approaches is less clear than it once was, but if a distinction had to be made it would be that an animal psychologist studies how animals solve artificial problems in a laboratory while an ethologist studies how they solve natural problems in the wild.

How behaviour develops was a point of controversy between ethologists and psychologists. Classical ethology stressed the inborn nature of behaviour while behaviorism, an animal psychology movement founded in America by J.B. Watson and B.F. Skinner, took the position that virtually everything mammals

5

do is based only on learning. Both extreme positions, like most extreme positions, were wrong, and the nature/nurture question of whether behaviour is innate or learned has become a dead issue, because it has now been shown beyond any doubt that the final form taken by all behaviour depends on the inextricable interplay of innate and environmental factors. The behaviour of every animal, including man, is partly innate, but mammals are the group in which 'nature' plays the smallest role.

Because this is a *field* guide it is about ethology rather than psychology, and function rather than development or causation.

Like all fields of interest, from cookery to computing, ethology has a special terminology, which is sometimes, admittedly, taken to extremes. Used properly this terminology does what it is meant to do; it provides a clear, concise, shorthand way of talking about important concepts. Used wrongly, as it all too often is, it becomes merely a source of confusion and misunderstanding. Some of ethology's special terms have fallen out of use as the concepts they applied to have been superseded by others. As far as possible I have avoided technical jargon but I have included a glossary of terms for readers who may find them used, or misused, elsewhere and wonder what they really mean.

THE HISTORY OF ETHOLOGY

The study of behaviour is nothing new. To eat and avoid being eaten, primitive human hunters had to know the habits of their prey and predators. The first step in the domestication of our farm and companion animals was to modify their behaviour by taming them.

The word 'ethology' was coined in 1854 to describe the study of how an animal's structure is related to its habits and habitats. Ethology now looks at how an animal's habits are related to its structure and habitat.

Despite the ancient roots of the study of behaviour, the foundations of what was to be built into modern ethology were not laid until the first half of the twentieth century when three researchers, Karl von Frisch, Niko Tinbergen and Konrad Lorenz, put the study of animals' natural behaviour on a firm scientific footing. Karl von Frisch worked on honeybees and his great triumph was to decipher the dance signals that a successful forager uses to tell her nestmates where nectar-laden flowers are to be found. Lorenz worked mainly with birds, concentrating on the innate building blocks of complex behaviour and on what triggers a particular behaviour at a particular time. His 'psychohydraulic model' was unquestionably an important stimulus for later work on motivation. Tinbergen worked on insects, birds and fish, designing elegantly simple experiments to demonstrate the causes and effects of their behaviour. The single most influential seed that Tinbergen planted, and then nurtured by his own example, was the idea that in order to understand an animal's behaviour we have to go out and see what it does in its natural habitat. The contributions of these three pioneers of ethology were honoured by the award of a Nobel Prize in 1973.

Von Frisch, Tinbergen and Lorenz worked mainly on insects, birds and fish – three groups whose behaviour is closer to the classical ethological concept than the behaviour of mammals. They worked in Europe, where almost all the surviving wild mammals owe their very existence, after centuries of persecution by man, to a secrecy and elusiveness that made them practically impossible to study with the techniques that were available in the first half of this century. Had Tinbergen and Lorenz worked in Africa, with its wealth of large mammals, who knows how differently ethology might have developed?

Paradoxically it was the intensive, systematic observation of animal behaviour in the wild advocated by Tinbergen that provided the impetus for a move beyond 'classical' ethology. When the behaviour of members of one species living under different circumstances was compared it could be seen that behaviour was flexible, and might vary as much within species as between them. In contrast, the classical ethological view was that a species' behaviour was as typical and invariant a feature as a colour pattern or the shape of a horn. This led in turn to studies that emphasised the functions of behaviour rather than its development or causation.

The 1960s saw a development in ethology that was to prove as important as the technical breakthrough provided by radio tracking (see Tools of the Trade, page 8). It was a change in approach rather than a development of new techniques or new interpretations; instead of looking at what large numbers of animals were doing at a particular time, attention was focused on a few individuals over long periods.

Obviously, longer studies provide more information. Gus Mills's 12-year stint in the Kalahari on the trail of brown hyaenas told us much more about them than anyone else's efforts, but a more important difference is the accelerating enhancement of the quality of the interpretations that are possible because all the new data are enriched by being interpreted in the light of the old. Observations of lions killing cubs made sense only once it was known that they had just taken over a pride, and that by hastening the cubs' mothers' return to breeding condition they were gaining a precious few extra months of reproductive opportunities. Before molecular genetic fingerprinting, family relationships could be worked out only if one knew which babies were born to which female by which male, and webs of interbreeding can stretch back for generations.

The success and importance of long-term ethology can be judged by the fact that the names of some of its pioneers have become well known even outside zoology. Many with a layman's interest in wildlife will have heard of Hans Kruuk, George Schaller, Jon Rood or Anne Rasa, to name a few of the groundbreakers who worked in East Africa.

The spotlight of long-term field studies has not fallen only on large and impressive species on the African savannas. The behaviour of a colony of rhesus monkeys that was introduced to Cayo Santiago off the coast of Puerto Rico has been studied continuously since 1938 except for a break between 1944 and 1956. Red foxes in Britain and Europe, feral cats in England, hanuman langurs in India, stoats and weasels in Sweden and red deer in Scotland have also had their ecology and behaviour followed over several generations.

How long 'long-term' needs to be depends on the subject animals' life histories; a small creature like a dwarf mongoose can be born, grow up, join a new group, rise in social status, breed and die in the time it takes an elephant calf to reach sexual maturity.

When animals are studied for substantial portions of their lifetimes it becomes obvious that dominance hierarchies and territoriality are not cases of weaker animals giving in so that the strongest can breed for the good of the species, but that subordinate animals and those without territories are, actually, biding their time until weakness and death among the upper ranks leave openings that they can move into. Animals that fight and run away live to fight, and more importantly to breed, another day.

In the 1970s theoretical ethology, and especially its sub-discipline sociobiology, came under spirited attack from some who felt that it undermined their sociopolitical viewpoints by telling them things they did not wish to hear, or to have others hear. Though more was read into it by a few of its proponents, and by many of its detractors, sociobiology was simply an attempt to see whether the general principles of biology – which apply to what an animal looks like, what it eats, where it lives and so on – could be applied to social behaviour. It contains no magic, either black or white.

As I write this at the beginning of the 1990s it seems likely that the next salient advance in mammalian ethology will be towards an understanding of the most important channel of mammalian communication; odour. Technological advances in chemistry have made it possible for the first time to unravel the chemical complexities of the odours of single scent marks and individual animals, so that we are closer than ever to being able to decipher the messages that mammals send by smell.

TOOLS OF THE TRADE

Ethology is, in essence, about watching animals in the wild – although, sometimes, this 'watching' draws as heavily on modern technology as any laboratory experiment.

Obviously it is important to be able to observe animals without disturbing their normal behaviour. What they do in a particular place, such as at a water hole or a den, can be watched from a hide. Hides are less effective with mammals than they are with birds, probably because mammals can smell if there is someone inside, and observation is restricted by the hide's location. In most conservation areas the wildlife is so used to vehicles that a car provides a convenient, mobile hide, with the advantage that it also offers some protection from the attentions of large, dangerous animals.

Binoculars and telescopes are invaluable aids, extending the range over which details can be seen without having to risk disturbing the animal by getting closer than it likes. If you already have a pair of birding binoculars they can be pressed into service for mammal watching, although a pair of binoculars specifically for mammals should have a high twilight factor for observations at dawn and dusk when many mammals are most active.

Many wild animals, especially those in undeveloped areas, are surprisingly unconcerned about being watched at night by the light of a spotlamp. Unfortunately an animal can be dazzled by a spotlight, affecting its chances of avoiding predators or catching prey. Hunters and hunted, and light-shy creatures can be spied on with infrared light using a 'hot-eye' scope. This converts the heat radiated by an animal, or reflected by it from the beam of an infrared lamp, into a ghostly, but quite detailed picture. Image intensifiers and star-scopes are similar to hot-eyes except that they work with whatever visible light the moon and stars provide.

Hand-raising young animals and then accompanying them into the wild was, at one time, a popularised approach but it leads inevitably to changes in the subject's behaviour, especially its social relationships. Many carnivores learn a large part of their hunting skills from their mothers. Deprived of their normal upbringing they may be inefficient hunters or may tackle the wrong sorts of prey, like the cheetahs introduced to Suikerbosrand Nature Reserve who attacked giraffe.

The most detailed, and the most exciting, observations are of animals that have become so accustomed to the presence of humans that they completely ignore them. Dian Fossey's gorillas and the Gombé stream chimpanzees are classic examples of the success of this approach. Taming like this works best with more intelligent animals because they learn more quickly that the human observer is harmless, and with social groups where safe approaches by one member encourage the rest of them. Suricates, which are both intelligent and highly social, will forage around the feet of a familiar watcher, and even use him as a lookout post.

Because the structures of mammal societies depend on each individual having a separate identity, an ethologist has to be able to recognise each of his study animals. While it is possible to mark animals with numbered or coded tags it is often better to identify them by their natural features. Animals with stripes and spots are easily recognisable because each has its own pattern. A rhino's horns, and an elephant's or warthog's tusks grow, and get broken, into individually distinctive shapes and, as it ages, every animal accumulates its own collection of scars from accidents, fighting or hair's-breadth escapes from predators. For long-term studies it is better to identify animals by features that they carry unchanged from infancy to death – the wrinkles on a black rhino's nose are a better long-term label than the shape of its horns, and the pattern of spots at the roots of a lion's whiskers stays the same throughout its life. Using differences like these, expert researchers are able to recognise over 100 individuals of some species.

Among the most interesting and important aspects of a mammal's behaviour are its movement patterns; for instance when, for how long, and how often it visits certain areas. Unless the animal is diurnal and large, and lives in open country so that it can be easily and repeatedly found, trying to study its move-

Individual animals can be recognised by the shapes of their horns or tusks, stripe patterns and scars such as the notch in the ear of the rhino on the right.

9

ments can become an exercise in futility. Early attempts to track the movements of small, nocturnal mammals were based on trapping them in different places, but it was impossible to set and reset enough traps and release captured animals fast enough to get accurate results. Trapping also disrupts the subject's normal behaviour – a rat that is sleeping off a meal of bait while waiting to be released is not filling its usual role in the local social system.

A similarly sketchy idea of a mammal's movements can be obtained by putting coloured plastic markers into baits and seeing where they turn up in droppings – showing that the animal must have visited both the bait station and the place where the marked droppings were found. It is often difficult, though, to determine which animal was involved, and when the movements took place.

The movement patterns of small rodents have been studied by catching the animals, dusting them with fluorescent powder and following their paths through dense vegetation and among rocks by searching with an ultraviolet lamp for the glow of the powder that has brushed off. A dusted mouse also sheds powder onto its grooming partners, fighting opponents and mates.

In the early 1960s two wildlife biologists in North America laid the groundwork for a technique that was to revolutionise the study of mammal behaviour in the wild. By tagging rabbits, racoons and striped skunks with small radio transmitters they were able to get detailed information on movement and activity patterns that simply could not be obtained in any other way. Radio tracking had been born.

Basic radio tracking involves tagging an animal with a miniature radio transmitter, usually attached to a collar or harness, that broadcasts a pulsed signal. An observer with a radio receiver can use a directional antenna to find out from which direction the radio signals are coming. Two simultaneous cross-bearings can locate the transmitter, and the animal carrying it – in an ideal world. In reality the radio signals are reflected from hillsides, bounced back and forward between the walls of krantzes, attenuated by thick vegetation, polarised by forests, and drowned out by static and interference, so that to obtain accurate fixes the tracker

While a radio-collared buffalo has its head down to feed, a switch in its collar is closed and its

must have an intimate knowledge of the radio landscape of the area in which his study animals live.

Just knowing where the animal is at various times shows the extent of its home range, which habitats it prefers and how it organises its movements. Special sensors can be added to the transmitter to measure temperature (which goes up when the animal is in its nest), to signal whether the wearer's head is up or down (which tells whether a buffalo is grazing) and to detect motion, which signals when the animal is sleeping or busy with other activities.

Ingenious special sensors have been used to study urine-marking by bushbabies. The transmitter was mounted on a belt rather than a collar, and when the bushbaby urinated two contacts on the belt were short-circuited and the transmitter's pulse rate changed. It is even possible to eavesdrop by adding a microphone and some extra circuitry to the collar.

A recent development in radio tracking is to transmit the signals to an orbiting satellite. This comes in most useful when the animals cover very large distances in difficult, featureless areas, as whales and seals do, or stroll unconcerned across the most sensitive of political boundaries, like the polar bears that circum-navigate the North Pole through American and Russian territory, and the Namibian elephants that trek into Angola.

To ensure that a radio-tagged animal is not inconvenienced by its transmitter the weight of the tag is kept to less than 3 per cent of its wearer's weight. This is roughly equivalent to the weight of a man's suit, or a well-stocked handbag, and slightly less, in proportion, than the weight of the receiver carried by the biologist. Thanks to developments in micro-electronics and battery technology, transmitters have been miniaturised to such an extent that a complete radio tag can be built with a weight of less than a gram, allowing even mouse-sized mammals to be tracked.

Radio tracking yields the most exciting results when it is used together with more traditional field craft. By following up a directional signal the ethologist can find his subject and see what it is actually doing – whether it is feeding, what it is

transmitter pulses faster than one on a buffalo with its head up.

feeding on, whether it is in the company of other animals and if so how they are reacting to one another, and even whether a carnivore is eating a fresh kill, or one that it has scavenged. When radio-tracking is used in this way the number of useful sightings of an animal can go up from one a month to one a day.

Another high-technology location system, radar, has been used to track the great clouds of bats that emerge from caves in tropical forests.

The use of modern technology and direct observation has complemented rather than superseded the field naturalist's traditional skills of interpreting tracks and other field signs. Tracking is as old as the study of behaviour and it can be as much an art as a science. Some signs, such as scent marks or bushes horned to shreds, are produced by animals as signals, but most, for example footprints and food remains, are just the incidental traces of the animal's activities. Field signs are, at best, only a second-hand record of where an animal went and some of the things it did; if they are to be used as the basis of ethological work they have to be interpreted conservatively – no more must be read into them than can be directly deduced from what is there. For example, jackal spoor on a lion's tracks does not necessarily mean that the jackal was following the lion; it could simply have used the same path hours later. Reading between the lines can tell an intriguing story, but it could be one with no real substance. To get the best out of tracking it helps to record what signs are left after something has been seen happening so that other tracks can be more accurately interpreted.

Some researchers have made use of the phenomenal tracking skills of an area's native inhabitants. The world's best trackers are the Kalahari San and their descendants, but their diplomacy is on a par with their skill at tracking and they cheerfully interpret field signs in the way they know will best please the zoologist they are working for. There is no substitute for direct observation.

It takes three times as long to analyse data as it does to collect them. Because ethology is based more on observation than on experiments, dozens of different, interacting influences have to be considered when trying to account for a particular set of results. To tease them apart needs statistical analyses of baffling and awesome complexity. These days a computer is an essential ally to an ethologist, but is not such a close friend as her binoculars and field notebook.

APPLIED ETHOLOGY

As a growing human population demands more food so more intensive forms of agriculture such as chicken battery farms and cattle feedlots become more important. These more intensive methods frequently put the animals under quite severe stress. This is undesirable not only from an ethical point of view; stress makes animals, as it does humans, less productive and more susceptible to disease. By using the ethological approach of analysing what animals actually do under various circumstances, it has been possible to design better cages for battery hens, and improved pens for pigs in which natural social groups and behaviour are maintained and stress is reduced.

Intensive agriculture with foreign stock species is not the answer to Africa's food shortage. The continent has the wrong soils, the wrong climate and too little water. The only ecologically rational long-term solution is to use Africa's own animals to feed her people, and that requires modifications to the animals' behaviour so that they can be easily and cheaply managed. Helping to bring about this behavioural domestication is one of the most vital contributions that ethology has to make.

Ethology also has an important role to play in wildlife conservation. When black wildebeest are introduced to a new area it is unwise simply to bring in a group of females and a single male. If the herd master has no male rivals against which to defend his mates he behaves aggressively towards the cows and calves, and breeding success is much lower than if a few extra males are present. Large, old buffalo bulls are not post-reproductive bachelors, as was once thought because they live apart from the large herds of cows, calves and younger males. Periodically they return to the herds to mate, and excessive trophy hunting of these old bulls, rather than removing an unproductive part of the population, gradually whittles away the genetic base of trophy-carrying buffalo. An impala ewe with no lamb at foot is probably not a barren cull but has simply left her lamb hidden safely from predators in a nearby thicket. The revolutionary success at De Wildt in breeding cheetah in captivity was achieved by mirroring the cheetahs' natural inter-sexual interaction patterns.

HUMAN ETHOLOGY?

Among the most important reasons why the behaviour of mammals is important is that we are mammals ourselves.

Nonetheless, although animal ethology may or may not be able to tell us how we can expect humans to behave in a particular set of circumstances, it has nothing whatever to say about how people *should* behave. Similarly, human moral standards are absolutely inapplicable to animals. To say that an animal should not behave in a way that offends against a human moral code is as much nonsense as to complain that water should not drown a careless swimmer. The complementary absurdity is to insist that animal behaviour be interpreted in ways that support standards of human morality. For instance, infanticide is morally wrong among humans and there is a school of thought that stoutly maintains that its occurrence in animals, no matter how common and widespread it has been shown to be, is aberrant and unnatural.

THE SENSES OF MAMMALS

An animal responds to its environment by reacting to stimuli that reach its central nervous system via external sense organs – each animal's best-developed senses are those that best suit its habitat and lifestyle. For instance, burrowers have very poor eyesight but are very sensitive to vibrations and draughts, while cats and bushbabies have excellent night vision and acute hearing for hunting nocturnal prey.

Antelope often seem to be in a continual state of nervous tension because their senses are so acute that they respond noticeably to stimuli too faint for most humans to detect. Their sensory abilities allow non-human mammals to communicate, navigate, find food and avoid enemies by signals that humans cannot

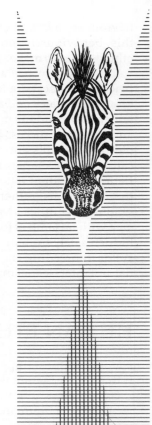

An animal with eyes in the front of its head has a wide field of binocular vision in which it can judge depth and distance, but it has a wide blind spot behind its head. With eyes in the sides of the head the field of binocular vision is narrower but there are no blind spots in which a predator can sneak up undetected.

even detect. With these abilities they have no need of mysterious 'extra-sensory perception' and there is not a shred of good evidence that they have it.

SIGHT

Humans are actually better than most other mammals at seeing fine detail in good light. It is when dusk falls that our visual abilities begin to lag behind; cats can see in light only a sixth as bright as that needed by humans. Even in bright light some diurnal mammals can see better than people; a suricate sentinel (see pp 100–2) can tell a dangerous eagle from a harmless vulture when both are only specks against the midday sky. At the back of their eyes nocturnal mammals have a layer of reflective crystals called the tapetum, which bounces light back through the retina's sensitive cells to increase the chance that it will trigger a nerve impulse. It is this reflected light that makes night mammals' eyes glow when a light is shone on them.

To see how far away something is needs binocular vision – the object must be seen by both eyes. Mammals to whom perception of depth and distance are important – predators and tree-climbing primates for instance – have forward-looking eyes in the front of the head, with a wide field of binocular vision where the visual fields of the two eyes overlap. Herbivores, both large and small, have their eyes on the sides of their heads so that they have a wide field of view in which to spot stalking predators, but they have only a narrow field of binocular vision directly in front of their faces. Because they have no depth perception over most of their field of view it is possible to get close to a herbivore by walking around it in a shallow spiral – it seems that they recognise that something is approaching by seeing that it is facing them rather than in profile.

Domestic cats and dogs can see colours, and their wild relatives and other carnivores can probably do the same. This is not to say that they make much use of their ability. Detecting small movements and judging speed and distance are much more important in catching prey than worrying about the precise colour of its fur. Primates on the other hand do use their colour vision to select food, to choose ripe rather than unripe fruit for instance, and for communication; a male vervet's red and blue genitals are one of the most striking visual displays given by any southern African mammal. Giraffes have at least some colour vision. Domestic cattle have partial colour vision – they cannot see red – and wild bovids are probably similar. Horses and zebras have full colour vision. Among rodents probably only the diurnal squirrels can see colours.

HEARING

Cats can hear frequencies of up to 78 000 Hertz (a Hertz, abbreviation Hz, is one vibration per second), dogs up to 40 000 Hz, and rats and mice up to 100 000 Hz. The upper frequency limit for some bats is 210 000 Hz. At the other end of the scale elephants respond to 20 Hz infrasound, of which humans hear even the upper harmonics only as a deep rumble. The sensitivity of nearly every mammal's hearing is way above that of the human ear, largely because their external ears are mobile cones that funnel sound waves down to the eardrum.

TOUCH

The whole of a mammal's skin is a sense organ, more or less sensitive to touch – although the armoured hide of a rhino, hippo or elephant is impervious to almost anything.

On their snouts many mammals, particularly carnivores, insectivores and rodents, have special long whiskers called vibrissae. Their roots are packed with nerve sensors so that they not only provide an exquisitely delicate sense of touch but can also pick up low-frequency sound.

SMELL AND TASTE

Most mammals live in a world of richly subtle odours that humans can hardly even guess at. In fact, for the majority of mammals the sense of smell is by far the most important. Mammals can detect odours at concentrations that are difficult to comprehend; one part in a thousand million million, equivalent to one drop in 10 million tons of water. Some animals respond intensely to substances that humans cannot smell at all, even at high concentrations, and domestic cats and dogs, and maybe their wild relatives, seem to be able to taste water itself.

A fruit bat selects the ripest fruit from a bunch on the basis of smell. Insectivores, invertebrate-eating small carnivores, and pigs are guided to buried food by their noses. Scavengers such as jackals, hyaenas and bushpigs can locate carrion by smell from kilometres downwind. Once a mammal has followed its nose to food and started feeding, its sense of taste takes over to warn it if the food is unwholesome; small carnivores are repelled by the poisonous and foul-tasting secretions of some millipedes and grasshoppers, and the number of termites an aardwolf can eat is determined by its tolerance of the taste of their defensive secretions. Browsers are repelled by the bitter taste of tannins because these chemicals disrupt their rumen bacteria.

Insectivores, bats, elephants, ungulates, carnivores and some primates have one sense more than man. In the roof of the mouth is the Jacobsen's organ, also called the vomeronasal organ, which seems to respond to both 'smells' and 'tastes' in a way that has no possible parallel in human experience. Jacobsen's organ connects to the nose or mouth, or both, and air- or liquid-borne chemical signals are pumped into it by muscular contractions whose outward signs are the curling of the upper lip and wrinkling of the nostrils which go by the German name (which has no English equivalent) of 'Flehmen'. Flehmen is most often seen when a male is testing whether a female is on heat by sniffing and licking her genitals and urine, and Jacobsen's organ is probably specialised for detecting sexual chemical signals.

The Flehmen grimace given by this zebra pumps chemical signals into his Jacobsen's organ, which lies between his mouth and nasal passages.

COMMUNICATION

Mammals communicate by sound, scent and taste, visual signals and touch, in ways that suit their various habitats and lifestyles.

SOUND

Sound signals can be changed quickly, and turned on and off abruptly, so they can transmit a good deal of information. They are the longest-carrying of mammalian signals; even a human can hear a lion roaring 8 km away, while whale songs carry for hundreds or thousands of kilometres underwater.

Most mammal sound signals are vocal calls, but many antelope also snort through the nose, warthogs champ their teeth, Damara dik-diks rasp their horns on vegetation, elephant shrews and rabbits thump their feet to signal danger, and porcupines rattle their quills.

Vervet monkeys (see pp 45–6), suricates and dwarf mongooses (see pp 100–2) use different alarm calls for different predators.

SCENT

Scent signals may be general body odours, like the smell of a waterbuck or a sable bull, or may be produced by special glands. Urine and faeces also carry scent signals; urine especially contains metabolic by-products that reflect diet and hormone levels. Nearly all carnivores have a pair of anal glands where bacteria process skin secretions into smelly brews that usually contain fatty acids and sulphur compounds. Most ungulates have preorbital glands that open just in front of their eyes and whose secretions, which are not always particularly smelly to the human nose, are wiped onto vegetation. Glands on the feet and legs, which mark the soil and vegetation as the animal walks, are also common in all sorts of mammals. Rodents have scent glands near their eyes and in the anogenital region, and urine is a particularly important odour carrier in these little animals. Shrews have glands on their flanks whose secretions rub off onto the walls of their tunnels and runways.

Scent marks have a unique property; they carry their messages into the future. The anal gland pastings of brown hyaenas and aardwolves still send scent signals weeks and even months after they are deposited.

Chemically, mammalian odours are amazingly complex, usually consisting of blends of dozens or even hundreds of different compounds. This gives them an enormous potential for carrying information; even a mixture of only 20 chemicals, each at three levels of concentration can produce over 5 billion different combinations. The messages that scent signals carry are probably limited by the ability of the nose and brain to detect and decipher their chemical subtleties. Even so, scent can inform a sniffer about the sex, age, diet, identity, species or subspecies, reproductive condition, group membership, social status and emotional state of the animal that produced the odour.

TOUCH

Touch only works at short range of course. It ranks in importance with smell for young animals still in the nest because it allows them to find their mother's nipples and to snuggle up to her for warmth. In turn a mother lets down her milk in response to the feel of sucking babies. Later in life allogrooming is the most common way of communicating by touch and it provides a sort of social glue that establishes and maintains friendly relationships within a family or social group. Lions rubbing their heads together, white rhino bulls pushing their horns against each other and elephants caressing one another with their trunks are all communicating by touch.

SIGHT

Most mammals are small and nocturnal and live where thick cover protects them from predators. In these circumstances visual signals cannot be very important.

Large, diurnal mammals that live in open habitats are the ones most likely to be seen and so they are the ones that use visual signals the most. Medium-sized and large antelope often have patches and bands of light or dark hair that accentuate the position of the head, horns, eyes and neck. Many of them have white tail scuts or rump patches that are flashed as visual alarm signals. The only mammals for which colour is obviously important are primates.

The striking black and white coat of a striped polecat, striped weasel or ratel is a warning that its wearer is not to be meddled with.

Open-country antelope have striking coat patterns for long-range visual signalling.

SOCIAL LIFE

The richness of their social lives is one of the things that set mammals apart from the rest of the animal kingdom. Even a mammal who lives alone is plugged into a local network of social communication via scent marks, long-range contact calls and occasional meetings with neighbours. There is no such thing as an asocial mammal. Of course, sociality is most conspicuous in group-living animals that spend a substantial part of their lives in each other's company.

LIVING IN GROUPS

The complexity of social organisation among southern Africa's mammals ranges from solo wandering, through pairs and family groups and loose aggregations of animals gathered in a favourable spot, to stable groups whose members collaborate to obtain food or avoid predators. It reaches a peak in the societies of dwarf mongooses, suricates and hunting dogs where individuals forfeit their own chances of reproduction to act as sentinels, guards, babysitters and nurses.

By looking at the circumstances in which groups form, and whether, or what, resources are involved, it is possible to identify some of the functions of grouping. For example, bachelor groups are obviously not mating aggregations but they do offer the protection of extra vigilant eyes and ears against predators.

A patch of fire-flushed grass or a tree full of ripe figs will attract animals from less favoured areas but within the patch each animal will mind its own business and what interactions there are will mostly be avoidance as personal spaces are infringed, or short squabbles over a particularly succulent titbit. When the animals disperse they do so one by one; the group's size and membership are unstable and it lasts only as long as the particular resource patch. These ephemeral, structureless, unstable groups are usually called aggregations.

Aggregations can form even where the habitat is uniform if several animals try to use one another as a screen from predators. As each potential victim tries to put another one between itself and a possible source of danger the animals in an area congregate in clumps, with those on the outside of each clump trying to get

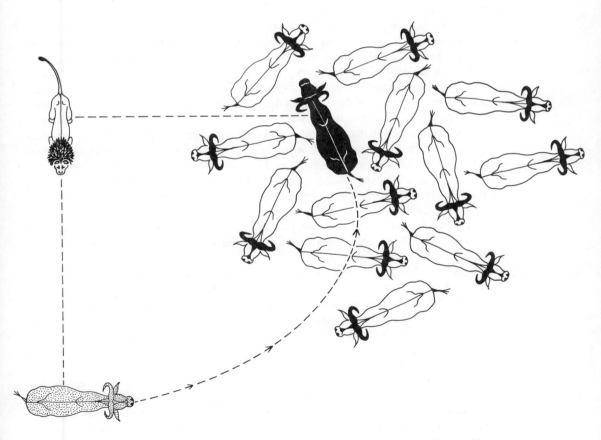

Herds can form simply because animals use each other as screens from potential attacks. The safest place is in the middle of the group.

into the middle. Large herds of ungulates probably accumulate like this; a wildebeest pursued by a predator does indeed flee into the centre of its herd, and eland calves and zebra bunch more tightly when danger threatens.

Truly structureless aggregations are actually rather rare among mammals; a much more common situation is for the members of a group to interact in ways that increase the benefits and cut down the deficits of a gregarious life-style.

The safety from attack by predators that is provided by extra eyes, ears and sniffing noses appears to be an important reason for herbivores to live in groups, while the group sizes are determined by their habitat and what they eat (see pp 180–1). Small, diurnal mongooses also live in groups to avoid predators, and they have an organised system of sentinels who take turns to stand guard (see pp 100–2). Zebra, large antelope, rhinos, elephants, bushpigs, vervet monkeys and baboons turn group living to extra advantage against predators by ganging up on them and counterattacking.

Being in a group can help with obtaining food. Lions, wild dogs and spotted hyaenas are able to tackle large, dangerous prey more effectively by hunting in parties. A banded mongoose that finds a patch of beetle-rich dung calls its companions to come and share the feast.

In highly social groups allogrooming is an important way of getting rid of external parasites, a compensation for the increased parasite transmission that social contact brings.

Group members also benefit by being able to learn from their companions – from generation to generation the knowledge of where to find water holes, refuges, dry season grazing and other resources is passed on from old, experienced members to the group's youngsters.

Living in groups has drawbacks as well as benefits; more competition for food and other resources, greater conspicuousness to predators or prey, and added risks of catching diseases or picking up parasites. Group living would be expected when its benefits outweighed its costs, and groups would be expected to contain roughly the number of animals that offered the best compromise between benefits and deficits. In fact groups will often be slightly bigger than the size that offers the best possible deal for all the members, because a lone animal gains more from joining a group than the established members lose from the increase in group size.

In complex societies the members have to be able to track continual changes in the social scene. They can certainly do so far more effectively than even the most assiduous human observer.

The most stable, persistent and richly patterned groups consist of animals who are close kin; a pride's lionesses are, on average, as closely related as cousins, while its males are often full brothers. That group members are usually blood relatives is a rule that survives the proof of its exceptions – unrelated immigrants that have to work their way gradually to acceptance by the group.

CO-OPERATION

For an animal to be altruistic by helping another at a cost to itself presented a puzzle for evolutionary models because, if the helper does worse than the helped, one would expect the behaviour to be weeded out by natural selection. Various explanations based on animals acting for the good of the group, the race, or the species have been put forward, but for any of them to apply in the real world would need special, and highly unlikely, combinations of circumstances.

Nonetheless co-operative, altruistic behaviour does go on in a wide range of situations, and it can be explained without special pleading.

Reciprocal altruism: 'you scratch my back and I'll scratch yours' can balance the accounts of costs and benefits among a group of animals that interact repeatedly – or even leave all of them with a profit if the favours have a low cost but a high value. Cheaters who received without giving: 'you scratch my back and I'll scratch my front', could prosper unless there was some way in which they could be excluded from the system. This can happen if animals recall unreciprocated favours and refuse further help to the cheater – a cheater loses more in the favours it no longer gets than it saves by being stingy. Such 'policed' reciprocal altruism does indeed occur among long-lived, intelligent, highly social animals like baboons.

Co-operative, altruistic behaviour between relatives was brought into line with the rest of biology by the theory of kin selection which, in outline, explains that an animal who helps a relative is bequeathing copies of its own genes to the next generation because close kin have more genes in common than two animals picked at random.

When group members are closely related, as they nearly always are, kin selection and reciprocal altruism reinforce and complement each other. For example, when a wandering suricate joins a new group it has to 'pay' for membership by babysitting youngsters who are not its relatives – but later those same youngsters will act as sentinels to the immigrant's benefit, and might even babysit its offspring one day if it rises to breeder status. Within vervet monkey and baboon troops interactions and patterns of co-operation are concentrated along lines of kinship and relatives support each other in social disputes.

DOMINANCE

In all mammal social groups, and often among solitary animals who meet each other regularly, it is far more common for disputes over resources such as food and comfortable resting sites to be settled by one animal deferring to another than by outright conflict. Such an arrangement is almost essential to group cohesion; no society could survive if every dispute was settled by a duel. The individual who is deferred to, and who therefore has privileged access to valuable resources, is said to dominate the other – and the network of similar interactions that runs through the group is known as a dominance hierarchy.

Dominance hierarchies in mammals are seldom linear 'peck orders'. There may be a single alpha animal or a pair, males and females may form separate or overlapping hierarchies and loops may form when one animal ranks high in some circumstances and low in others.

Status can depend on being a member of a particular class. In buffalo herds, for example, all bulls dominate all cows, regardless of individual identity, and within each sex there are dominance hierarchies in which rank depends on fighting ability, which in turn depends on size and strength. Any buffalo can decide whether to defer to another simply by seeing which sex it belongs to, and how big it is. Every so often an animal's status will be tested by a real fight – and its relationship with its opponent may then come to be based on their mutual recognition of each other's abilities.

In elephant family groups and the more richly structured carnivore and primate societies the whole dominance hierarchy is based on individual recogni-

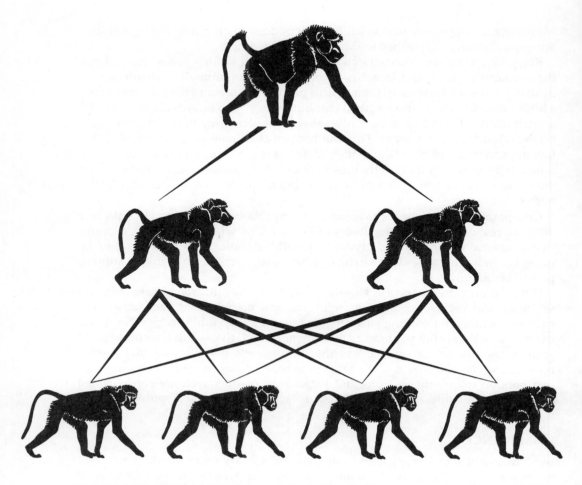

In pyramidal dominance hierarchies an alpha individual or pair outrank a series of progressively larger lower classes.

tion. Each group member comes to know its place by remembering past encounters. Because the subordinates are conditioned to defer to a particular individual it can retain its dominant position even when it has passed the peak of physical condition that originally allowed it to climb in rank.

By far the most common situation is for an animal's rank to depend on its fighting ability and for it to have to enforce its position every so often by giving a painful lesson to a challenger from the lower ranks. When the dominant animal's fighting abilities decline it begins to fail these tests and so sinks lower in the hierarchy.

Dominance hierarchies tend to be self-reinforcing – a high-ranking animal eats better, sleeps more comfortably and suffers less stress than those below it and so stays in better physical condition than likely challengers.

The more valuable the resource the more likely it is that there will be a real fight – most of the battles that occur are between males over females.

As with threat and ritualised fighting (see 'Conflict' below) both parties in a dominance-subordination relationship come away from each interaction better off than they would have if the relationship had not existed, so there is no need to invoke 'good of the group' or 'good of the species' arguments to explain why dominance hierarchies exist. For a weak, subordinate animal, deferring to a dominant one is better than being attacked and losing anyway. For a strong, high-ranking animal pulling rank saves energy, and is less risky than having to fight every time. Benefits to the group there certainly are, because less fighting leaves more time for social bonding and vigilance against predators, but these are fringe benefits, not the driving force behind the development of dominance hierarchies.

Once two animals have sorted out their dominance relationship the signals of superiority and submissiveness that pass between them may be very subtle – it may take no more than a glance from a dominant male baboon to move a subordinate away from a comfortable resting spot. Fighting is a sign that dominance has not been established, or that new relationships are being worked out.

CONFLICT

Both attack and defence are called 'agonistic' behaviours. The animal that initiates an agonistic encounter is the one that is behaving aggressively.

Despite the numerous occasions on which animals have both motive and opportunity for it, fighting is rather rare, full-scale battles rarer still, and fights to the death so rare that they call for special notice. Most conflicts are settled by threats, or cursory tests of strength in which there is not much chance that either opponent will be injured.

Threat can be offensive or defensive. Offensive threat means something like 'if you do not back down I am going to attack you' while defensive threat is 'if you attack me I will defend myself with violence'. Defensive threat is not the same as submission, which says 'I dare not retaliate'.

Postures that display weapons such as horns and teeth, or emphasise the size of the body, such as standing broadside on, fluffing up the hair, hunching the shoulders and standing tall are usually threats. Crouching, sleeking the hair, and de-emphasising weapons are submissive signals.

Both parties to a conflict gain by threatening and limited fighting rather than all-out combat. The weaker of the two gains by avoiding a thrashing and the stronger gains by winning without having had to fight. Both benefit from avoiding the energy and time costs, and risk of injury, of battling it out.

One of the most persistent 'good of the species' myths is that submissive postures expose the subordinate's most vulnerable parts, an invitation to attack that the dominant animal declines for the good of the species. If this argument was sound it would be the subordinate of a pair of vervet males who flaunts his colourful genitals at the dominant – surely an invitation to attack a vulnerable spot if ever there was one. But it is the dominant monkey who signals in this way, and the subordinate does not attack because he dare not.

If faced by an opponent whose displays show that he would be hard to beat, a challenger would do well to find himself a weaker opponent. It could be that displays by resource holders serve to convince challengers not so much that the holder cannot be beaten but that an easier conquest can be had elsewhere.

The importance of ritualised 'fighting by the rules' in intraspecific combat has probably been exaggerated. That neither combatant goes for a reckless all-out attack is more likely to be because, while each is doing his best to inflict enough damage on the other to beat him off, at the same time he is carefully avoiding injury himself. A kudu bull who carefully locks his horns against a rival's is not

23

sportingly ensuring that he cannot injure his challenger, but prudently making as certain as he can that the challenger cannot injure him. When two seals fight most of the bites land on their protected necks – because that is the only part that can be attacked without leaving an opening for dangerous retaliatory bites to rump and flippers.

SPACING

An animal's home range is simply the area in which it goes about its normal business. It may be a definite area in which the animal spends all its time, with regular movements from one place to another, as in the case of thick-tailed bushbabies for example, or a diffuse region through which the resident wanders with no clear pattern. The borders of a home range may encompass areas where the resident never goes because the habitat there is unsuitable for it – lakes and rivers within the home ranges of terrestrial mammals are an example that springs readily to mind. Of course space itself is not particularly useful; the *real* resources are the food, water, females etc. that are more or less scattered through it. An animal can have a well-defined home range that it uses on a regular basis only if the areas resources are sufficiently rich and reliable.

A home range becomes a territory if the resident animal or group keeps the area's resources for itself. This usually happens when the resources are rich and reliable enough for home ranges to be well defined and regularly used. If resources are poor, scattered or unpredictably distributed then defence, if it is possible at all, costs more than the benefits that come from exclusive use. At the other end of the scale, resources so abundant that everyone has enough are also not worth defending; it makes no sense to look after something that nobody wants to steal.

A territory has to contain at least enough resources to keep the holder going for as long as he stays there. The resource is not always food; male impalas stake out exclusive areas during the rut but they spend so long in courting, mating and defence that they hardly get a chance to feed – the resource they are defending is females, not food.

With rare exceptions, such as seals that set up seasonal territories in dense populations, the chances of seeing real defence occurring in enough different places to enable one to map territory boundaries are slim enough to deter even the most optimistic observer. Using scent marks, middens, display sites and so on to map boundaries requires one to ask whether these are really used for defence and whether they actually keep other animals out. For scent marks and middens at least, the answer is usually 'no'. Consequently, in mammals, the most practical definition of a territory is that it is an area where an animal can dominate others who dominate it elsewhere.

Territoriality does not often take the form of attacking and driving off all intruders. Even the most careful vigilance and determined expulsions cannot keep all intruders out all of the time. Intruders that do not deplete the defended resources are quite likely to be tolerated as long as they defer to the resident – immature males may enter breeding territories and the holder of a riparian area may allow others to come to drink. A very common situation among mammals is for a territory to be labelled by scent marks or something similar, which tells an intruder that the area is not available for squatting. The marks themselves do not keep intruders out but they are backed up by the threat of violence from the resident if an intruder chooses to ignore them.

Only in areas with rich, reliable resources can animals stake out territories. Where resources are sparse or unreliable, overlapping home ranges will be established.

PLAY

Play is easy to recognise but, for the ethologist, infuriatingly difficult to define. Play involves exaggerated movements, rapid changes of behaviour and role, and incomplete behaviour patterns. In short it simply looks 'playful'. Obviously it is important that each participant in a social play bout 'knows' that the other is 'only playing', otherwise one of them might get hurt. Playful approaches are clearly signalled by postures and facial expressions, and it is probably because of this need to signal playfulness and to interpret the signals that play is so easy to recognise.

The purpose of play is probably training – muscles are exercised and fighting, prey capture and social skills are practised. Youngsters play in ways that suit their adult lifestyles – predators stalk, pounce on and 'kill' their playmates, young squirrels dive into holes and young antelope practise sprinting and dodging.

MATING

Sexual styles in southern African mammals range from prolonged mating (30 to 40 minutes in rhino), through short, repeated copulations in lions to momentary, single contacts in some antelope.

Because female mammals feed their young with milk, the males of most species are free to leave the raising of the family to the mother while they go off looking for other mates without worrying that their offspring will die of neglect. Consequently only about 5 per cent of mammal species have members who are monogamous: aardwolves, elephant shrews, black-backed jackals, Damara dik-diks and other small antelope are southern African mammals whose males usually stay with one female and help her to raise their offspring. Group living does not preclude monogamy; in wild dogs, suricates, dwarf mongooses and porcupines only one pair in the group breeds.

By far the most common mating system among mammals is for a male to mate with as many females as he can, and then leave them to their own devices in bringing up the young. Males may search for, court and couple with individual females as they come on heat, as in white rhinos; they may actively collect a harem of females before they come on heat, as fur seals and many antelope do, or they may monopolise access to a group of females that has formed for some other reason. Dominant male rock dassies defend rocky outcrops where colonies of females and youngsters dwell, and coalitions of male lions live with groups of females.

It is nearly always the male that initiates courtship and mating but in the case of porcupines, and in lions in the late stages of the female's receptive period it is the female who does the prompting.

CULTURE

Culture is the transmission of information from animal to animal either through or across the generations, and humans do not by any means hold the monopoly on it. Cultural transmission of movement patterns, territory borders, feeding habits and knowledge of the locations of water, food and refuges is very widespread among group-living mammals. Some wild dog packs have specialised hunting techniques that are passed from generation to generation (see p 89). Young vervet monkeys take four years to learn the alarm calls and responses for different sorts of predators from the older monkeys in their troop. Stock-raiding jackals learn from each other how to avoid traps and poisoned bait (see p 86). Even man-eating can become a tradition in a lion pride (see pp 76–7).

The learning is nearly always a passive process: one animal imitates what another is doing, or remembers a route as it follows the rest of the group. Although the youngsters learn, the adults do not teach, unless by example. Dwarf mongooses are an exception; experienced sentinels actively teach juveniles their guard duties.

PART 2
SPECIES ACCOUNTS

Order INSECTIVORA
Insectivores

Family   **SORICIDAE**
Shrews

There are sixteen species of shrews in southern Africa, representing four genera. So little is known about their behaviour that the following generalisations have to be applied to the whole family.

All shrews are continually, frenetically active in their search for food. They need to eat one- to two-thirds of their body weight each day to fuel the energy demands of keeping such small bodies warm. Small bodies chill much quicker than large ones because they have proportionally more surface from which heat escapes. Because shrews have rapid metabolisms, small stomachs, and a fast throughput of food, they are able to go without eating for only a few hours at a time. This is why they alternate periods of one to four hours' sleep with similar periods of hunting and feeding in a continuous cycle throughout the day and night.

All shrews have poor eyesight, but their hearing is good and their sense of smell is excellent. They hunt mainly by sniffing out their prey and feeling for it with the whiskers of their distinctive and incessantly mobile snouts.

Shrews communicate by odour, touch and high-pitched, even ultrasonic, squeaks. When fighting they rear up on their hindlegs and slash at each other with their teeth.

All shrews are solitary except at mating time and while families are growing up. Musk shrews (*Crocidura*) are known to be territorial, and at least some of the others probably are as well. Males and females defend separate areas except for the few hours when a female is sexually receptive, when she will tolerate intrusions by males. All species have flank glands whose secretions rub off against vegetation and other objects as the shrew moves around, thus marking its territory. The glands are especially large in shrews of the genus *Crocidura* and produce the smell from which they get the common name of musk shrew. The taste and smell of the flank glands usually dissuades predators from eating shrews but not from killing them.

Shrew courtship consists of persistent approaches by the male, which are at first fiercely rejected, and finally tolerated, by the female. During mating the male bites the female at the back of her neck.

Musk shrew (*Crocidura*) and dwarf shrew (*Suncus*) mothers lead their offspring around by caravanning; one baby grips the mother's rump fur in its teeth and the rest of the family forms a line with each gripping the fur of the one in front.

Lesser red musk shrews (*Crocidura hirta* No. 14) and greater musk shrews (*Crocidura flavescens* No. 12) are known to lick their everted rectums, a habit known as refection, in order to recycle intestinal bacteria and to obtain extra vitamins.

31

Family   ERINACEIDAE
Hedgehogs

Hedgehog   *Atelerix frontalis* No. 16

Hedgehogs are usually nocturnal but can sometimes be seen during the day, and quite commonly at dusk and dawn. They move slowly while foraging but can run at 6 or 7 km/h. They find food by their keen sense of smell, snuffling into debris and under rocks and logs. A hedgehog is noticeably noisy and seems to make no attempt to conceal its presence, relying instead on its prickles to protect it from predators. When it is alarmed a hedgehog rolls itself into a ball and special muscles pull the spiny skin on its back down over its head, legs and underside and then pinch the opening closed so that the rolled hedgehog presents a uniform ball of springy, interlocked spines to an attacker. At the same time it gives a rhythmic, puffing hiss, presumably imitating a snake.

Communication is mainly by odour.

A rolled hedgehog.

Hedgehog courtship is noisy and prolonged. The male and female circle each other with much sniffing and snorting. During mating the female flattens the spines on her rump and the male, who has a particularly long penis, holds himself in position by biting the spines on her shoulders.

Young hedgehogs forage with their mother from an age of about six weeks.

During the cold, dry, winter months when their insect food is scarce, hedgehogs hibernate in well-insulated nests for periods of a few days or a few weeks, punctuated by brief sessions of activity.

Family   CHRYSOCHLORIDAE
Golden moles

All golden moles are specialised burrowers who only occasionally emerge onto the soil surface. Except for Grant's golden mole (*Erimitalpa granti* No. 23), which 'swims' through loose sand just below the surface, covering about 5 km in a

32

night, they construct elaborate, permanent burrow systems and forage in temporary tunnels just below the soil surface. A hottentot golden mole (*Amblysomus hottentotus* No. 30) has a burrow system that may contain 240 m of tunnels, with refuge chambers, a grass-lined nest for the young, and latrine chambers. A golden mole detects its prey of invertebrates and, for Grant's golden mole, small lizards, by sound, touch and probably, by smell; its eyes are completely covered by skin. It will defend its burrow systems against other golden moles but will share them with rodents. Soil from tunnel systems is pushed up into molehills, and the tunnel beneath the hill is plugged with soil. Occasionally golden moles emerge onto the surface to catch prey or to travel to new areas.

Order MACROSCELIDEA
Elephant shrews

Family **MACROSCELIDIDAE**
Elephant shrews

All elephant shrews are active during the day. Four-toed elephant shrews (*Petrodromus tetradactylus* No. 32) also come out at night, and round-eared elephant shrews (*Macroscelides proboscideus* No. 33), short-snouted elephant shrews (*Elephantulus brachyrhyncus* No. 35) and rock elephant shrews *Elephantulus myurus* No. 38) are active at dawn and dusk too. They eat mainly insects, which they locate by sight or sniff out from crevices with their long, incessantly mobile snouts. They may search actively for prey or, like rock elephant shrews, sit in a shady spot and dash out to capture what passes by. In captivity at least they enthusiastically tackle well-armoured insects such as large grasshoppers and dungbeetles. They are extremely alert; continually watching, listening and smelling for signs of prey or danger, and are fleet and agile when pursued. Four-toed elephant shrews maintain networks of crisscrossing paths with bare patches every 70 cm to provide safe footing for the elephant shrews when they are bounding at high speed, an arrangement that favours the elephant shrews over any pursuer with a different stride length.

Crannies under roots, logs or dense undergrowth, hollow logs and termite mounds, or burrows that the elephant shrews dig themselves or annex from rodents are used as nest sites and refuges.

Four-toed elephant shrews, bushveld elephant shrews and rock elephant shrews produce an alarm signal by stamping their hind feet.

Four-toed elephant shrews are territorial, but how the others organise their use of space is unknown. While moving around a rock elephant shrew regularly rubs its belly on firm surfaces, presumably depositing scent marks.

33

Order CHIROPTERA
Bats

Many aspects of bats' behaviour reflect their status as the only mammals capable of powered flight.

Although the bats are the second most diverse order of mammals in southern Africa, accounting for about a quarter of the mammal species in the subregion, their nocturnal activity and aerial habits, the rarity of many species and the difficulty of keeping them in captivity make them difficult to observe and mean that much is still unknown about specific details of their behaviour.

Bats can occasionally be seen flying in daylight but they are usually active only when darkness protects them from predatory birds.

Suborder   **MEGACHIROPTERA**

Family   **PTEROPODIDAE**
Fruit bats

All eight of the southern African fruit bats eat the soft fruits of a variety of indigenous and orchard trees.

Fruit bats use their keen eyesight for navigation, only the Egyptian fruit bat *Rousettus aegyptiacus* also uses echolocation. Once they have found a fruiting tree they locate the ripest fruit by smell.

A female fruit bat carries her single young until weaning.

Peter's epauletted fruit bat   *Epomophorus crypturus* No. 43

Up to a few hundred may roost together on the thinner twigs of trees with dense foliage. Each bat defends its roosting spot by slashing at others with the claws on its first and second digits. A male gives repeated musical barks, usually while resting but sometimes in flight. He has white, glandular hair tufts on his shoulders, presumably for display. These bats eat the softest fruit direct from the tree and pick off harder fruits and carry them in their mouths to a twig where they can hang and handle them with claws of the first and second digits.

Wahlberg's epauletted fruit bat   *Epomophorus wahlbergi* No. 40

Roosts in colonies of up to a few dozen in evergreen trees. The bats commute up to at least 4 km between roost and feeding site, and roosting sites are moved according to where food is to be found. Males have glandular patches on their shoulders covered by long white hair which can be everted to form rosettes.

Straw-coloured fruit bat   *Eidolon helvum* No. 45

South of the Zambezi these bats are seen only when migrating in search of food.
They settle in an area where food is abundant and move on when the supply runs
out. They rest singly or in colonies of up to 30, and each bat clambers around in
the roosting tree until it finds a suitable place to hang. A straw-coloured fruit bat
eats flowers and freshly sprouted leaves as well as fruit, and it holds food with its
feet while hanging from the claws on its wings.

Egyptian fruit bat   *Rousettus aegyptiacus* No. 46

Egyptian fruit bats are able to roost in caves, where they form colonies several
thousand strong, because they can echonavigate in pitch darkness. When flying
outside they navigate by sight. They forage up to at least 24 km from their roost.
They fly around fruiting trees, hover near promising bunches and make a final
selection by smell after landing. When feeding together they squabble over the
choicest fruit. Fruit is eaten on site, or carried in the mouth to a better roost where
the bat hangs by one foot and holds the fruit with the other, or hangs by its wings
and holds the food with both feet. They hang by one foot when resting.

Mothers recognise their babies by smell, and roost neighbours carefully sniff
each other.

Suborder   MICROCHIROPTERA
Insect-eating bats

Although they are definitely not blind, all the Microchiroptera use echolocation
rather than sight to navigate, to locate roosting spots and to capture their prey
(see pp 36–7).

Unlike most fruit bats insectivorous bats roost in sheltered spots, ranging from
crevices under tree bark to caves, where they are protected from the weather and
safe from predators.

Because their full acrobatic skills are needed for prey capture nearly all mic-
rochiropteran mothers, with the exception of common slit-faced bats (*Nycteris
thebaica* No. 98), leave their babies in the roost when they go out to hunt. Mother
and young probably find, and recognise, each other by sound and scent when
the mother returns.

Nearly all Microchiropterans live on flying insects but large slit-faced bats
(*Nycteris grandis* No. 95) and common slit-faced bats (*Nycteris thebaica* No. 98)
also take grasshoppers from vegetation and scorpions and solifugids from the
ground. Large slit-faced bats also eat fish, frogs, and even birds and other bats.

Insects attracted by lights provide easy pickings for bats, and yellow house bats
(*Scotophilus dinganii* No. 88), hairy slit-faced bats (*Nycteris hispida* No. 94) and Hildebrandt's horseshoe bats (*Rhinolophus hildebrandtii* No. 100) even hunt inside
houses. Several species can be seen hunting as they swoop into the clouds of termites fluttering around street lamps.

Insectivorous bats probably obtain most of the water they need from their
prey, and those that live in damp caves can lick up seepage and condensation.
Sundevall's leaf-nosed bats (*Hipposideros caffer* No. 111) and Egyptian free-tailed
bats (*Tadarida aegyptiaca* No. 63) drink on the wing from open water.

Bats with short broad wings, for example horseshoe bats (Family
Rhinolophidae) and slit-faced bats (Family Nycteridae) fly slowly, but are very

LISTENING IN THE DARK
BAT ECHOLOCATION

Bats are creatures of the air and of the night. The Megachiropteran fruit bats have excellent eyesight and they face no great challenges in finding and handling their vegetable diet. On the other hand the insect-eating Microchiroptera have to locate and capture small, moving prey, usually in flight, in the dark. Their solution to the problem is to use ultrasound – the bat produces pulses of very high frequency sound and listens to the echoes that bounce back from objects in its path. The further away an object is the further the outbound pulse and the returning echo have to travel, and the bat gauges distance from the time lag between call and echo.

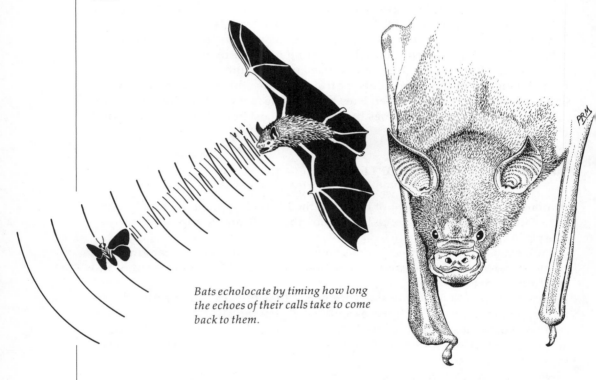

Bats echolocate by timing how long the echoes of their calls take to come back to them.

A bat's noseleaves are sound reflectors which beam its echolocation pulses forward.

During each pulse the sound frequency may remain constant, which helps to pick out an insect's regular wingbeats against a background of wind-stirred foliage, or may sweep, nearly always downwards, so that the pitch at one end of the pulse is two to three times as high as at the other. This probably helps the bat to identify different targets from the way they reflect certain frequencies. Some bats use pulses with both fixed frequency and sweep components.

Most people can hear vibrations of 20 to 20 000 Hz (Hz is an abbreviation for Hertz, the unit of frequency of one vibration per second), whereas bats hear frequencies of 100 to 210 000 Hz. A typical bat's echolocation pulse sweeps between 45 000 and 90 000 Hz, most work between 20 000 and 80 000 Hz, a few go as high as 210 000 Hz and some as low as 4 000 Hz. The calls are emitted as a stream of short pulses that can last for as little as 1/5000 of a second. When bats are foraging together in a limited airspace each adjusts its call frequency so that its neighbours' calls do not get confused with the echoes of its own. The squeaks that you can hear when bats are flying overhead are social calls, not echolocation pulses.

At the frequencies used by bats sound has a wavelength of less than a centimetre, so that they can pick out small targets; longer wavelengths just bend around small objects rather than echoing back. Sound audible to humans has a wavelength of 15 to 20 m and so will only echo from very large surfaces.

Because ultrasound attenuates very quickly in air an echolocating bat has to shriek at a sound intensity that is difficult to imagine. The noise level 5 to 10 cm in front of a bat is often around 170 decibels (db), and can be as high as 300 db even 15 cm away. For comparison the sound pressure of a gunshot is 110 to 140 db, and a lion's roar reaches a paltry 114 db. Bats that fly low, or in dense vegetation, do not need far-carrying calls and they whisper at less than 54 db. High, fast flyers call loudly; 103 db has been recorded from a greater horseshoe bat (*Rhinolophus ferrumiquinum*).

When flying high and fast where there are no obstacles a bat gives a loud pulse about once a second, probably to check its height above the ground. A cruising bat orientates itself with sound pulses between 0,2 and 100 milliseconds long (a millisecond is a thousandth of a second). Its cruising pulse rate of about 10 per second goes up to 20 to 50 per second if it hears something interesting, and climbs to 200 per second as it closes in on its prey. As the pulses come quicker and quicker the echo from one is coming in while the bat is giving the next one. To counteract this the pulses may be shortened to leave more time for listening in between.

The insect-eating Michrochiroptera produce their echolocation sounds in the larynx. Egyptian fruit bats (*Rousettus aegyptiacus*) are the only Megachiroptera that echolocate, and they do it rather crudely using sounds produced by tongue-clicking.

The noseleaves on a bat's face beam the sound forward as an ultrasound 'search-light' and keep the very loud, outbound pulses away from its ears. The ear tragus may also help to deflect away the direct sound of the call. By exploiting its ears' directionality a bat can pick out the echo of its own calls from background noise that is 2 000 times louder. Some long-eared bats apparently home in on prey by listening to the noise it makes itself.

Insects that taste nasty warn bats off by ultrasonic clicks. Some moths jam the bat's sonar by noises that mimic the echo of a large solid object. The pursuing bat, faced abruptly with the prospect of flying full tilt into a tree trunk instead of catching a moth, swerves away and the moth escapes.

The Doppler effect is what makes the pitch of a car's hooter seem to change as it speeds past. Bats use Doppler shifts in sound pitch to judge how fast an object is moving towards or away from them – the echo from an approaching object is shifted to a higher pitch, and when the object is moving away the echo's frequency is lower. The bat may adjust the pitch of its calls to keep the echo at the frequency to which its ears are most sensitive.

The echolocating abilities of bats are astonishing. Most species can locate a metal wire 0,2 mm thick, a greater false vampire bat can locate one 0,08 mm thick (about the same as a human hair), and a Mediterranean horseshoe bat can pinpoint wires only 0,05 mm in diameter. A little brown bat (*Myotis lucifugus*) detects a 3-mm wire at 2 m, a 0,28 mm wire at 1,15 m and a 0,18-mm wire at 1 m, and can echolocate a fruit fly 0,5 to 0,75 m away. *Pteronotus parnelli* can locate a fruit fly from a distance of 3,3 m.

Bats can discriminate between targets of different shape, size and texture, and between wood and metal. They can tell when a target 12 mm away has been moved back 1 mm from the 25 microsecond difference in the time it takes an echo to come back (a microsecond is a millionth of a second), when a target at 58,7 cm is moved back to 60 cm, and can pick up a 0,8-mm difference in the depth of small holes 8 to 9 mm deep. The best testimony to the effectiveness of echolocation is the ability of some bats to catch 5 000 gnats in an hour.

The oldest bat fossil has a skull that shows that bats were already echolocating 50 million years ago. Echolocating allows bats to use secure roosts in the pitch darkness of deep caves, where they are protected from the elements and safe from predators. Large bat roosts containing upwards of 50 million animals are the most populous aggregation of any mammal.

agile and usually hunt close to the ground, or amongst vegetation. Those with long, narrow wings like the sheath-tailed bats (Family Emballonuridae) and free-tailed bats (Family Molossidae) fly fast and high, well away from obstacles. Midas free-tailed bats (*Tadarida midas* No. 54) need a free drop from their roosts to become airborne.

In their roosts bats may either crowd together like Schreiber's long-fingered bats (*Miniopterus schreibersii* No. 67) or space themselves out by fighting and squabbling like Commerson's leaf-nosed bats (*Hipposideros commersoni* No. 110).

Tomb bats (*Taphozous mauritianus* No. 49) roost in pairs on the vertical surfaces of rocks, trees or buildings where there is shade and shelter from the weather. Their eyesight is better than most bats', they keep an alert watch for intruders and if disturbed they clamber or fly to another roost. Egyptian tomb bats (*Taphozous perforatus* No. 50) roost in crevices between rocks and boulders in groups of up to eight.

Hairy slit-faced bats (*Nycteris hispida* No. 94) roost in dense bushes as well as in holes in the ground and in caves. Exotic tastes are shown by banana bats (*Pipistrellus nanus* No. 75), which hang in the rolled-up leaves of bananas, strelitzias and similar plants, and by Damara woolly bats (*Kerivoula argentata* No. 92), who use old weaver nests.

Flat-headed, free-tailed bats (*Sauromys petrophilus* No. 52), Cape serotine bats (*Eptesicus capensis* No. 86), yellow house bats (*Scotophilus dinganii* No. 88), Damara woolly bats (*Kerivoula argentata* No. 92) and large slit-faced bats (*Nycteris grandis* No. 95) tuck themselves away alone or in small groups in crannies between rocks, under bark or inside buildings.

Little free-tailed bats (*Tadarida pumila* No. 59), Egyptian free-tailed bats (*Tadarida aegyptiaca* No. 63), common slit-faced bats (*Nycteris thebaica*), Hildebrandt's horseshoe bats (*Rhinolophus hildebrandtii* No. 100), Dent's horseshoe bats (*Rhinolophus denti* No. 108), Commerson's leaf-nosed bats (*Hipposideros commersoni* No. 110) and Sundevall's leaf-nosed bats (*Hipposideros caffer* No. 111) form colonies of a few dozen or a few hundred which need the more spacious quarters provided by caves, mines, large hollow trees or the roofs of houses.

Schreiber's long-fingered bats (*Miniopterus schreibersii* No.67), Geoffroy's horseshoe bats (*Rhinolophus clivosus* No. 102) and Cape horseshoe bats (*Rhinolophus capensis* No. 106) swarm together in thousands or tens of thousands in caves, cellars, mines and roofs.

Order PRIMATES
Bushbabies, monkeys and baboons

Family   **LORISIDAE**
               Bushbabies

Both southern African species of bushbaby are nocturnal and arboreal, with the astonishing ability of leaping in darkness between branches 2–3 m apart. A lesser bushbaby (*Galago moholi*) has been recorded to jump 2,22 m, over 15 times its body length, straight up, and to cover 6 m in a downward leap.

To gather as much light as possible a bushbaby's eyes are so large in relation to its head that they cannot move in their sockets. The bushbaby shifts its gaze by turning its head, and is able to look directly backwards over its shoulder.

In line with their nocturnal habits bushbabies make heavy use of scent signals. They have an unusual and elaborate way of scent-marking, called urine washing; balancing on the foot and hand of one side they dribble urine over the other hand and foot, rub them together, and then repeat the performance on the other side. Then they leave a trail of damp, smelly foot- and hand-prints along their pathways through the branches. The sticky urine also gives them a better grip. Both sexes of bushbabies have chest-glands; they are bigger in the males than in the females and are used to mark branches and members of the bushbaby's social group.

Using its large ears a bushbaby can locate prey by sound so precisely that it can snatch flying insects from the air.

A bushbaby mother carries her baby around with her from the time it is a few days old, and leaves it clinging to a twig while she forages nearby.

Thick-tailed bushbaby   *Otolemur crassicaudatus* No. 114

Thick-tailed bushbabies live in groups of two to six, consisting of an adult male with females and their young, who share a home range. Sometimes a male's range encompasses those of more than one female group. They sleep together in thick foliage up to 12 m above the ground but forage alone, using established routes among the branches to search for gum, fruit and insects. Thick-tailed bushbabies walk along branches whereas lesser bushbabies hop and jump more freely. Territories are labelled by scent marks and loud, wailing calls that carry well and may be answered by neighbours.

Thick-tailed bushbabies communicate over short distances with a chattering noise, and they have a shrill alarm call. Their long-range, territorial call sounds just like a squalling human brat.

Young males disperse while females stay in their mother's range. To avoid competition from her daughters a female will give birth to more sons; the sex ratio among newborn thick-tailed bushbabies is 133–170 males for every 100 females.

Lesser bushbaby

Lesser bushbabies sleep during the day in dense foliage, old birds' nests and holes in trees. Both in trees and on the ground they move by hopping rather than walking.

The females live in groups of relatives that defend and scent-mark a territory. A dominant male holds mating rights over one or more female groups. Males fight savagely and a loser that cannot escape may be killed.

Dominant animals scent-mark more than subordinates, and males more than females. Urine-washing and chest rubbing are especially associated with courtship. Apparently scent marks inform a group's members of the extent of their territory, but do not keep intruders out and are not used to mark trails.

Lesser bushbabies have a repertoire of at least 25 calls. The wailing screams from which the name bushbaby comes, and a croaking yelp, are used to advertise that a territory is occupied. Intruders are clucked and chattered at. The alarm call is a shrill whistle and males cluck when following a female on heat.

Group companions greet each other by nose-to-nose sniffing and males check the reproductive condition of females by sniffing their genitals. A female on heat calls for three or four nights but aggressively repulses the male's first approaches. When she does finally allow it, mating takes place repeatedly for about five minutes every two hours.

A mother stays continuously with her babies for their first three days. The young are weaned at six weeks and are independent at two months. Young males disperse a few kilometres from their birthplace while females often remain in their natal group.

Family	**CERCOPITHECIDAE**
	Baboons and monkeys

Chacma baboon

Baboons live in troops of up to about 100, from which they get the benefits of shared knowledge about their environment, shared vigilance, and strength in numbers against the attacks of predators. A troop's social structure is maintained by a complex repertoire of interactions among its members.

Each troop occupies a home range that overlaps those of other troops. Each home range needs to contain refuges for sleeping, sufficient food, and a source of water. The sizes and shapes of the ranges depend largely on where these resources lie in relation to each other. Cliffs, caves and large trees, which are relatively secure against predators are used as night-time refuges. Troops may use one site more or less permanently or switch erratically between sites. Large cliff refuges may be shared between troops.

Most baboons drink regularly and if their water supply fails they commute from their home ranges to reach an alternative source. In the Namib baboons manage to go for as long as 20 days between drinks by selecting food with a high water content.

Young baboons learn the location of refuges, water and food sources from the old, experienced members of their troop.

Troops that share the use of an area tend to avoid each other. When meetings do occur they are usually at watering or refuge sites. Although these meetings may be tense and involve much barking and chasing, actual fighting is rare. When fights do occur, however, they can be extremely violent and involve all troop members from the adult males to the juveniles. An adult male baboon's canines are longer and sharper than those of a lion and can inflict fearful wounds. They serve as weapons of attack in fights between baboons and of defence against predators.

Within a troop the adult males form a dominance hierarchy that is established by fighting and maintained by staring, displaying dental weaponry by gaping with the lips drawn back to expose the canine teeth, and chasing. A submissive animal opens its mouth only slightly, and pulls its lips back in a grin. A dispute between two males often sets off a chain reaction of squabbles, chases and fights in the rest of the troop. The highest-ranking male is the most aggressive member of the troop, and also its most assiduous defender; other troop members present their rumps more often to him than to each other, and females with babies still in their black, natal coats tend to stay near him. Low-ranking males occasionally form coalitions with one or two partners and gang up against dominant males. Males play with and groom infants, sometimes as a way of avoiding aggression from dominant animals. A high-ranking male gets first choice of feeding site and other adults keep clear of him, but he will tolerate approaches by the babies of his female social partners.

There is also a hierarchy among a troop's females, but it is fluid because each female's status depends on her reproductive condition, which male she is with, and whether she has a baby. A female baboon inherits her mother's status and each troop contains a number of matrilines that are hierarchically arranged relative to one another. In social conflicts females support their offspring and grand-offspring, and males support their offspring.

Baboons eat almost anything except carrion. They are carnivorous if they get the chance; rabbits, birds up to the size of Egyptian geese, and antelope lambs who are lying out are grabbed opportunistically as the troop forages. The dominant males do most of the hunting and eat almost all the meat. A baboon that strikes a rich food patch hastily stuffs as much as it can into its cheek pouches, which hold as much as its stomach, so that it can move to a safer place to chew and swallow at leisure. A youngster learns what is good and safe to eat, and how to go about getting it, by watching its mother and the other members of the troop, who also learn from each other. New food sources are usually discovered by young baboons, and the knowledge spreads quickly to the rest of the troop.

Baboons usually leave their overnight refuges at first light, assemble and then move off together. In a day's search for food a troop may cover between two and fifteen km. In hot weather they take a midday siesta. They begin to forage back towards their sleeping site in mid-afternoon and reach it well before dusk, probably so that they have time to find an alternative refuge if the first is already occupied or if danger threatens.

A foraging troop spreads over a wide area with its dominant males in front and at the rear and other adult males on the flanks. Old females, and adult males of all ages pause in their foraging to sit and watch for danger. A baboon troop that takes fright when refuges are easily accessible scatters in apparent disorder, but if alarmed in open country the troop bunches together and flees for the nearest refuge or vantage point with younger males on the flanks and the largest, most dominant males guarding the rear. When approaching a dangerous area, such as a water hole where predators might be lurking, the dominant males form a van-

A female baboon's swollen, red rump signals that she is on heat.

guard. Concerted action by these guardians is enough to deter even the largest predators.

A female baboon can come into oestrus at any time of the year. The most obvious sign of her receptivity is the swollen, bright red sexual skin on her rump – and it has to be red to stimulate the males. She solicits mounting, quite often unsuccessfully, by presenting her rump to males or by flashing her white eyebrows at a male some distance away. During the early part of her receptive period a female may mate apparently promiscuously with several of the troop's low-ranking males, but mating late in the cycle, when the chances of conception are highest, is reserved for the dominant male. On the other hand a female may consort with a single male for several days during which they sleep and forage close to one another and the consort male aggressively drives off other suitors. These consorts are usually favoured social partners with whom the female has built up a stable, long-term friendship.

A baboon that smacks its lips while narrowing its eyes and keeping its ears back, or one who grunts softly, is in a friendly mood. One who yawns with its eyes shut is relaxed and happy, as when being groomed for example. If it yawns widely with its eyes open it is slightly tense and excited. It signals mild aggression by opening its mouth and drawing its lips back slightly without exposing its teeth. A stronger threat is given by thrusting the body and head forward with the eyebrows lifted and the mouth closed, and shaking grass or branches. The most serious threat signal is a wide yawn that displays the fangs.

Besides its use as an invitation by sexually receptive females, presentation of the rump is also used as a conciliatory signal by baboons of both sexes.

Baboons have an enormously wide range of vocal signals that can be graded into one another, and combined with each other and with visual signals, in complex and subtle social communication. Their well-known 'bokkum' double bark is an alarm signal and an aggressive signal against other troops. It is given

A relaxed and happy baboon.

most often by the high-ranking males. The rank and file's alarm call is a shrill, single bark. A bark like a dog's is given when one part of a troop rejoins another. Grunts with subtly different intonations can signal contentment, desire for contact, or mild aggression. Baboons screech when frightened and 'yak' when withdrawing from a threat. Youngsters chatter while playing and babies whimper and scream when distressed.

A baboon baby that has graduated to jockey-riding after clinging underneath and then riding crossways on its mother's back.

Baboons are socially sophisticated enough to use deceitful signals. A youngster screams in apparent distress to incite its mother to attack another female who has some food that the youngster wants. False alarms or false alarm reactions, or panic at a minor disturbance, are used by subordinates to distract attacking dominants.

Baboon troops can sometimes be seen moving around with impala or other antelope, each apparently benefiting from the vigilance of the other.

A mother baboon carries her newborn baby clinging to the fur beneath her belly, after a few hours it can cling without help. When it is old enough to walk, at about five weeks, it rides on her back, at first crossways and face down and later sitting up and using the mother's raised tail as a backrest. During alarms the baby reverts to an earlier riding stage than the one it usually uses. If its mother refuses to give it a ride a baboon baby will throw a tantrum just like a human child.

When her baby is about two months old a mother begins to let other baboons play with it, whereas previously she will have limited contact to brief touches, and it will often hitch rides from its adult companions. High-ranking males are especially interested in babies less than four months old. They carry them, play with them and protect them from the boisterous play of older juveniles.

A young baboon whose mother dies will be tended by subadult and young adult males and females and, as long as it is at least six months old so that it can eat solid food, it will probably survive.

A baby baboon and a baby vervet monkey (*Cercopithecus aethiopicus*) have been seen playing together, but baboons also sometimes eat vervets.

Females stay in the troop they were born in, but some males emigrate when they are seven or eight years old and move from troop to troop, staying in each troop for months or years.

Vervet monkey   *Cercopithecus aethiopicus* No. 119

Vervet monkeys live in small troops of up to about 20 animals. If more are seen together it is likely that different troops have aggregated around a localised resource such as a water hole or a tree full of fruit. Such meetings are not always peaceful because vervet troops are sometimes territorial. In meetings between troops high-ranking males and females are more likely than the lower ranks to be aggressive.

Within each troop there are separate dominance hierarchies among the males and females. A young vervet inherits its mother's rank. Mothers and their offspring, grand-offspring and even more distant relatives support each other in disputes, and members of kinship groups interact more with each other than with the rest of the troop. Threats and attacks are influenced by kinship, and even by the interactions of one monkey with another's relatives. Dominant males are favoured as mates by the females, and dominant females get better access to resources. When a dominant vervet threatens or bites a subordinate the victim does not retaliate but instead attacks a monkey lower in the hierarchy. A low-ranking vervet can be recognised by the bite marks on the base of its tail. Aggression and wounding are more common among all ranks in troops that raid human food than in those living under natural conditions

Vervets use at least 36 calls. They 'wrrr' and grunt if they spot another troop and 'chutter' during inter-troop conflicts. A baby gargles or gives a drawn-out 'wor-hor-hor' to attract its mother and screams if it is lost or hungry. Females

Relationships in vervet troops are patterned along lines of kinship.

squeal-scream to repel unwanted sexual advances. Lip-smacking signals submission, and chattering low-intensity aggression. Harsh grunts which sound
alike to humans, but which the vervets can distinguish, are given by a subordinate approaching a dominant, a dominant approaching a subordinate, as the
troop moves away from cover and when another troop is seen. There are six different alarm calls for different predators. 'Uh!' is given for mammalian predators
that are not very dangerous to vervets, such as hyaenas and wild dogs, and when
it is given the other monkeys watch the predator or move slowly away. A chirp is
a leopard alarm; on hearing it the troop looks where the caller is looking to locate
the danger, and flees into the trees. 'Nyow!' signals a large owl in flight. Males
bark and females 'braup' for eagles; the response is to look up and flee to dense
bushes. The snake alarm is a chutter which makes other monkeys stand up and
look around, they are especially wary of poisonous species and pythons. Where
vervets fear humans they chutter for them as well, but the call is slightly longer
and lower than that given for snakes.

Young vervets learn the appropriate calls for each predator, and how to respond to them, during their first four years. Dominant adults are much more reliable sentinels and alarm callers than the rest of the troop. A dominant male will
sit in a conspicuous position in a tree near where his troop is foraging; as long as
they can see him they know they are safe. When the sentinel spots approaching
danger he simply leaves his perch; the troop notices he is gone, and moves
quietly away. The guard gives an alarm call only if there is a sudden threat close
to his troop.

Vervet monkeys also respond to the alarm calls of birds.

Visual signalling is just as important as sound in vervet social life. It is most obvious in the dominance-subordination displays of adult males. An adult male vervet's bright red penis and blue scrotum are an unmissable and unmistakeable signal of his sexual maturity and social status as he walks with a swagger that flashes his colourful genitals as his tail swings from side to side. A dominant male curves his tail up, lowers his bright blue scrotum and displays his scarlet penis while walking broadside past or around a subordinate, while the subordinate male retracts his scrotum and penis. A pregnant vervet female has a swollen, red vulva. An aggressive vervet flashes its white eyelids by raising its eyebrows and holds its head forward and down with its mouth closed. As it gets more aggressive it opens it mouth and pulls its lips back to expose its teeth. The submissive response is a grin with eyes half closed. The vervet friendly greeting is a kiss with pursed lips.

Vervets scent-mark their home ranges by rubbing their chests and cheeks onto the branches of trees.

Allogrooming is used to maintain friendly relationships within a troop. Sometimes one vervet simply starts grooming another, otherwise one who wants to be groomed lies down in front of a prospective groomer. During grooming, parasites, bits of dead skin and salt crystals are picked off. Females initiate more grooming than males.

Vervets sleep huddled together in tall trees or on cliffs and begin foraging in the early morning. They rest during the hottest part of the day, which is when they do most of their socialising. They spend more time in play and socialising when food is plentiful. They have a varied diet of fruit, flowers, buds, gum, insects, birds' eggs and nestlings, reptiles and so on. New food sources can be discovered by any member of a troop, but the knowledge does not spread as fast as it does among baboons.

The unmistakeable signals of a dominant male vervet's status.

Baby vervets are cared for by all the females in a troop, even the immature ones, and although the males usually take no notice of babies the whole troop will rush to rescue one that is in danger.

Females tend to stay in their natal troops while the males emigrate.

Aggressive threat from a vervet monkey.

Samango monkey   *Cercopithecus mitis* No. 120

Samangos live in troops of between 13 and 21, and sometimes up to 34 individuals. A typical troop contains one adult male, six to eight females and an assortment of youngsters. They sleep in trees and, if the weather is right, they sunbathe first thing in the morning. They forage in short bouts during the day, nearly always staying up in the trees, and take a midday rest in the sun or the shade depending on the temperature. Most of the time is spent resting. They finish foraging at about 16h00 and move to a roost tree.

The troops are territorial, avoiding one another in response to deep 'boom' calls by adult males, which also attract straying troop members. Adult males also give a loud, repeated, sharp 'nyah nyah' alerting call, followed by a chuckling noise for more serious alarms. Samango females and young males twitter when disturbed. A croak is used to keep contact with troop members. Screaming, chattering and squealing signal that a female or juvenile is in danger. The threat signal is to push the head forward with the eyebrows raised and the mouth in an O shape.

An adult male samango keeps his troop under protective surveillance, checks the route ahead for danger, leads the troop forward and then sits watching as they pass.

Relationships within samango troops are usually peaceful; one may threaten another by a forward thrust of its head with eyebrows raised but serious fights usually only occur when males compete for females. During the mating season unattached males try to invade established troops.

Samango monkeys take a wide range of plant food, of which fruit is the most important, and also birds' eggs and insects. An unusual item in the diet is the meringue-like foam nests of tree frogs, which the samangos dunk into water to soften them. They lick water off leaves or drink from tree holes.

Samangos are pests in pine plantations because they gnaw the bark off trees.

Samango babies become independent when they are two months old.

Pangolins usually walk on their hindlegs.

Order PHOLIDOTA

Family   **MANIDAE**
Pangolins

Pangolin   *Manis temminckii* No. 121

Pangolins usually move around after dark but can sometimes be seen during the day. They sleep in aardvark or springhare holes, or buried in piles of vegetation.

A pangolin's usual pace is a slow walk with the weight of its body and tail balanced on its hindlegs. It only occasionally touches the ground with its front feet.

It locates ants, which are its favoured food, by smell, scratches open their nests with its front claws and licks them up with its long, sticky tongue.

Pangolins produce a stinking anal gland secretion, which is presumably used for chemical communication or as an extra deterrent to predators.

Although a pangolin is not particularly stealthy it is alert. At the first sign of danger it freezes, and if it is approached it will run away, every so often standing high on its back legs and tail with head vertical to sniff the wind. A pangolin that is unable to escape rolls itself into a ball with its head and legs tucked safely under its heavily armoured tail. A roughly handled, rolled-up pangolin tries to trap its molester's hands or paws between its sharp-edged scales by sliding its tail sideways across its body. If the pangolin is successful it can inflict serious cuts in this way.

A baby pangolin rides crossways on its mother's back with its front claws hooked under her scales. If threatened the mother rolls herself around her baby.

Although a pangolin's scales and rolling behaviour are an excellent defence against predators they unfortunately lead to numbers of pangolins getting tangled in, and killed by, electrified game fences.

Order LAGOMORPHA
Hares and rabbits

Family **LEPORIDAE**
Hares and rabbits

Cape hare   *Lepus capensis* No. 122

Scrub hare   *Lepus saxatilis* No. 123

Both species of hare are nocturnal, but they can be seen during the day in cool weather. They do not make burrows or nests but lie up during the day in 'forms', which are simply hollows pressed by the animal's body into the soil in the cover of grass or bushes.

When approached a hare sits tight in its form until the last moment, when it dashes off on a sharply zigzag course. Flat-out a hare can reach 70 km/h. Cape hares run with their ears up, except at top speed, and may hide in holes, whereas scrub hares run with their ears back and have not been seen to use holes.

Both species eat grass and Cape hares also browse on Karoo bushes.

Both scrub hares and Cape hares breed at any time of the year. Males fight over females by boxing and kicking. Boxing also occurs during courtship.

Hares do not build nests for their young, which are born fully furred, with all their senses operating and can run to escape from predators when only a few hours old.

Left: a Cape hare runs with its ears up. Right: a scrub hare runs with its ears down.

Red rock rabbits

Smith's red rock rabbit   *Pronolagus rupestris* No. 124

Natal red rock rabbit   *Pronolagus crassicaudatus* No. 125

Jameson's red rock rabbit   *Pronolagus randensis* No. 126

All three species of red rock rabbit are nocturnal and spend the day in forms under overhanging boulders or tucked away in rock crevices. They do not dig burrows but the females line the above-ground nests in which they have their young with vegetation. They lie tightly in their forms when approached and they are most likely to be seen as they dash away after being unexpectedly flushed.

Rock rabbits are solitary, if groups are seen they may be males attending an oestrous female, a female with well-grown young, or an aggregation of rabbits at a rich food source such as a patch of fire-sprouted grass.

Red rock rabbits defecate in middens.

Riverine rabbit   *Bunolagus monticularis* No. 127

These rare rabbits are nocturnal, solitary and probably territorial. During the day they lie up in forms in the cover of vegetation. They eat fresh, green grass in the summer and turn to a diet of the leaves of shrubs in winter. Females dig shallow burrows lined with grass and fur in which to have their babies.

Riverine rabbits are slow runners and so are easily hunted with dogs – a factor that has contributed to their precarious conservation status.

The young are weaned when they are a month old.

Order RODENTIA
Rodents

Family   **BATHYERGIDAE**
                  Molerats

All molerats lead subterranean lives and, in the wild, their behaviour can be observed only on the rare occasions that they emerge onto the surface, and second-hand in the molehills and tunnels they produce. The molehills made by Cape molerats (*Bathyergus suillus* No. 129) are distinctively large; up to 75 cm across and 50 cm high. The mounds of the other species are rarely more than 50 cm across and 20 to 30 cm high; the actual size depends on the type of soil and the pattern of the molerat's burrowing. Soil is pushed up into the molehill as solid plugs with the same diameter as the tunnel. If a molerat's tunnel is opened the resident soon detects the damage by changes in air currents and speedily repairs it as long as there is no disturbance in the surrounding area. Cape molerats' burrows are from 15 to 22 cm across and 40 to 65 cm deep, common molerats' (*Cryptomys hottentotus* No. 132) burrows are 5 to 7 cm across and less than 35 cm below the surface. Both species can have more than 400 m of tunnels in their burrow systems.

Family   **HYSTRICIDAE**
                  Porcupines

Porcupine   *Hystrix africaeaustralis* No. 134

Porcupines are nocturnal, and almost the only time they are seen in daylight is when they sunbathe just outside the sanctuary of their burrows. As refuges they use existing rock crevices, caves and cavities among tree roots, or take over burrows already made by aardvarks or springhares. They also dig their own burrows, which sometimes consist of elaborate systems of interconnecting tunnels and chambers.

Refuges are shared by family groups of up to six, even when there are empty holes nearby. Group members forage alone except when an adult (usually a male rather than a female), accompanies a youngster in order to protect it from predators.

The home ranges of neighbouring porcupine groups overlap, but meetings between neighbours are not necessarily peaceful.

Porcupines scent-mark with urine and the strong-smelling secretion of their anal glands. The chemicals produced by these glands change as the females go through their reproductive cycles.

Porcupines eat almost any sort of vegetation, moving up to 16 km from their burrows along established pathways to reach favoured feeding sites. They are serious pests in farmland because they are such wasteful feeders; a porcupine will take a single bite from a dozen pumpkins before it finds one ripened to its taste. They carry food back to their burrows and build up substantial stores. They also collect bones, which they gnaw to obtain phosphorus and calcium, and can be seen feeding from carcasses for the same reason.

With their hollow spines buoying them up porcupines are strong swimmers.

Porcupines make little attempt to conceal themselves and the noise of their sniffing, gnawing and quill-rattling can be heard from several metres. Their senses of hearing and scent are keen, and a porcupine that hears or smells anything suspicious freezes while sniffing and listening. If a predator approaches the porcupine tries to escape by running away, but if it is cornered it brings its armoury of quills into play. A porcupine carries quills only on its rear half, and because it cannot protect its head by rolling up like a hedgehog, it defends itself by erecting its quills and pointing them towards its attacker and manoeuvring to keep its head away from danger. At the same time the porcupine shakes its tail so that its thick, hollow quills produce a dry, hissing rattle, stamps its feet to rattle the quills, and gives a growling roar. If the attacker is undeterred by this display and approaches closer, the porcupine dashes backwards or sideways at it, trying to plant quills into its paws or face. If the porcupine succeeds its quills pull out of their loose attachment to its own skin and stay buried in its enemy. The quills are not barbed but if they break beneath or near the skin their victim is unable to pull them out. The quills are always dirty and they set up infections that can be fatal. Porcupines cannot shoot their quills, although the speed of their movements and the number of loose quills lying around after an attack give the impression that they can. Although a porcupine's defence is impressive it often fails against a determined predator that continues harassing the porcupine until it is exhausted. A porcupine that cannot find a hole stands little chance against more than one attacker because it can only keep its quills aimed at one of them at a time, leaving its head vulnerable to attack by the other.

A porcupine's defensive rearguard.

In each porcupine group only one pair breeds. The others mate but do not conceive – probably their low social status and chemical signals from the breeding female have something to do with this. A female initiates mating by backing towards a male with her tail held up. The male stands almost vertically behind her, supporting himself with his paws on her back and ejaculates once after a short burst of thrusts with his exceptionally long penis. After mating the male and female groom each other. The porcupine is one of the very few animals that indulge in sex outside the female's fertile period, which is probably an important factor in keeping the group together.

One baby is born at a time. It is suckled for three months, and eats its first solid food at about a month. During weaning it forages under the protection of its parents.

Family   **PEDETIDAE**
             Springhares

Springhare   *Pedetes capensis* No. 135

These large, aberrant rodents are strictly nocturnal. They spend the day alone in burrows that they dig themselves, and leave to feed only well after sunset. The burrows have at least two, and maybe as many as 11 entrances, and can be up to 45 m long. Once the springhare is inside it usually plugs up the burrow with soil to keep small predators out.

A springhare can be recognised at night by the distinctive way in which it bobs its head when a light is shone on it.

A springhare will move up to about 400 m from its burrow to feed on roots and fresh grasses. It will not move as far in cold, wet weather or on bright, moonlit nights. Several animals may congregate in particularly rich food patches. There is a record from East Africa of two springhares scavenging at a road hill.

A springhare's senses of sight, hearing and scent are all keen, and to avoid predation it relies on early detection of danger and an ability to flee at speeds of up to 25 km/h, with hops up to 3 m long powered by its muscular hindlegs. If captured it uses its sharp hind claws as dangerous defensive weapons. Hopping is the usual way of getting around, while a springhare uses its front feet for digging, moving slowly within a food patch and grasping food while it nibbles.

One baby is born at a time, and it first emerges from its burrow when it is six to nine weeks old. By this time it can run almost as fast as an adult.

Family   **SCIURIDAE**
             Squirrels

Ground squirrel   *Xerus inauris* No. 140

Ground squirrels are diurnal and therefore easy to observe. They are strongly terrestrial; cautious clambering into low bushes is the closest they come to climbing. They live in colonies of related females and their young, in complicated warrens whose tunnels they continually add to and modify. The soil thrown out of the burrows accumulates to form a distinctive, low mound onto which the burrows open. Adult male ground squirrels move among several colonies, setting up temporary residence in those where there is a receptive female.

Each group defends its warren from intrusion by other ground squirrels; the dominant female does most of the chasing. Within groups the relationships are usually friendly except that the dominant visiting male may be chased around by the colony's dominant female, and may displace others from food by an open-mouthed threat display. Infants and young adults chase each other and mock-fight in spirited play.

The area immediately around a warren is marked with its residents' urine, a secretion from their anal regions and by secretions from their lips, which they rub on nearby stones. Smell is also apparently used to recognise colony members because ground squirrels greet each other with nose-to-nose sniffs and anal sniffing.

A ground squirrel spends about six or seven hours a day on the surface. Its activity is strongly influenced by the weather. Pouring rain and strong winds keep it in its burrow all day and on a cold, cloudy morning it will get up later than in warm sunny weather. To escape the midday heat it takes a siesta in its burrow or in the shade of a bush. In cool weather ground squirrels sunbathe spreadeagled on the ground, and if the weather is too hot they lie in the same position in the shade. They use their bushy tails as parasols and flick sand over themselves to keep cool.

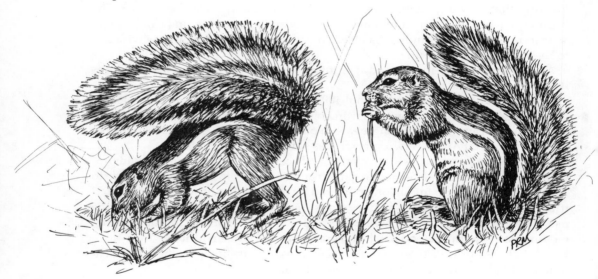

A ground squirrel's tail serves it as a parasol.

A ground squirrel uses its claws, teeth, tongue and lips in fastidious grooming. It will also nibble and lick the fur of its colony mates.

Ground squirrels are mainly herbivorous, taking any part of a plant from its roots to its flowers, but when vegetable fare runs short they supplement their diet with termites. They feed as close as they can to the refuge of their burrows, stripping the plant cover down to bare soil and digging out the roots.

Because their diurnal habits and open habitat make them so vulnerable to predation, ground squirrels are continuously on the alert and will flee from a predator that is still as much as 50 to 80 m away. When suspicious they jerk their tails up and down and give an alarm whistle that intensifies to a scream as the danger increases. When they hear an alarm call all of a colony's squirrels go on the alert, locate the source of the danger if they can and dash back to their warren with their bodies held low and their tails straight out.

Unless taken by surprise ground squirrels on the surface have no great fear of snakes. Rather than fleeing they mob the snake and harass it with sideways swishes of their tails until it leaves the area.

Ground squirrels have mixed relations with small mongooses. They may share their burrows with either yellow mongooses or suricates in a state of amicable mutual tolerance but will also chase away yellow or slender mongooses. The changes in behaviour may be connected to the presence of vulnerable baby ground squirrels, or the degree of familiarity between individuals of the different species. Cohabiting ground squirrels and mongooses benefit from extra anti-predator vigilance and readily respond to each others' alarm signals.

Baby ground squirrels emerge from their burrows at about four weeks of age and for the next two or three weeks they keep strictly within 10 m of home. Young males disperse as yearlings, whereas females tend to stay in their natal groups.

Sun squirrel *Heliosciurus mutabilis* No. 142

Sun squirrels are diurnal and arboreal. They live alone or in pairs and use holes in trees or tangles of foliage and creepers as nests. When alarmed they give a clucking call, flee to the highest branches and lie along them so that they cannot be seen from below.

Red squirrel *Paraxerus palliatus* No. 144

Red squirrels are diurnal. Males and females have overlapping home ranges, and only the area directly around the nest is defended from intruders. Associations between a male and a female may be stable but they are not permanent. Like all the other squirrels red squirrels use tail flicking to signal excitement and they have a wide repertoire of vocal signals. Murmuring signals a desire for contact – females use it to call infants, a dominant males uses it when he sees an intruder whose identity and status he wants to check, and the males chasing a receptive female murmur to her. If a red squirrel does not want to be approached it grunts and growls, and under stress it hisses and growls. A red squirrel that is alert to the presence of a predator or an intruder gives click calls which, in high intensity mobbing or territoriality, run together into a trill. A baby red squirrel calls its mother by ticking sounds. Imminent danger elicits an alarm bark.

Red squirrels scent-mark with urine and by anal rubbing.

When surplus food is available red squirrels bury small hoards of large, hard seeds.

Tree squirrel *Paraxerus cepapi* No. 14ᵣ

Tree squirrels live in small, territorial family groups but are usually seen alone because they forage solitarily. Group members share a common odour that they spread by sleeping together and allogrooming and by marking each other with their anal glands. Squirrels that do not carry the proper group odour are chased away, most often by the resident males. Territories are marked by the secretions of lip glands, urine, and anal wiping.

Tree squirrels sleep and have their young in tree holes or, quite commonly, in the attics of houses.

Vocal communication is very important in tree squirrel groups. Murmurs are used by the males chasing a female on heat, who attracts suitors from neighbouring groups with bouts of loud, high-pitched calling. A series of clicks increasing in strength and running together to a harsh rattle signals the presence of a predator and calls the group together to mob it. A tree squirrel that is very frightened gives a high-pitched whistle. A loud, repeated 'chuck-chuck' call increasing in intensity and running together, given by a tree squirrel sitting in a prominent spot and flicking its tail, is probably a long-range territorial advertisement.

Tree squirrels frequently forage on the ground, when they become particularly alert. At any sign of danger they dash to the nearest tree and, leaping from tree to tree over distances of up to 2 m, head back to their nest.

Tree squirrels sunbathe in sheltered spots in cold weather. They are fastidious groomers. They are expert handlers of small seeds and fruits. Excess food is buried in small caches.

Oestrous females are chased through the branches by groups of males but it is not known how many of them finally mate. There is a record of a male tree squirrel killing babies, possibly as part of his taking over a new group.

Family   THRYONOMYIDAE
Canerats

Greater canerat   *Thryonomys swinderianus* No. 147

Greater canerats sleep during the day in nests of grass among dense reeds or grass, or in holes. They become active around sunset, moving to feeding areas along established runs. They eat a wide variety of vegetable food, especially sprouting reeds and grasses that they cut off near the base and bite into short pieces which are chewed up separately. Piles of discarded stems mark their feeding places.

Greater canerats are noisy feeders, and their grunting and chewing can be heard several metres away. They have very acute hearing and if there is a suspicious sound they freeze to listen. If threatened they dash noisily away into heavy cover, then suddenly freeze, making it difficult to keep track of their movements.

While greater canerats can be found in groups it is not certain that these are really social units or whether they are simply aggregations in suitable areas. That they thump their feet, whistle and give 'boom' calls when alarmed suggests alarm signalling, which would be expected in a social group. They also squeak in submission and threaten by growling.

As would be expected for a swamp-dweller, greater canerats are expert swimmers.

Families   CRICETIDAE AND MURIDAE
Rats and mice

Brants' whistling rat   *Parotomys brantsii* No. 150

One of these diurnal rodents is usually detected first by the fine, high-pitched alarm whistles it gives as it disappears into its burrow at the approach of an observer. The burrows are dug in areas of firm sand, often under bushes whose

Brants' whistling rat babies cling to their mother's nipples for their first few days.

lower branches are buried by the accumulated soil from the whistling rat's tunnels. If watched quietly from a few metres a whistling rat that has fled into its burrow will reappear at the surface from one of the many entrances that most burrows have. At first it will dive for cover at the slightest movement or sound but after a while will become used to being watched.

Whistling rats are territorial and they prefer to eat near the security of their burrows. Food plants growing any distance away are harvested and carried home to be eaten, and inedible remains can be found around the burrow entrances.

For the first few days of their lives baby whistling rats cling to their mother's nipples so tenaciously that females can be seen dragging from one to three babies around as they forage.

Vlei rat   *Otomys irroratus* No. 156

Vlei rats are active in short bouts throughout the day. They live alone, in pairs, or in families in thickly vegetated, wet areas. They do not make burrows, which would probably become waterlogged, instead they build domed grass nests on patches of higher, drier ground or in grass tussocks, or use the holes that other species dig in dry ground. The regular pathways they use radiate out to their feeding grounds, which are littered with short pieces of discarded grass stems. They prefer green vegetation to fruits and seeds.

Vlei rats have home ranges but whether they defend territories is uncertain – they do use a vocal threat; a metallic 'chit' delivered while sitting upright.

To help digest its vegetable food a vlei rat eats some of its own faeces directly from its anus, and the fresh faeces of other vlei rats. This habit is particularly important for establishing the correct bacteria in the guts of weanlings.

For the first two weeks of their lives a female vlei rat carries her litter of between one and four babies clinging to her nipples.

Striped mouse   *Rhabdomys pumilio* No. 163

Striped mice are active during the day, especially in the early morning and late afternoon. They dig their burrows beneath bushes or clumps of grass, or build slightly flattened nests about 12 cm across from pieces of grass 5 to 8 cm long, low down in grass clumps. Striped mice are most easily observed as they glean fallen seeds from bare soil or sand. When foraging like this they are very alert and dash back to cover at the first suspicion of danger. They prefer fruits and seeds to green vegetation, and are also partial to insects.

Striped mice fill an important role as pollinators of proteas. The mice are dusted with pollen as they feed on the succulent bracts and style bases of the flowers, and as they move from bush to bush they carry the pollen with them to cross-fertilise the flowers.

Water rat   *Dasymys incomtus* No. 165

These rats are mostly crepuscular but may be seen at any time. They are good swimmers and readily take to water when their runs through the vegetation are flooded. They build grass nests on sloping banks with boltholes underneath that may lead into the water, with the exit beneath the surface.

Multimammate mice
Mastomys natalensis   Mastomys coucha No. 174

Even if one compares specimens close-up these two species are indistinguishable. Because they are nocturnal they are most likely to be seen when they move into houses or other buildings, where they nest in sheltered corners or in spaces inside walls. They eat almost anything, including each other if food is scarce.

M. natalensis is more excitable and active than *M. coucha*.

Although the two species live in the same areas they do not interbreed. Mates of the appropriate species are recognised by ultrasound and odour.

Tree mouse   *Thallomys paedulcus* No. 177

A tree mouse is most likely to be seen from below by torchlight, which reflects off its white belly, as it climbs out onto the finest twigs to harvest fresh leaves, shoots and seeds, which it sometimes carries back to its nest to eat. The nest is built in a hole in a tree, from which it sometimes overflows as the tree rat keeps adding more leaves. Strange objects hung in a tree where tree mice live are cautiously and thoroughly investigated.

Giant rat   *Cricetomys gambianus* No. 195

Although giant rats are mostly nocturnal they sometimes come out at dusk or in the early morning. Their eyesight is poor but they have very good hearing and a keen sense of smell.

A giant rat is a great hoarder and it will accumulate kilograms of fruit, seeds, the inedible remains of food, and even things like stones and pieces of metal. Hoarding allows it to spend long periods in its burrow, away from inclement weather and hungry predators.

A giant rat is rather slow-moving and although it is fond of various sorts of fruit its movements in trees are limited to cautious clambering rather than agile climbing.

It lives alone in a complicated burrow system conveniently close to reliable food sources. It may dig short, temporary burrows near particularly productive food patches and will seldom forage more than 150 m from home.

Order CARNIVORA
Carnivores

Family   **HYAENIDAE**
Hyaenas

Brown hyaena   *Hyaena brunnea* No. 245

Although they are mostly nocturnal, brown hyaenas can be seen in the early morning or late afternoon, especially if the weather is cool.

Brown hyaenas are usually seen singly as they forage but they live in groups of between two and ten which share a den in a large burrow or a cave. Most of a group's members may congregate at a large carcass but they nearly always take turns to feed singly. Each group maintains a territory that is heavily scent marked with anal gland pastings (see pp 62–3). In the Transvaal the territories cover between five and fifty km², in the Kalahari 200 to 500 km² and in the Namib 100 to 220 km². In the Namib, despite the unlimited food available at the seal colonies on the coast, the territories contain huge empty areas, because the hyaenas keep up the tradition of visiting abandoned human settlements where presumably their predecessors once scavenged garbage. Some brown hyaenas travel enormous distances; one released near Rustenburg in the Transvaal disappeared from its known haunts and four months later was shot for sheep raiding 530 km away in the Smithfield district of the Orange Free State. Another moved 650 km from Wolf's Bay to the Orange River. Occasionally brown hyaenas or their signs are seen in the suburbs of even large cities; in Lüderitz they regularly enter the town to scavenge at rubbish dumps.

Unlike spotted hyaenas, brown hyaenas carry food back to the den for their cubs, their powerful forequarters enabling them to carry heavy loads over long distances. The average distance over which they bring in food is 6,5 km but Gus Mills saw one carry a 7,5 kg load for 15 km in the Kalahari.

Brown hyaenas are specialist scavengers, as they lack the speed, agility and co-operative behaviour of successful hunters. In the Kalahari they get only about 5 or 6 percent of their food by hunting. Some individuals become pests by specialising in the hunting of farm animals, which are more vulnerable than wild species. A brown hyaena can sniff out carrion from over a kilometre downwind and it listens for the sounds of a kill or of predators and other scavengers at a carcass. The brown hyaenas that exploit the seal colonies on the Namib coast regularly wade out into the sea to obtain carrion floating just offshore.

A brown hyaena has awesomely powerful jaws and teeth; only the heaviest bones of the largest species are immune from its attentions and the carcasses of medium-sized antelope can be consumed completely.

Brown hyaenas do not always make the long trip back to their group's den at the end of a night's foraging. If they find a rich food source they may make a temporary camp by scooping out a hollow in the soil under cover of long grass, bushes or trees.

Brown hyaenas are independent of drinking water, as they obtain what they need from their food and fruit like wild melons (tsamas).

When group members meet they sniff each others' heads, backs and anal regions to establish identity. The younger of the two presents its anal region for sniffing with its head low and its ears flattened sideways, and whines like a cub begging for food. Brown hyaenas of different sexes from neighbouring groups greet each other in the same way and such meetings are usually peaceful. Meetings between neighbours of the same sex involve threat displays in which they make themselves look bigger by erecting their manes, and which might escalate to neck biting which draws blood. Full-scale fighting is rare.

A brown hyaena's massive forequarters enable it to carry heavy loads over long distances.

A common interaction within groups, especially among the subadults, is muzzle wrestling. The two animals try to bite each other on the cheeks, jowls or the sides of the neck. If one gets a grip it may give the other a shake but the interaction, which can go on for an hour, appears to be restrained and friendly.

Within a brown hyaena group there is a weak dominance hierarchy apparently based on age. Subordinate animals defer to their superiors by a crouched posture with the ears flattened backwards and the mouth open, and by whining and squealing.

Brown hyaenas defecate in middens, which are concentrated near territory boundaries.

Vocal communication is important for brown hyaenas. High-pitched screams, squeals and whines indicate fear or submissiveness in adults, while cubs whine harshly before sucking and softly while being groomed. Growls are given by frightened brown hyaenas, especially in encounters with spotted hyaenas or lions, or during muzzle wrestling. Aggressive adults hoot and fluff up their manes. Brown hyaenas do not have an equivalent to the spotted hyaena's whooping long-range contact call.

A brown hyaena that finds a particularly rich source of food, such as a nest full of ostrich eggs, stores what it cannot eat at one sitting in scattered caches hidden in vegetation or down holes.

The resident males of a brown hyaena group check the females' reproductive conditions by licking, sniffing and Flehmen of their genitals. Courtship lasts from one to four hours and may be aggressive. While mounting the male holds the female with a gentle neck bite and they mate repeatedly at intervals of about 10 minutes. In the Kalahari the brown hyaenas have a most peculiar mating system, although a group's resident males check the females they do not mate with them; that task falls to nomadic males. Surprisingly the residents still help to look after the cubs. Female brown hyaenas may be seen carrying small cubs from den to den, possibly to avoid predators or parasites. The cubs live on milk for the first three months, begin eating solid food at four months, are weaned at nine months and begin to forage independently at 10 to 15 months. All the members of a group contribute to the cubs' upbringing by delivering food to the den.

Spotted hyaena   *Crocuta crocuta* No. 246

Spotted hyaenas are most active at night but it is not unusual to see them during the day, especially in cool weather. They are fond of lying in shallow water to cool off.

Spotted hyaenas are social creatures; they live in clans of up to 80 animals whose stable core of members consists of a dominant female and successive generations of her daughters and their offspring. Clans also contain resident males, and immigrant males who have been accepted to membership after as long as four weeks of cautious approaches and abject subordination, with the immigrant bearing the brunt of the clan's aggression without retaliating.

Within a clan there is a dominance hierarchy; females are larger than males and dominate them, cubs dominate males and, once they have been admitted to the clan, immigrant males outrank resident males. Dominant animals are usually bigger than subordinates, but whether large size brings dominance with it, or dominance allows large size due to freer access to food is not certain. Cubs inherit their mothers' rank. When a female is on heat males follow her in rank order but only the highest-ranking immigrant male actually mates. When nursing cubs high-ranking females have the best positions; those closest to the den. A subordinate hyaena initiates greetings and is more likely than a dominant to extend its penis or clitoris.

Spotted hyaena clans are territorial. They mark their area by anal gland pasting (see pp 62–3), especially near the borders, by defecating in large middens and by pawing the ground to deposit smelly secretions from glands on their feet. Most pasting near the den is done by males and young, low-ranking females. High-ranking females and males paste near kills and after aggressive encounters, and all clan members paste along their territory border. Latrines seem to be information sites and a spotted hyaena may visit one in order to sniff around rather than to defecate. Groups of spotted hyaenas patrol territory boundaries, systematically scent-marking and adding to latrines. Encounters between spotted hyaenas from different clans take many different forms – from the intruder's withdrawing without meeting the resident, through meetings with apparent recognition by sight and smell, and chases with no contact, to pitched battles in-

SIGNALLING BY SCENT
IN HYAENAS AND AARDWOLVES

Aardwolves, both species of hyaena in southern Africa, and the striped hyaena that lives further north, make heavy use of scent signals to help maintain their territories. Faeces are used for this purpose by all three southern African species and spotted hyaenas lay down secretion from glands between their toes by scratching the ground. The scent marks that are produced most often, and are most characteristic of the hyaenids and aardwolves, come from their anal sacs. These sacs lie between the tail and the rectum, and have a muscular lining that squeezes them outwards for scent-marking and during social encounters.

The three species differ slightly in where and how they deposit their marks and in what the marks look like.

An aardwolf walks over a grass stem, squats slightly and with a quick sideways wipe rubs its extruded anal sac on the bent-over stem. The marks are thin smears of greasy black or dark brown secretion about 1 cm long.

Spotted hyaenas mark with their anal sacs on clumps of grass as well as on single stems. The hyaena walks over the grass, squats and extrudes its anal sac, which it dabs against the grass leaving smears of white secretion 2 to 5 cm long.

Pasting by brown hyaenas is one of the most elaborate scent-marking procedures seen

62 *A brown hyaena's elaborate pasting behaviour produces a double mark on a single grass stem.*

among mammals. The hyaena selects a single grass stem and walks over it, bending it down in the process. When the stem is between its hindlegs the hyaena crouches and extrudes its fist-sized anal sac. Running up the surface of the extruded sac is a groove which the hyaena carefully manoeuvres down onto the stem. The sides of the groove close around the stem to leave a neat blob of creamy, white paste, then, as the anal sac retracts, the grass receives a thinner smear of a dark brown or black secretion from another part of the sac. The finished mark has two separate parts; the blob of white paste about 1 cm long and about 1 cm above it, the brown smear, also 1 cm long. Such a bipartite mark is unique.

In the Kalahari, brown hyaenas deposit an average of 2,6 pastings for every kilometre of their nocturnal wanderings. Each animal covers around 30 to 40 km a night, so if there are six animals sharing a group territory their combined efforts will stud their territory with 500 to 600 scent signals every night. The pastings can quite certainly be smelled by a hyaena for at least a month, so the number of marks actively signalling that the residents are at home is 15 to 18 thousand.

Spotted hyaenas paste much less frequently than brown hyaenas, travelling an average of about 2,5 to 7,5 km between marks. They concentrate their marks at significant places such as the site of a large kill.

Aardwolves cover 8 to 12 km per night and paste 10 to 20 times per kilometre as they search their territories for termites. They increase their pasting rate near their territory borders, setting up an olfactory boundary line. The odour of an aardwolf's pasting is amazingly persistent. Marks exposed to the air keep their smell for at least nine months. Aardwolf noses are certainly more acute than human ones, and each pair's territory could be showered with as many as 100 000 active marks. The black smear of a brown hyaena pasting loses its smell (to the human nose) after about seven to 10 days; the white blob lasts for four to six weeks, by which time it has turned brown. The difference could be because the two parts send different messages. The short-lived black paste could remind a hyaena, or tell its group mates, that it foraged through an area too recently for a return visit to be worthwhile, and the longer lasting white paste might be to provide a warning to neighbours and itinerants that they are trespassing in an occupied area.

Aardwolves and both species of hyaenas defecate in middens. One reason why aardwolves do this may be because their faeces smell strongly of termites and if they were scattered around they might distract the aardwolf from its foraging. Spotted hyaena latrines can become very large and if they are near territory borders the accumulations of hundreds of bright white scats act as boundary markers. Brown hyaena latrines in the Kalahari are concentrated near territory borders. For some reason, if a midden is near a shepherd's tree it is never to the north of it.

Scent marks can play more than one role in maintaining a territory. At the least they warn an intruder that others have been in the area. The fresher the marks the more recently they were there, and the more marks there are the more frequently the area has been used and the greater the chance of a potentially dangerous encounter. The safest course for an intruder is to avoid freshly, and heavily, scent-marked areas. The territory holders thus benefit from scent-marking because it tends to keep intruders away from their resources.

Obviously scent marks do not always act as simple repellents; animals frequently trespass into others' territories despite sniffing the owners' scent marks. In these cases the role of the scent marks may be to establish the status of the territory's residents. Intruders should be more wary of meeting residents than of encountering other individuals who are just passing through, and more ready to behave submissively or to flee if they should happen to meet. Residents will fight fiercely to keep what they already have because they have put time and energy into defending their territory and because they know their area better than an interloper does. They have more to lose by being ousted from their territory than the intruder has to gain by taking it over. Residents can be recognised if their odours match the smell of the scent marks in the surrounding area; because each individual has a unique odour an animal that smells like the scent marks must have done the marking, and to do that it must have been resident in the area.

volving all members of the two clans, in which those losers unable to flee are savaged and killed.

Spotted hyaenas are renowned and highly effective scavengers. They find carcasses by scent, by the noises made by other predators, and by watching vultures. On a one-to-one basis they can displace any predator except a lion from a kill, and even lions give way when outnumbered by spotted hyaenas. A large pack of wild dogs can keep spotted hyaenas at bay and can seriously injure a lone hyaena.

Spotted hyaenas are accomplished hunters and they get up to 75 per cent of their food from their own kills. They usually go for large and medium-sized antelope and select young or weakened targets, but have been known to tackle anything from mice to baby elephants, and adult hippos trapped in mud pools. They are the predators most likely to attack humans sleeping outside. Spotted hyaenas are less skilled stalkers than cats and rely instead on their speed and stamina to run down their prey. They can sprint at 60 km/h and keep up a speed of 40 to 50 km/h over 4 or 5 km. Most healthy, adult antelope can still escape from a single hyaena but by collaborating, the hyaenas dramatically increase their hunting success. Hunting as a group is especially effective against prey that is able to defend itself. If two hyaenas hunt wildebeest calves they are five times as successful as one operating alone, because one of the team can distract the mother while the other grabs the calf. Even adult gemsbok fall prey to a hyaena group's ability to attack from several directions at once. Hyaenas hunting gemsbok in the Namib herd their prey away from gravel areas onto soft sand where their padded feet provide better footing than the gemsbok's hooves.

Spotted hyaenas' prey dies from shock and loss of blood as it is torn apart.

Spotted hyaenas kill their prey by biting chunks out of it as it runs and tearing it apart once it is pulled down. The victim dies from shock and loss of blood.

Where spotted hyaena clans are large and there is competition from other predators, the hyaenas gorge themselves as fast as possible. One spotted hyaena can eat 15 kg of meat, about a week's average supply, at a sitting. A clan of 21 ate a 100 kg wildebeest in 10 minutes and a clan of 31 finished off a 200 kg zebra and a 150 kg foal in 36 minutes. During such frenzied feeding hyaenas are very noisy and chase each other around, but they do not fight over food.

In the Namib, where hyaena clans are small groups of about four animals and no other large predators occur, feeding is less frantic. Each hyaena takes a turn at the carcass; priority depends on dominance, backed up with teeth. The high-ranking adults get nearly 9 kg of meat at a meal, the lowest male only about 2 kg.

In the smaller clans where high rank brings privileged access to food females eat better than males, who compensate by travelling further in their search for food and by making do with poorer fare.

A spotted hyaena that is harassed at a kill by superior numbers of other predators may cut its losses by tearing a piece off the carcass and carrying it away, perhaps for more than a kilometre. Surplus food is sometimes stored in caches, a favourite site for which is shallow water where jackals and vultures are unable to get at them.

Spotted hyaenas are great travellers, they may cover 40 km in a night and do a 70 km round trip in two nights.

The spotted hyaena's most puzzling feature is that all of them, females as well as males, seem to have male genitals. A female spotted hyaena has an erectile clitoris as large as a male's penis and a false scrotum filled with fat. This puzzling state of affairs is probably related to the females' exposure to testosterone at a critical stage of their foetal development, which might also explain their dominating aggressiveness and large size.

If you can get a good look at a spotted hyaena it is possible to tell its sex. A female's pseudoscrotum is less deeply lobed, and more hairy, than the genuine article of the male. An adult female will nearly always be in milk, and so her teats will be visible, and a female's belly curves up less sharply than a male's. If a male approaches a female to sniff her flank or rump he will look frightened. These interactions only rarely happen between animals of the same sex.

Spotted hyaenas' prominent genitals are sniffed during the elaborate greeting ceremony. The one on the left is a female.

However it arose, a female spotted hyaena's strange genital anatomy now plays a role in the complex greeting ceremony that clan members use to reinforce social bonds. The hyaenas recognise each other by sight, each usually briefly sniffs the side of the other's mouth and head, or they may stand head to tail alongside each other, lift the inside back leg and carefully sniff and lick the partner's erect penis or clitoris. One or both of them may give a soft, deep groan. Sniffing and licking usually takes 10 to 15 seconds, or maybe as long as 30 seconds, and when it is finished the two drop back onto all fours and walk away.

An aggressive spotted hyaena curls its tail over its back, pricks its ears forward, keeps its mouth closed and may evert its anal gland. A frightened one holds its ears low, opens its mouth, tucks its tail between its legs and slinks away in a crouched posture. Grinning and laying the ears back is a submissive greeting. Spotted hyaenas also have a rich repertoire of vocal signals. Cubs whine when they beg for food or milk. A high-pitched yell is the hyaena for 'Ow!'; they give it when they have just been bitten. When chased off a kill they giggle. A series of short, quiet grunts is given by a hyaena that is surprised and frightened, and louder grunts when a clan is advancing into battle against other clans, or lions. Grunts and growls signal an imminent attack, and a growl precedes retaliation in kind for being bitten.

Their most distinctive call is a long 'whooo-oop' rising in pitch towards the end. The calls are very loud, carrying for more than 5 km, and it is very easy to locate their source, which suggests that they are long-range signals to inform clan members of each other's locations. Fast whoops are used to attract members to carcasses and to recruit them for confrontations against lions.

Spotted hyaena cubs are born in litters of one to four in dens that may be converted aardvark holes, caves or drain culverts. When they are about three weeks old their mother may carry them to a different den. If more than one female in a clan has a litter each feeds only her own cubs – allosuckling has been reported only once. Unlike brown hyaenas, spotted hyaenas rarely carry food back to the den. Cubs are suckled until they are old enough to go along on foraging trips at about 14 months, before which they get little solid food. The cubs live on milk alone for six to nine months, then they begin to visit kills and take solid food, and they are weaned at 10 to 14 months.

Cubs only six weeks old go through the motions of pasting on grass stems near their den. They are probably picking up bacteria from the marks of the clan's adults to inoculate their anal glands, which at that stage are undeveloped.

Family   PROTELIDAE
Aardwolf

Aardwolf   *Proteles cristatus* No. 244

Aardwolves are nocturnal except in winter, because the harvester termites that make up nearly all their diet also come out only at night in the hotter months. An aardwolf sleeps the day away in a disused aardvark or porcupine burrow. It emerges around sunset and makes a beeline for the nearest midden where it digs a hole, defecates and buries its faeces. The faeces can be 10 per cent of the aardwolf's own weight and consist mostly of the sand that it licks up while feeding on termites. The middens are areas of bare, dug-over soil about 2 m across, containing the remains of droppings. The faeces smell strongly of the tur-

WHY DO LARGE CARNIVORES LIVE IN GROUPS?

Southern Africa has six species of large carnivores; lions, leopards, cheetahs, spotted and brown hyaenas and wild dogs. Four out of the six; lions, cheetahs, spotted hyaenas and wild dogs live in groups and sometimes (cheetahs), usually (lions and spotted hyaenas) or always (wild dogs) hunt communally. Brown hyaenas live in groups, but they forage alone, and leopards are entirely solitary.

What, then, explains why some large carnivores live in groups?

Young male lions form coalitions to give themselves a better chance of taking over a pride by ousting the resident males, while lionesses team up against infanticidal, invading males; but this probably only affects group size rather than being the primary reason why lionesses live together.

Only in wild dogs does protecting the young seem to be one of the purposes of group living; they leave a guard with the puppies while the group is on a hunting foray. Newborn lion cubs are not protected by the pride, because the lionesses go off alone to give birth. In both species of hyaenas babies seek refuge in small tunnels at the back of the clan's den where nothing big enough to harm them can get at them. Group-living cheetahs are most often males, and they have nothing to do with raising cubs.

Killing efficiency is unquestionably an important reason for spotted hyaenas to hunt in groups. They even change the size of their hunting parties to suit the prey they are after; one or two go for gazelles, an average of two to three for adult wildebeest and an average of 11 for zebra. Lions also do better when they hunt in groups and although the improvement in success does not keep pace with increases in the size of a hunting party, being a member of a hunting group provides meals more regularly than operating alone.

Male cheetah who share a territory may also hunt together and be able to down more formidable prey than they could tackle alone.

Wild dogs always hunt in packs but the chase is usually led by the alpha male or female and the other dogs actually play a role only if the prey circles, when they gain on it by cutting the corner, and once the leader has caught up with it, when they pile in for the kill.

In none of the four species where hunts are collaborative does teamwork help with prey detection, or even very much with its capture. It is at the kill itself that extra sets of teeth and claws make a positive contribution – pulling down and killing large, dangerous prey more quickly, and with less danger of retaliation, than a lone predator would be able to manage.

In contrast, foraging cannot be the reason why brown hyaenas live in groups because they search for food singly. What does favour group living is the provisioning of growing cubs with food by all members of a social unit, most of whom are as closely related as half siblings.

Another reason to live in a group is to stop others from stealing your food – and to be able to steal theirs if the opportunity arises. Lions and spotted hyaenas score on this account by stealing regularly from each other and from other predators. This is probably why clans and prides, which defend and steal food, are bigger than hunting parties that only have to catch and kill it. In one-to-one contests over food the ranking is lion, spotted hyaena, leopard and brown hyaena, wild dog, cheetah but the tables can be turned by strength in numbers – a pack of wild dogs can put a lioness off a kill.

The only benefit of group living that is common to all the social, large carnivores is that the duties of territory defence – whether fighting, scent-marking or patrolling – are shared by the whole group, thus cutting down the burden falling on any one member. Probably only in the case of cheetahs is this the primary reason for groups to form – in the others groups that have formed for some other reason are able to hold territories where single animals could not.

pentine-like secretions of soldier termites, and it could be that the aardwolf buries them in one place so that their smell does not distract it while foraging.

An aardwolf finds columns of harvester termites by smelling and listening, and feeds by licking them off the soil surface. How many termites it can obtain from a column depends on how fast it can feed before too many foul-tasting soldiers arrive, and the licking action of an aardwolf's tongue is faster than the eye can follow. Aardwolves do not eat anything bigger than a grasshopper. They show no interest in catching mice, let alone lambs, and in any case their cheek teeth are so small and widely spaced that they are useless for chewing meat.

Aardwolves live in pairs that share a territory whose size depends on the number of termite mounds. The territories are fiercely defended against intruders and are demarcated by scent marks (see pp 62–3).

An agitated aardwolf erects the mane of long hair on its neck and back to make itself look almost twice as big as normal. At close quarters it gives a sharp bark, a deep growl or a surprisingly powerful roar. It uses its sharp canine teeth for fighting and for defence against predators, especially jackals, from which parents have to protect their cubs for the first three or four months. The male and female take turns at babysitting and going off to forage.

During the midwinter mating season a male aardwolf roams widely, scent-marks profusely to advertise his presence and fights fiercely with other males for opportunities to mate.

Aardwolf cubs are born in the spring. They emerge from their den when they are about a month old and join their parents on foraging trips after about another month. By the time they are four or five months old they are foraging independently. They share their parents' territory until they are almost a year old, and about three-quarters grown, then disperse to try to find a vacant area to settle in.

Family   **FELIDAE**
Cats

Cheetah   *Acinonyx jubatus* No. 247

Because they hunt by sight cheetahs are active during the day, especially in the cool of early morning and evening. They have also been known to hunt by a full moon's light.

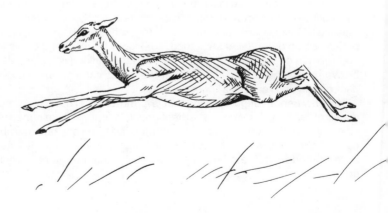

Male cheetahs label their territories with scent marks of sprayed urine.

Adult female cheetah are usually solitary, but their cubs stay with them for at least a year, and families can be mistaken for groups of adults. Male cheetah quite often live in small groups with strong, stable social ties reinforced by allogrooming and head rubbing. In the stock-farming areas of Namibia, where large carnivores have been eliminated, cheetahs thrive and groups there are bigger and more common.

Some males hold territories for up to four to six years, while others are wanderers. Coalitions are more successful at establishing and holding territories than are single males. Territories are scent-marked with sprayed urine, but if the

A cheetah can accelerate to 70 km/h in two seconds.

marks are more than a day or two old intruders ignore them and so some areas are used on a 'time-share' basis. Nevertheless, trespassers who do get caught are savagely attacked, mauled and sometimes killed. Large rocks and trees provide traditional marking sites that are frequently visited by residents and itinerants seeking information on the local cheetah social structure.

Cheetahs use surprisingly high-pitched, almost bird-like chirrups as greeting and short-range contact calls. In friendly social encounters they give a loud, rumbling purr. Mothers 'churr' to call their cubs. When threatened they give a loud, barking spit, often slapping the ground with their forepaws at the same time.

Cheetahs are highly specialised for a particular style of hunting; a stalk followed by explosive acceleration to a full-speed 100 to 120 km/h chase that lasts for up to 600 m. They can reach 70 km/h within two seconds of a standing start; better acceleration than a sports car. They can keep up full speed for about 500 m, after which they have to give up the chase.

A vantage point such as a termite mound or an easily climbed tree is used to keep a lookout for prey. If cover is available cheetah use it when stalking, in the same way as other cats, but a cheetah will also stalk across open ground by moving slowly forward when the prey looks away or lowers its head to feed, and freezing when it looks around.

A cheetah tends to select the least vigilant prey on the fringes of a group. If it is seen by its prey before it gets within about 100 m the cheetah gives up the stalk because it depends for success on the element of surprise. If it can get within 100 m the cheetah will charge if the prey flees, but the cheetah's chances of success are better if it can attack from less than 30 m while its prey is still unaware of its presence. The cheetah can then be up to full speed while its quarry is still getting into its stride. The most common cause of failure in cheetah hunts is that the prey sees the cheetah before it charges. Once charging a cheetah is successful in about two out of seven attempts.

A cheetah that catches up with its prey hooks at it with one or both forepaws, getting a hold with its dew claws. These are sharp and catlike, in contrast to the others, which are blunt and permanently exposed to give better traction when running. The prey is knocked or pulled off balance, giving the cheetah a chance to grab it by the throat and throttle it, which may take several minutes. If there is cover nearby the cheetah will probably drag its kill there to escape the notice of vultures, which are not only competitors in their own right but also attract the attention of lions and spotted hyaenas, which frequently steal cheetahs' kills.

With its lighweight teeth and skull a cheetah has difficulty biting through the skin of even small antelope, so it usually starts feeding at the groin where the skin is thin. It eats the meat off one thigh, then the belly, the other thigh and the forelegs. They do not eat the skin and intestines of their prey and can chew up only small bones with their weak teeth.

Although they do not usually scavenge, cheetah will eat carrion that has escaped the notice of more effective scavengers.

Cheetahs' favourite prey are smallish antelope like springbok and impala or the young of larger species. They also eat hares, springhares, porcupines and birds. Hunts for large antelope are successful only when a group of cheetahs operate together; two males in the Nossob riverbed in the Kalahari made their living by catching adult gemsbok. Three males introduced to Suikerbosrand Nature Reserve successfully tackled young giraffe. Group hunting is also used for calves and lambs with protective mothers, while one cheetah draws the mother's attack the other chases the infant.

A female cheetah that is about to come on heat is detected by males from the smell of her urine. Their first approaches are aggressively rebuffed and they respond in kind. During this period the males spray-mark heavily and fight among themselves. They also scratch up small mounds of loose soil and urinate or defecate on top of them. After one to two weeks of such courtship the female becomes receptive and aggression among the males reaches a peak, with mating rights going to the winner. The female invites copulation by crouching in front of a male, who mounts from behind with a neck bite. Mating is not as frequent as in other cats.

A young cheetah cub may look enough like a ratel to deter potential attackers.

Cheetah cubs are born blind and helpless and are carefully hidden by their mother in thick cover. The cubs are very vulnerable to predation and so they frequently move to new refuges. Up to an age of about six to eight weeks the mother carries them between sites. The cubs get their first solid food at about six weeks and are weaned at three months. At four to five months their mother brings them live prey to practise on, at six or seven months they begin to make their own kills and they regularly hunt with their mother at a year of age.

For their first three months cheetah cubs have a mantle of long, grey hair. It may just be extra camouflage but it has also been said that it makes the cubs look enough like the ill-tempered ratel to dissuade other predators from risking an attack.

71

Leopard

Leopards frequently move around during the day in National Parks and remote areas where they are not hunted. Their nocturnal habits in developed areas may be a response to human pressures. To escape the midday heat they rest in heavy cover, among rocks, in caves, or draped along thick tree limbs.

Leopards are very solitary; the only times they associate with each other are when a male consorts with an oestrous female and when a female has cubs. They defend territories against other leopards of the same sex but the territories of males overlap those of females, the larger territories of the males encompassing three or four females' areas. Occupation of a territory is advertised by marking with urine and faeces, clawing the bark of trees and by vocal signals. Leopards have astonishing powers of navigation and homing, a capacity that has bedevilled attempts to relocate stock raiders to areas away from human settlement. Such homing leopards have probably been kept on the move by the territoriality of the residents in the areas through which they have travelled.

Leopards have a distinctive contact call that sounds remarkably like a thin plank of wood being cut with a coarse saw. This call probably allows territorial neighbours to keep away from each other, and males and females to find each other. Leopards growl when aggressive, spit and snarl when threatened and purr when contented. A quiet 'pfff-pfff', made by blowing air through the nostrils, is a friendly contact call. Hungry cubs give high-pitched 'aow' calls.

Leopards are very agile climbers and also readily take to water.

Almost any vertebrate, including reptiles, fish, and mammals ranging in size from mice to kudu, may fall prey to a leopard. They eat more predators than do other carnivores, being especially partial to jackals and domestic dogs. In farming areas individual leopards may become stock raiders, as they are capable of killing anything from chicken to cattle. Man-eating leopards are rare but not unknown (see pp 76–7).

A leopard's stalk brings it close enough to its prey for a rush-and-pounce attack.

The leopard's usual hunting technique is classically feline. When it sights a potential target it stalks forward with head low and legs bent so that its belly almost brushes the ground. It makes clever use of cover, and crouches motionless if the prey looks up. In open country where leopard and prey can see each other over long distances the leopard detours behind thick vegetation, a river bank or a sand dune before it begins serious stalking. A leopard will stalk a target that moves slowly away over distances of a few hundred metres, or wait in ambush if the target moves towards it. Once it is within range, usually within 10 metres, the leopard settles itself with small stepping movements of its hindlegs, dashes forward and uses the five sharp, hooked claws of each forepaw to grab the prey and pull it down. The killing bite is directed at the nape of the neck or, if the victim has horns, at the throat. Small prey such as mice, rats and small birds are swatted to death with one paw. An alternative hunting strategy that can be brought into play is to flush small animals from patches of heavy cover and pursue them in the open.

If its victim has horns a leopard kills with a strangling throathold.

If its prey is dassie-sized or larger a leopard disembowels it before eating, and may scratch earth over the guts of large prey before it begins its meals. It uses its incisor teeth to pluck birds and furry mammals such as rabbits. Excess food is stored to be eaten later, and more kills may be made in the meantime. If there are no other large predators or vultures in the area, the leopard will leave its kill on the ground covered with loose soil, leaves or branches. If protection from scavengers is needed the prey is carried up into a tree and wedged among the branches. The strength of leopards is demonstrated by their ability to carry carcasses weighing more than 50 kg up vertical tree trunks. Leopards are outranked only by hyaenas in their willingness to eat rotten meat and will feed on a stored carcass over several days.

Leopards scavenge if they get the chance and can steal kills from cheetahs, lone hyaenas and any of the smaller carnivores.

A female leopard on heat attracts males by the smell of her urine. The male and female may stay together for several days, even sharing food, and they mate repeatedly over a few days. Leopard cubs are born in caves, hollow trees or holes in the ground, and their eyes open after six days. Their mother may move them to a new den every two to three days to avoid predators. She brings solid food to her cubs when they are about six weeks old, at four months she takes them hunting with her and they make their first kills about a month later. Families may stay together for 18 months to two years, and even after they have split up meetings between them remain friendly.

Lion   *Panthera leo* No. 249

To avoid the heat of the day lions are most active at night. Nevertheless they show their full behavioural repertoire in daylight as well, especially in the cool of the morning and evening. They are mostly ground-living but will climb trees to take advantage of cool breezes and to get away from flies.

Lions are the only cats in which close-knit social groups are almost universal, and the only ones that regularly hunt in groups. The basic unit of lion social life is a pride, which consists of two groups, one of four to 12 closely related females and their cubs, and another of one to six males who are often closely related to each other but not to the females. The females form the stable core of the pride while the males are exchanged every few years. Most prides contain about a dozen adults, but groups are smaller where conditions are less favourable, e.g. the Kalahari, and larger where prey is abundant and reliable. The members of a pride do not always move around together and individuals or small sub-groups may operate independently for days or weeks.

Lion prides with a rich, reliable food supply can afford to be territorial. Where their prey are migratory lions tend to follow the herds, and where the food supply is sparse and unpredictable the prides have huge home ranges that are too large to defend. In all these cases encounters between lions from different prides are hostile, but actual fighting is rare, one party leaving the scene under the watchful eye of the other.

Both lions and lionesses signal their pride's occupation of an area by scent-marking with urine and faeces and by roaring. The urine's strong, tomcat smell hangs in the air of places heavily used by lions. Roars can carry for a good 8 km and are also used to attract straying members of the pride. A richly-resonant grunt is used as a close-range contact call.

Lions eat almost any animal from termites to elephants. Their favoured prey are medium and large antelopes in the 50 to 300 kg range. They do not always simply catch the most common prey, wildebeest seem to be popular and waterbuck are not favoured. Such preferences may be passed on as a pride tradition. Lions can, and do, hunt successfully alone but when they hunt as a group for medium-sized prey their success rate goes up from one successful stalk in five to six, to one in three. With larger prey such as buffalo, single lions do not even bother to attack. The degree of co-ordination among the hunting lions varies with circumstances, and probably from pride to pride. Typically a group of the pride's females stalk in line abreast of a single animal or a herd. When within range one of the lionesses charges, which is a signal for the rest to close in on the flanks. A lone target thus finds at least half its escape routes blocked by lionesses, and the panic reaction of a herd, which effectively confuses a single hunter, is as likely to send its members dashing into danger as out of it. In a hunt aimed at a herd of smallish antelope such as impala, each lioness in the team may select and pursue

Group hunting enhances lions' success in securing large dangerous prey.

her own victim. If a larger, tougher animal is the quarry the combined efforts of several lions may be needed to pull it down and kill it. More advanced co-oper-ation can be seen when one lioness moves to the opposite side of the quarry from the rest of the group and flushes it towards them.

Lions can run at 58 km/h which is too slow to catch antelope in an open chase. Attacks are seldom launched from more than 20 m and chases longer than 200 to 300 m are rare, although much longer ones sometimes occur.

Lions often lie in ambush at water holes, especially ones like those on the fringe of the Etosha Pan, which are the only reliable source of water in a large area.

All else being equal lions hunt more successfully in long grass and thick bush, when the quarry is alone, when they are able to stalk close, and on very dark nights.

Pride males do not usually hunt, as their manes and large size make them more conspicuous and less successful than lionesses. Instead they live off the efforts of their females, using their dominant status to appropriate food. Males have to fend for themselves both before they take over a pride and after they have been displaced from one. Young males may form small bachelor groups that hunt to-gether but lone males are restricted to smaller, easier prey such as warthogs and porcupines and the young of other species. Old, solitary males are often pep-pered with black spots marking the scars from porcupine quills.

A lion usually kills by a strangling throat hold or by clamping its mouth over its prey's muzzle. Lions in the Kalahari have a specialised way of dealing with gemsbok; they first cripple them by leaping onto their hindquarters, biting into the back and jerking upwards to break the spine at a weak spot. The Kalahari lions are also accomplished hunters of porcupines, whose prickly defences they overcome by attacking from two directions at once. Lions may dig warthogs out of shallow burrows.

Lions readily take carrion. They can locate kills by either smell or sound and by watching vultures. Unless they are heavily outnumbered they can displace any other carnivore from its prey.

When plenty of food is available lions gorge themselves into near immobility. Males swallow up to 35 kg, and females up to 22 kg which is 15 per cent of their body weight, at a sitting. This is five times their average daily needs. They are extremely aggressive while feeding; snarling, pawing and snapping at one another. The pride males dominate the females, and may drive them off the kill, but they are more tolerant of the cubs who are their offspring. Even so, in the scrum around a kill the cubs usually fare badly, and starvation is their main cause of death. Cubs that are too young to accompany the hunt are brought to the kill by their mother after she and the rest of the pride have fed and little, if anything, is left over.

Although lions groom themselves and each other they are not as thorough as small cats, and most of them are infested with ticks and bloodsucking flies.

AFRICAN MAN-EATERS

Although they have not achieved the infamy of the notorious man-eating tigers and leopards of the Indian hill country, Africa has had, and still has, its share of large carnivores who turn to people as easy prey.

Most historical records of man-eating are mixed up with tales of ritual murders by mysterious lion cults, and of malign spirits in predators' bodies.

'Man-eaters' of course also eat women and children; one male lion who operated around Msandile actually concentrated his attacks on children, presumably because they were easier than adults to catch and not as dangerous, but even then he only managed to kill two of them.

Perhaps because Africa is not as densely populated, or cases are not as well reported, the lists of victims of individual African man-eaters are much shorter than those of Indian man-eating tigers and leopards. 'Chiengi Charlie' took at least 90 human victims, and Namvelieza, 'the cunning one' took 43 around Kasawa in Zambia. A man-eating leopard in the Golis Mountains claimed 100 human victims and the Chambisi (Zambia) leopard killed 67.

Most man-eating lions have been single individuals but between 1900 and 1910 a pride of man-eaters took a toll of 10 lives per year from the Mporokose area. The most terrible devastation was wrought by a man-eating lion pride, which killed around 2 000 people in the Njombe district of Tanzania between 1932 and 1947.

The two Tsavo man-eaters plagued the labour gangs building the railway from Mombasa to Uganda for the last nine months of 1898. Man was their preferred prey, and they ignored live baits until all humans were made inaccessible in wagons or on top of water tanks. At one stage they were striking once or twice a night and work on the railway ground to a halt for three weeks. The lions' victims were in unprotected camps scattered along 13 km of track, and through repeated exposure to humans, and successful hunts, the lions lost all fear of man and ignored attempts to drive them away with sticks, stones and firebrands. They were finally shot over bait by Lieutenant-Colonel J.H. Patterson when their tally of known human victims stood at 28.

In 1900 at Kima station about 70 miles from Nairobi, a man-eating lion tried to break in through a tin roof. Later he ate a railway worker and broke into a carriage and killed one of three hunters sitting up for him. In a sort of poetic justice he was finally caught in a cage trap.

A lioness becomes sexually receptive for two to four days about once every two years if she raises her cubs to weaning. If she loses her cubs she comes into heat within as little as four weeks. The pride males detect her condition by scent and begin to associate closely with her. Between the males within a pride there is noticeably little sexual rivalry but savage and sometimes fatal fights occur if an intruding male is encountered. Either the male or the female may intitiate mating, the male by testing the female's odour and showing Flehmen, by grooming her, or by simply mounting, and the female by crouching in front of the male or by rubbing against him. Mating occurs about four times an hour over a period of one to two days and lasts for less than a minute each time. The male uses a somewhat ritualised neck bite only in the final moments of mating and the female's reaction to his withdrawal, though agonistic, is less violent than in other cats. After mating both male and female may roll on the ground, groom or rub against each other. As the number of matings increases the initiative passes more and more to the female, who may turn her attentions to one of the other pride males when the first one is worn out. It is this superabundance of sexual opportunities that keeps inter-male rivalry at low levels.

When it is time to give birth a lioness leaves her pride and has her cubs in thick

Leopards turn man-eater much more rarely than lions – possibly because they are smaller and better able to keep themselves fed in areas where large game has been displaced by agriculture. They very rarely become specialist man-eaters; human flesh is just one of the items in their varied diet of large and small herbivores and small carnivores. There is one intriguing thing about man-eating leopards – of 152 of them, 94 per cent were males.

Spotted hyaenas have the nasty habit of eating without killing. They bite a chunk from whatever part of a sleeping human they can conveniently get at and then flee.

Until they have become seasoned man-eaters it is extremely rare for wild carnivores to break into closed dwellings – they even stay out of tents. Open doors are an invitation to trouble though, and a leopard can easily get through the average lavatory window, and just as easily through an open car window. If you are in an unfenced camp it is safest to sleep in a tent with the door zipped up, or in a vehicle with the windows just ajar. If you have to sleep outside it is best to post a guard.

By no means are all man-eaters old or crippled animals forced to turn to people because they can no longer kill more worthy prey. The Tsavo man-eaters were prime males, probably waiting for a chance to take over a pride. The man-eating lion prides of Mporonkose and Njombe had nothing remarkable about them except their diet. On the other hand a lion that turned on and ate some children who tried to chase it away because they thought it was a hyaena, was a large female who had been injured in a fight. A starving two-year-old lioness killed five people in two days in the Kruger National Park where, overall, about half the man-eating lions have been old or in poor condition. Man-eating leopards are nearly always fit and healthy.

Man-eating is a behavioural aberration; in all respects except their choice of prey man-eaters are indistinguishable from thousands of other predators that stick to wild meat. What makes a particular predator turn to human prey can never be known for certain. Hunger and disability are obvious contributing factors in many cases. Otherwise a youngster might learn from its mother or group-mates, or a human killed in anger or fear might be sampled and found tasty. Sometimes man's own activities provide both motive and opportunity to formerly ordinary predators and scavengers. The casualties of war or famine provide both carrion and defenceless prey. Recent problems with man-eating lions in the Tunduru region of Tanzania have arisen when natural game has been forced out by farming, and lions who have had to turn to domestic stock for food have attacked people as well.

Lions mate four times an hour over one to two days.

cover where they remain hidden for one to two months before being introduced to the rest of the group. A mother may carry her cubs to a new refuge every so often – probably to avoid predators. The cubs' introduction to the pride will be delayed if cubs are already present who are more than about a month older and who would dominate the newcomers in competition for their mother's milk. All the lactating females in a pride suckle cubs indiscriminately, showing no favouritism for their own offspring. Thus one lioness may be seen suckling cubs of obviously different sizes. This collaborative behaviour probably stems from the close genetic relatedness among a pride's females, each lioness is enhancing her own genes' success by helping to raise her sisters' offspring. Cubs start to eat meat at about three months and are weaned at about six months.

Cubs stay with their mothers for about two years, by which stage they have joined the pride's hunting trips. Females stay within the pride all their lives but males either leave of their own accord or are driven off by the pride males at two to three years of age. If a small group of males can leave together they are able to hunt as a group and stand a better chance of being able to take over a pride. After one to two years of nomadic life these young males drive out the resident males of a pride and take over the females. At this stage savage fighting occurs which is not uncommonly fatal. The displaced males seldom live long since they no longer have lionesses to hunt for them. After a takeover the new males kill any cubs in the pride so that their mothers come quickly back into breeding condition. The loss of their cubs is obviously detrimental to the females and there is evidence that females prefer their pride to be controlled by a large coalition of males whose strength in numbers will give them a longer tenure. Single males manage to hold onto their prides for an average of a year, coalitions of two for one and a half years, coalitions of three for three and a half years, and of four to six for four to eight years. The longest known tenures are about ten years.

Caracal

Caracal are quite strictly nocturnal and solitary; males and females associate only for mating and families split up as soon as the young are able to fend for themselves. It is not certain whether they are territorial – in conservation areas they occupy stable home ranges but in farming districts their high mortality in control operations tends to disrupt their spatial organisation. Caracals of both sexes spray urine and either bury their faeces or leave them exposed on tracks and pathways, probably to show that an area is occupied. They leave visual and scent signals when they sharpen their claws on wood or bark. Adult males are usually battle-scarred but whether the fights are over territories or females is not known.

Caracal hiss, snarl and spit when threatened and purr when happy. Its black markings and the black backs of its tufted ears make a caracal's face strikingly expressive, especially when its ears are turned down or back in aggressive or defensive threat.

A caracal's threat expression is emphasised by its black facial markings.

Caracal are typically feline in that they take a wide range of food from insects to small antelope, and capture their prey by stalking to within about 5 m, then chasing and pouncing. They kill by biting either the nape of the neck or the throat. Larger prey are usually attacked at the throat and death is caused by haemorrhage as much as by strangulation. Caracal, especially adult males, are very solidly built and strong for their size and are easily capable of handling adult sheep and goats and antelope up to the size of mountain reedbuck and springbok. Their long back legs give them great jumping powers and in captivity at least they are able to snatch flying birds from the air. Whether they use this technique in the wild is unknown. Caracal have been known to engage in mass killings, probably in response to the presence of large numbers of frightened, fenced-in targets.

Caracal do not usually scavenge but in areas where they are not disturbed they will return to feed again on a large kill, perhaps having covered it with vegetation or debris. In farming areas they rarely do this, possibly because the behaviour has been selected against by generations of poisoned carcasses or because of the disturbance that follows the discovery of predator-killed stock. They do not eat the guts of large prey, concentrating instead on the meat of the hind legs and shoulders. Both the skin and stomach of dassies are discarded.

Caracal are agile climbers, which makes them more difficult to control than black-backed jackals because they can easily climb over ordinary fences, and overhangs or electrified strands are needed to keep them out.

Males are attracted by smell to females on heat. A caracal mother has her young in a cave, rock crevice, or thick vegetation but the course of their upbringing is not yet known. Older cubs go with their mother on hunting trips and it is most likely at this stage that prey preferences are passed on, influencing whether the youngsters will grow up to be stock raiders or not. It is also possible that a young caracal learns how to avoid traps by watching its mother. When they become independent, young female caracal disperse over relatively short distances and establish home ranges. Young males travel much further, often tens of kilometres, and it is mainly these itinerant animals that get trapped – the residents in an area manage to survive there only because they know how to avoid such hazards.

Because they kill small stock caracal share with black-backed jackal the dubious distinction of being the most serious pest of sheep and goat farming in southern Africa. Although the caracal's behaviour has never been studied in enough detail to be certain, comparisons with other carnivores suggest that stock killing is a specialisation of individual caracal while others in the same population stick to a diet of rodents, dassies and so on. Prey preferences, and thus problem behaviour, may be passed on from mother to offspring. The most economical way of controlling damage by caracal would be to remove only the stock killers, leaving the rest to carry on reducing the numbers of problem herbivores that compete with farm stock for grazing. To develop efficient ways of aiming control only at problem individuals more detailed information on caracal behaviour is needed.

African wild cat   *Felis lybica* No. 251

Although it conducts most of its business at night there is a good chance of seeing a wild cat during the day, especially in the cool of early morning or in the evening. They rest in any convenient hole in the ground, in hollow trees, among rocks, or in dense vegetation. Wild cats live alone nearly all the time, and families and mating pairs are the only groups that can be expected to be seen.

Whether or not African wild cats are territorial has never been investigated; one male which was tracked by radio in Kenya had a home range of 1,6 km². Depending on how rich the food supply is, and how many cats are in an area, they are probably more likely to live in overlapping home ranges than in territories. Both male and female African wild cats spray-mark with urine and they may bury their faeces, leave them exposed on tracks and pathways or accumulate them in middens. All these behaviours probably have some connection with their use of space.

An African wild cat's vocal signals are virtually the same as a domestic cat's. It purrs when happy, mews to establish contact, and growls, snarls, hisses and spits in defensive threat. Its facial expressions and body postures are also the same as a domestic cat's.

An African wild cat hunts and kills in typical felid fashion by stalking up close to its prey, rushing at it, pouncing to secure a grip with the claws of its front feet, and delivering a killing bite either to the back of the neck, chest and head, or to the throat. The size of the prey determines where it will be bitten – throat bites are used on larger species. An African wild cat can kill mammals up to the size of dassies and rabbits and even the young of small species of antelope such as steenbok, as well as birds up to about guinea fowl size, but small rodents and arthropods are its usual targets. Whether or not it will eat carrion is uncertain.

A male wild cat probably locates females on heat by the smell of their urine. The male leaves after mating and does nothing to help raise the kittens.

African wild cats living in Egypt from 3 000 to 4 000 years ago were the ancestors of domestic cats. Even today domestic cats and African wild cats are so similar that they interbreed with complete freedom and are considered by some authorities to be the same species. In fact the most serious threat to the genetic integrity of wild cat populations is interbreeding with domestic cats.

The adjustment of the wild cat to life with man has involved changes not so much in size and shape as in behaviour. It is quite likely that the wild cats moved into farms and villages of their own accord to feed on the hordes of rats and mice that plagued ancient granaries. Under these conditions cats that tolerated human disturbance and the presence of other cats would have fared better than those that were more nervous and less gregarious. In time the populations of cats around human settlements would have become behaviourally domesticated, probably before they became visibly different from their wild forebears. Even by the time the cat came to be revered as a deity by the Egyptians, its skeleton was still the same as the African wild cat's.

Artificial selection by man for particular coat colours and body shapes has probably occurred only over the past few hundred years and the domestic cat is more uniform in size and shape than any other domestic animal. Their social behaviour is much more variable. They are as solitary as their wild ancestors and relatives when food is scarce, while under the right conditions of concentrated, rich food sources they form tightly knit social groups that outdo lions in the complexity of their interaction patterns.

Small-spotted cat   *Felis nigripes* No. 252

Except that they are nocturnal and solitary, almost the only thing that is known about this tiny cat's behaviour in the wild is its reputation for using holes in termite mounds as dens.

Serval   *Felis serval* No. 253

Serval are nocturnal but they can sometimes be seen in the cool of early morning or late afternoon. Male and female servals sometimes hunt together, presumably as a prelude to mating and young servals accompany their mother on hunting trips. The rest of the time they are solitary. They live in overlapping home ranges which, for males, cover two to three square kilometres. At least some of their faeces are left exposed, probably as a signal of the serval's presence.

Various aspects of a serval's behaviour reflect its specialisation for hunting small rodents in thick grass. A hunting serval uses its large ears to locate its quarry by sound, and pounces in a high, curving leap that carries it above the intervening grass and down onto its prey with enough force to stun or kill it. It

The high, curving leap of a serval's pounce carries it above the long grass of its usual habitats.

may also scoop up its quarry with one paw and catch it in mid-air in its mouth. This contrasts with the usual felid pounce, which is an almost horizontal thrust with the hind paws remaining firmly on the ground. It also attacks with a hard downward slap of a forepaw. When hunting vlei rats and canerats, which live in swampy areas, a serval will paddle about in water up to 8 cm deep.

Female serval apparently prefer clumps of vegetation to holes as places to have their kittens. If they can they carry the kittens away when danger threatens.

Family   CANIDAE
Wild dogs, foxes and jackals

Bat-eared fox   *Otocyon megalotis* No. 255

Bat-eared foxes are active at any time of the day or night, although they prefer to spend the hottest hours in burrows or the shade of bushes. They dig their own burrows or take over and adapt springhare and aardvark holes.

They live in closely bonded pairs that sleep and move around together. Neighbouring pairs have widely overlapping home ranges and they congregate peacefully at large patches of food.

Bat-eared foxes get about 80 per cent of their food from insects, especially termites, although they also eat other sorts of arthropods, small rodents, reptiles and fruit. Their speciality is to hunt for succulent, subterranean beetle larvae. A bat-eared fox locates these by sound; it meanders along, turning its head and huge ears from side to side until it hears something promising. It fixes the position of the sound source and approaches with its ears pricked forward and its head lowered. As it gets closer it almost touches the ground with its nose and the tips of its ears and it can locate the grub so precisely that it can dig directly down to it. The digging action is a fast scratching with alternate front paws, which leaves an economically narrow hole. Food on the soil surface is probably also located by sound rather than sight – something that stays still and quiet will often escape notice. Inanimate food such as berries must be located by sight and smell. A bat-eared fox that finds a rich patch of food calls its mate with a high-pitched whine.

A bat-eared fox greeting another holds its head slightly down with its neck extended and ears back and points its muzzle at the corner of the other's lips. The recipient stands with its head high and tail down. Mutual lip nuzzling is a common, friendly interaction. A submissive bat-eared fox crouches with its tail flat on the ground. Bat-eared foxes threaten jackals and African wild cats by fluffing up their fur and arching their backs and tails. They mob jackals and brown hyaenas and give a high-pitched bark to attract mates and neighbours to join in the harassment.

Bat-eared foxes are unusual in that they are playful as adults in the wild. The members of a pair will play-chase or fight with fierce-sounding growls, or one of them will play with some object, perhaps throwing a stick or vigorously attacking a tuft of vegetation.

Both sexes of bat-eared fox scent-mark with drops of urine. This may be a signal to other bat-eared foxes that an area is occupied, or a record for its own use of the marker's movements. In captivity they mark unfamiliar objects once they have established that they are harmless.

Bat-eared foxes have their cubs in the burrows they use for general refuges. Up to an age of about three weeks the babies stay underground. Both the mother and the father begin to bring them solid food when they are about four weeks old and the young then start to make short trips away from the den under the watchful eye of their parents, who growl to call them back. From an age of about three weeks the cubs emerge from their burrow when the parents are away but flee

A bat-eared fox locates buried grubs by sound.

back to it at the slightest sign of danger. If a cub is attacked by a predator it gives a high-pitched, chattering alarm call which brings its parents running to its assistance. Bat-eared fox cubs first go with their parents on hunting trips when they are about 10 to 12 weeks old. At this stage the family becomes nomadic, shifting every few days to a new den, possibly to avoid predators or to find better feeding grounds. The cubs leave their family when they are about seven months old.

Black-backed jackal   *Canis mesomelas* No. 259

In areas where they are not disturbed, jackals can be seen at all times of the day and night. They are most active in the early morning and evening and they tend to avoid the midday heat by lying up in holes or in the shade of vegetation. This activity pattern matches that of their small mammal prey. In settled areas jackals become strictly nocturnal because of control measures to keep their numbers down. They are less active at the full moon or the dark of the moon.

Black-backed jackals live alone, or in small groups. Usually they are solitary or live in pairs that stay together for life. The large numbers that gather at carcasses are temporary aggregations with no lasting social structure. Family groups can be seen foraging together.

In line with their wide habitat tolerance and varied diet, black-backed jackals' movement patterns are also very variable. They live in overlapping home ranges or territories of up to nearly 20 km². Mated pairs are territorial and some individuals are wanderers, moving over 80 km in four nights. Settled jackals cover seven to 12 km in a night's foraging.

In territorial pairs the female chases out intruding females and the male deals with intruding males. Home range and territorial boundaries tend to break down when food is scarce or when it becomes very abundant in a particular spot, such as with the death of a large herbivore, or at the seal colonies on the West Coast. In

An agonistic interaction between two black-backed jackals. The one on the left is dominant and more aggressive while the one on the right is defensive.

A black-backed jackal's pounce is a typically canine curving leap.

farming areas the rapid turnover of jackals due to control measures keeps their spatial organisation in a state of continual flux.

Both male and female black-backed jackals scent-mark with urine. A male and female who are foraging together mark the same places.

A black-backed jackal's most distinctive call is a drawn out, almost siren-like 'yaaaaa-aa-aa', which advertises its presence and may be answered by its neighbours. Each family is attracted only to the contact calls of its own members. Under threat they 'gekker' and the puppies whine when they are hungry. Adults give a rumbling growl, or bark, to warn their puppies to get back to the den.

Black-backed jackals also communicate by facial expressions and body postures. An aggressive jackal points its ears forward, wrinkles the skin on its snout and exposes its canines by lifting its lips. A submissive one flattens its ears back, narrows its eyes and exposes its teeth by pulling the corners of its mouth back. These signals intergrade with each other to produce a wide range of expressions of the jackal's feelings. A jackal also signals with its tail, tucking it between its legs in fear or submission, swishing it tensely from side to side in aggression and arching it upwards when excited.

A group of jackals around a carcass provides a good opportunity to watch these social interactions.

Despite their reputation as scavengers jackals in most areas catch nearly all their own food – otherwise they would not be able to survive where there are no large carnivores. They eat anything from fruit through insects, rodents, birds and reptiles to small antelope. They even catch catfish and mullet in drying pools and lagoons.

When after small prey a black-backed jackal walks slowly, looking and listening carefully. When prey is located the jackal pounces with a high, curving leap, pins it down with its forepaws and bites it across the back – a style of attack seen in nearly all canids. Hares and baby antelope are bitten with a chopping snap across the back and shoulders, whereas larger prey is attacked at the throat or may be disembowelled. Canids do not have the same precise killing bite as cats. A single jackal is usually unsuccessful when hunting baby antelope because in five out of six hunts the mother chases it off. Operating as a pair the jackals' success rate goes up to two in three because one jackal decoys the mother while the other deals with the baby. On the Namib coast single jackals kill seal pups up to five months old and older pups are tackled by jackal pairs. Packs of jackals in Botswana will select an old or sick impala from a herd, bring it to bay and kill it by biting the large veins of its neck and belly.

Black-backed jackals can locate carrion by smell from a kilometre downwind, and probably from even further away by the sounds of large carnivores squabbling over their food, and by watching vultures. How jackals behave around a carcass depends on circumstances – if food has been abundant in the recent past they usually wait for the larger carnivores to move off before feeding – but then they have to contend with vultures. A jackal that has been short of food may dash in, grab a portion of meat and carry it away to feed. Jackals are fast and very agile and can usually dodge any counterattacks from larger species. If the jackals are persistent a large carnivore may waste more time chasing them off than it spends in feeding and they may then grudgingly be allowed to share the carcass. A jackal who is fortunate enough to have a food surplus may bury some of it for later consumption. On the Skeleton Coast the jackals have favourite feeding spots in the shelter of hummocks of vegetation, where the remnants of their unselective scavenging accumulate.

Jackals drink if they can, but they can survive for weeks without water by eating moist fruits. In the Namib they lick settled fog.

Jackals are unusual in that they form stable pairs in which both parents contribute significantly to the care of the young. Females use holes in the ground, usually dug by aardvarks, as dens for their pups. Until the pups begin to wean the male helps to guard them and brings food to his mate. During weaning both parents regurgitate food for the pups and at two to four months the youngsters accompany their parents on foraging trips. In southern Africa young jackals disperse when about two years old, but in stable jackal populations in East Africa young jackals from previous litters may stay to help raise their baby brothers and sisters. This is probably because the helpers cannot breed until they secure a territory of their own, and they make the best use they can of the time they have to wait for one to fall vacant.

Black-backed jackals are notorious stock predators, especially in sheep and goat farming areas. They are difficult to control because they readily learn to avoid human activity, and traps and poisoned baits. Some stock killers have become so skilled at avoiding control measures that they have become known as 'super jackals'. A black-backed jackal is able to learn by watching other jackals – if it sees another sniff and reject a poisoned bait it will do the same, or try a small portion that will make it sick but not kill it, and so drive the lesson home. Such transmission of learned behaviour is probably especially important between mates, and even more so between mother and offspring. A super jackal mother will, therefore, raise her cubs as super jackals who will thrive at the expense of their less skilled neighbours who fall foul of blanket control measures. The proportion of super jackals in the population will then increase, as indeed it is already increasing in parts of the Cape Province and Namibia, and the number of jackals and the damage they cause will become more and more difficult to control by the blanket methods that caused the problem in the first place.

Side-striped jackal
Canis adustus No. 258

The behaviour of side-striped jackals has not been studied in nearly as much detail as that of the black-backed jackal. Side-striped jackals are quite strictly nocturnal; they live alone, in pairs or family groups or, exceptionally, in packs.

Side-striped jackals are omnivorous with a leaning towards plant foods. Their hunting activities and behaviour at carcasses are probably similar to those of black-backed jackals. They follow baboon troops to glean the fruit that drops from the treetops.

Side-striped jackals are less vocal than black-backed jackals, although they yap, and chatter under stress. Hungry puppies whine. Both males and females scent-mark with urine; the male cocks his leg to do so and the female half-crouches.

Side-striped jackal puppies are born in converted aardvark burrows, but if there is serious disturbance the mother carries them to a new site.

Cape fox
Vulpes chama No. 257

Although nearly all their activity is at night these little foxes can quite often be seen near their den entrances in the early morning or resting in the shade during the day. Except for females with cubs they are solitary and live in overlapping home ranges that are heavily urine-marked but, apart from a small area around the den, not defended.

They are active hunters of small rodents and arthropods and also take wild fruits and berries. They dig mice out of their burrows and lick termites from the soil surface. They seldom take carrion. Excess food is cached in holes in the ground and covered with soil, which the fox carefully tamps down with its nose.

A Cape fox will give a high-pitched howl, probably as a long-range contact call, which another may answer with a bark. Barking is also an alarm signal. Under threat a fox snarls and spits. As its level of excitement rises so does its tail, until it is curled forward over the fox's back. The tail's black tip makes its movements more obvious. The Cape fox also has black tips on its ears, which signal stress and aggression. A fox that is about to attack another lays its ears back and holds its head low with its mouth open.

The black patch near the root of a Cape fox's tail covers its caudal scent gland, the function of which is unknown.

A female Cape fox always squats to urinate, whereas a male sometimes squats and sometimes cocks a leg.

Cape fox cubs are born in holes in the ground, often expropriated springhare burrows.

Wild dog
Lycaon pictus No. 256

Wild dogs are active during the day because they hunt by sight, although they sometimes take advantage of bright moonlight to hunt at night. Like most animals they tend to rest in the shade during the hottest part of the day.

Wild dogs live in packs whose close-knit social structure is one of the peaks of mammalian social organisation. A pack can consist of anything from two to over 50 dogs, but most of them have about a dozen adult members. Each pack occupies an enormous home range, about 450 km^2 in the Kruger National Park and in East Africa up to 4 000 km^2. A pack's movements around its range are probably governed by the location of prey. While its puppies are too young to travel a pack operates from a fixed base. Occupation of an area is signalled by scent-marking, which allows neighbouring packs to avoid meeting. On the rare occasions that meetings do occur they range from friendly to aggressive, though actual fighting is very rare. How two packs react to each other probably depends on their familiarity and genetic relatedness and on how good the hunting has been.

A wild dog pack is headed by a dominant male and female who, in the vast majority of cases, account for all the breeding activity. The rest of the pack consists of the offspring of the current or previous alpha pair with, exceptionally, an immigrant female. Wild dogs are unusual in that it is the females who disperse while the males remain in their natal pack to become helpers while they wait for the loss of the dominant male to give them a chance to breed.

Below the alpha pair there is no definite hierarchy; submissiveness, not aggression, is the deciding factor in wild dog competitive interactions. A wild dog who wants a piece of meat that another is eating begs for it with head and forequarters flat to the ground, hindquarters raised, tail arched and maybe wagging, ears flattened to its head and lips drawn back. Similar fawning serves as a friendly greeting when the pack sets out to hunt.

A friendly greeting between wild dogs.

Wild dogs are purely carnivorous. They are specialised hunters of medium-sized antelope such as springbok, impala and blue wildebeest but also take animals as small as rabbits and as large as kudu and zebra.

It is in the hunt that the pivotal role of the pack in the survival of wild dogs comes to the fore. They hunt by sight, usually in the cool of early morning or evening and alter their hunting behaviour to suit the prey and the habitat. On the short-grass plains of the Serengeti the dogs make no attempt at concealment; a pack approaches potential prey openly at a trot, or at a careful walk with their heads low and ears back, and breaks into a run only when the prey flees. They may rush a herd to panic it into flight and then stand watching to see if one member of the herd is slower than the rest. The leading dog, who is usually the dominant male or female, selects a particular target and pursues it single-mindedly even if apparently easier victims are passed on the way. The rest of the pack strings out behind the leader; occasionally one of the other dogs chooses a victim of its own and leads some of the dogs on another chase. In the bush of the

Transvaal lowveld dog packs use roads as sight lines and for easy travelling while hunting, pack members split off and comb through the bush alongside the road and may snap up and eat mice and other titbits as they go along. When prey is sighted the dogs sneak up slowly behind bushes. If the quarry scatters, as the most common prey, impala, usually do, the pack splits up and multiple kills may be made.

Wild dogs can reach speeds of 65 to 70 km/h, too slow to catch a medium-sized antelope in a short chase – for that the cheetah's leaping acceleration to 100 km/h is needed – and they depend on their stamina in long pursuits to wear down the prey. Most chases cover 1,3 to 3 km but if they have to the dogs can keep up a speed of 60 km/h for 4 to 5 km. They do not run in relays, which would be impossible anyway because they all start from the same place, but if the prey runs in a curve, as territory holders often do in order to stay on familiar ground, the trailing members of the dog pack gain on it by cutting the corner. The dog that catches up with the prey grabs it and pulls it down if it is small enough or, if not, runs alongside and slashes at its rump or shoulder to slow it down until more dogs catch up. They bite chunks out of the prey and disembowel it so that it dies of shock and loss of blood. Some packs develop specialised hunting techniques that are passed down from generation to generation. In some East African packs a zebra or wildebeest that has been run down is immobilised by one dog holding its nose, which affects it like a twitch on a horse, while the others disembowel it. In the Kruger National Park the wild dogs have no such techniques for dealing with large and dangerous prey and both wildebeest and zebras will stand their ground when dogs approach.

Once a chase starts the prey has only one to three chances in ten of escaping the wild dogs' relentless pursuit compared to a six to eight in ten chance of evading an attack by lions or hyaenas.

When a kill has been made the juveniles rather than the adults are allowed to feed first. Carcasses are consumed quickly without the snarling and bickering that goes on at lion and hyaena kills. This reduces the risk that the carcasses will be stolen by larger predators or vultures. A pack of wild dogs is usually able to keep hyaenas at bay because some of the dogs concentrate on guard duty while the others feed. On the other hand there is a record of a golden jackal, and of warthogs, displacing wild dogs from a kill.

The most important part of the wild dog's hunting and feeding behaviour is the division of the spoils after a carcass has been eaten. A dog that has remained behind at the den to guard the puppies, lost the trail of the hunt or stood guard at a kill, begs food from other members by whining, nudging and nibbling their lips and licking their faces. In response, dogs that have fed regurgitate lumps of meat, sometimes directly into the supplicant's mouth. Weaning puppies are also fed in this way by all the pack members, even by those who have had to beg for the food that they give to the youngsters. So strong is the urge to share food that a single chunk of meat may pass from one dog to another through as many as four or five stomachs. Sick and injured wild dogs also receive a share of meat for as long as they remain with the pack.

Besides the tactile signals used in food begging wild dogs also communicate by sound, scent and visual signals. When they are excited, such as before a hunt or just after a kill, wild dogs give a high-pitched giggly twitter. Their long-range contact call is a tuneful 'hoo-hoo' that carries for 2 to 3 km; they also whine when begging and growl and bark threateningly. Their alarm call is a deep, gruff bark.

Urine scent marks are used to show that an area is occupied and by the dominant female to advertise that she is sexually receptive. The dominant male immediately urinates on top of her scent marks, presumably to deter competitors. Only the alpha male and alpha female cock a leg when urinating. A wild dog's notoriously strong smell probably helps those that have lost their pack to track their way back to it.

Wild dogs do not have expressive faces, but they do communicate by body posture and tail position. A slinking posture with the tail tucked between the legs signals fear and submissiveness, a friendly wild dog has an upright posture and it curls its tail up over its back, an an aggressive one is rigidly upright with its tail stuck out behind.

Wild dog mothers have their pups in holes in the ground, usually in old aardvark diggings. Normally only the dominant female breeds, and if another female also has young the dominant female will harass her and kill her pups. This may be because raising one litter at a time keeps the time for which the pack has to hunt from a fixed base to a minimum. Because males stay in the pack and help raise subsequent litters the sex ratio at birth is 59 males to 41 females. The pups begin to wean at only two weeks of age, when all the pack members regurgitate meat for them. If the mother should die the pups are raised on meat by the rest of the pack. Wild dogs are so attentive to pups that when a cage of captive-bred pups was put out in an attempt to integrate them into a wild pack, the wild adults regurgitated meat and pushed it through the cage bars. Weaning is complete at 10 weeks and by three months the cubs are old enough to leave the den and travel with the pack as its takes up its interrupted nomadic lifestyle. They join in their first hunts when they are about 14 months old.

Family	MUSTELIDAE
	Otters, ratel, polecat and weasel

Cape clawless otter _Aonyx capensis_ No. 260

Cape clawless otters are nearly always seen near or in water, in which they catch most of their food. The water bodies they use range from the sea to strings of shallow pools in the stream beds of dry areas such as the Karoo and northern Cape.

Cape clawless otters are crepuscular with some activity at night and during the day. They make resting places, known as holts, in holes in the ground, among rocks or in the shelter of vegetation. They live singly, in pairs or in groups of up to five which are probably families.

Cape clawless otters live in overlapping home ranges; females use about 14 km of coast and males about 20 km. Within its home range an otter has several holts that it uses for a few days at a time, probably moving on in response to changes in food supply. Small latrines containing faeces (called spraints) and anal gland secretions are a sign that otters are active in an area.

Although it occasionally takes waterfowl, reptiles, small rodents and insects a Cape clawless otter gets nearly all its food under water in the form of crustaceans, frogs, fish and octopus. It swims around on the surface making dives up to about 30 seconds in duration. It hunts fish by sight, swimming after them with great agility, using its hind feet for propulsion and its tail as a rudder. For obvious reasons it does best with slow-swimming species such as barbel and suckerfish.

Cape clawless otters eat fish from the head backwards.

Prey such as crabs and octopuses, which hide in holes, are felt for with its very sensitive and dexterous forepaws. Except for bony-headed barbel a Cape clawless otter eats fish from the head backwards, unlike spotted-necked otters which start at the tail. Crabs are crunched up and eaten shell and all, whereas water mongooses leave the carapace. When carrying food out of the water a Cape clawless otter holds it against its chest with one paw, whereas a spotted-necked otter carries things in its mouth. A Cape clawless otter which has just finished a meal carefully washes its face and paws in the water.

After a swim a Cape clawless otter dries itself by shaking vigorously and then rubbing itself on rocks, sand and vegetation.

Cape clawless otters are playful even as adults. They chase and play-fight in the water or play with things such as sticks, stones or freshly caught prey.

Female Cape clawless otters have their babies in burrows near water.

Spotted-necked otter   *Lutra maculicollis* No. 261

Spotted-necked otters are crepuscular, with limited activity in darkness or during the day. They are much more dependent on substantial bodies of water than are Cape clawless otters and do not move very far from them. They are even better swimmers than Cape clawless otters and when patrolling they spend about half the time on the surface and half submerged. They hunt by sight for fish, frogs, freshwater crabs and molluscs. Their webbed feet and claws are not well adapted to catching things by feel. Fish are eaten from the tail forwards, the opposite direction to the Cape clawless otter. On land a spotted-necked otter carries food in its mouth. It may carry on fishing after it has eaten its fill and then play with what it catches.

Spotted-necked otters usually live alone but up to five or six may be seen together. These are probably families. Members of such groups groom one another. They probably live in overlapping home ranges. Spotted-necked otters defecate in latrines near the water's edge. A female holds her tail horizontal when defecating and a male holds his vertical.

Under stress a spotted-necked otter discharges a strong-smelling secretion from its anal glands, which probably helps to deter predators.

91

Female spotted-necked otters choose deep, inaccessible holes and crevices or dense reed beds in which to have their young.

Striped weasel   *Poecilogale albinucha* No. 263

Striped weasels are small, secretive and rarely seen. They are intermittently active throughout the day and night, resting up in burrows that they dig themselves or annex from small rodents, probably after eating the original occupant.

Striped weasels are solitary most of the time but pairs, probably a male and female, and females with their young can also be seen moving around together. These family parties may 'caravan', with each animal keeping its nose close to the anal gland of the one in front.

How striped weasels organise their use of space is unknown. In captivity they defecate and urinate in middens; if they do the same in the wild it could have some connection with scent-marking a home range or territory. Striped weasels have anal glands which, besides their social function, are used to produce a defensive spray of strong, unpleasant, clinging, odorous secretion.

Although they readily eat insects striped weasels are apparently specialised for hunting by scent for molerats and other small rodents in their burrows.

Striped polecat   *Ictonyx striatus* No. 264

Striped polecats are nocturnal and solitary. They rest in holes in the ground, in rock crevices, under fallen trees or in dense vegetation. They hunt by sound and smell, sniffing in debris and under loose stones for arthropods and small rodents. Their usual pace is a fast trot with nose to the ground and tail held out behind. They live in home ranges.

If a striped polecat is disturbed it will run to whichever of its refuges is the closest. If hard pressed it fluffs up its long black and white hair, curls its tail over its back and turns away from its opponent while spitting, growling and screeching. As a last resort it squirts a stream of oily secretion from its anal gland. The secretion's odour is shockingly foul and irritating, and it provides a completely effective defence against any mammalian predator. Unfortunately, large numbers of striped polecats are killed on the roads because they stand their ground and spray at approaching cars.

Honey badger or ratel   *Mellivora capensis* No. 262

In undeveloped areas ratels are active at any time of the day and night but they become nocturnal where there is human disturbance.

Ratels are nearly always solitary although sometimes pairs, probably a male and a female, can be seen together. A hunting ratel meanders slowly along, sniffing for prey with its nose close to the ground. When heading for its hunting grounds it travels with a rolling trot. How ratels organise their use of space is unknown, but they probably have overlapping home ranges. They sleep in rock crevices or in holes in the ground that they dig themselves or take over from other animals.

A ratel will eat almost any arthropods and small vertebrates, including rodents, reptiles, amphibians and ground-nesting birds, that it can get hold of. It will clamber into trees to get at birds' nests and bees' honey. A ratel is extremely

THE HONEY BADGER'S HANGERS-ON

A ratel's foraging may be interrupted by a dry, rattling call from a small, greyish bird flying around and frequently settling on nearby branches. The bird is a greater honey guide (*Indicator indicator*) which, so the story goes, has found a bees' nest and needs the ratel to come and break it open. The ratel associates the bird with honey and bee grubs and so follows it. When they reach the hive the ratel breaks into it and plunders the comb, protected by its thick, tough skin from the attentions of the bees. The ratel's messy eating habits mean that plenty of grubs and wax are left over for its honey guide so that both parties benefit from the arrangement. Some doubt has been cast on whether ratels actually follow honey guides. Human honey hunters certainly do, but more observations of honey guides and honey badgers operating together are needed to resolve the issue.

A ratel digging for mice, shadowed by a pale chanting goshawk and a black-backed jackal.

Although they are exceptionally strong, ratels are not particularly fleet of foot, and a resourceful rodent being dug from its burrow can make its escape by dashing past its pursuer. In the Kalahari, hunting ratels are shadowed by pale chanting goshawks (*Melierax canorus*) waiting to snatch up rodents that evade the ratel. More rarely, a black-backed jackal may hang around a ratel that is busy digging up mouse holes; a rather risky undertaking even for an animal as fast and agile as a jackal given the ratel's reputation for ferocity when angered.

Since a ratel can only catch the mice that it can corner in their burrows, the hangers-on are not competing with it for food, and the ratel tolerates their activities. In the case of the pale chanting goshawks there is not much it could do to keep them away.

strong and it uses the long, knife-edged claws of its front feet to dig rodents, scorpions and baboon spiders out of even the hardest ground, and to tear apart rotting logs to get at grubs and beetles. Ratels are notorious for raiding beehives, both natural and domestic, to obtain the bee grubs and pupae as well as the honey. They also break into chicken runs. In their search for bees ratels are reputedly guided by a honey guide bird (*Indicator indicator*) (see p 93), and a ratel digging for mice may be shadowed by other small predators.

Ratels are renowned for their courage and ferocity. Their distinctive black and white pattern is undoubtedly a warning to other animals to stay clear. They have been recorded as killing a blue wildebeest, a waterbuck and a 3 m python, and of putting up savage resistance against a lion. Nevertheless a ratel that pressed home an attack on a retreating python was killed by it. The antelope victims bled to death after having the scrotum torn off.

Under threat a ratel gives a surprisingly high-pitched growl, and may release a foul-smelling secretion from its anal glands. That it uses this secretion to gas bees is probably a myth.

Family   VIVERRIDAE
Genets, civet and mongooses

Small-spotted genet   *Genetta genetta* No. 267

Large-spotted genet   *Genetta tigrina* No. 268

The habits of these two species are as similar as their appearance.

Genets are strictly nocturnal; they do not become active until about two hours after sunset. They are solitary as adults, though family groups can be seen, and probably live in overlapping home ranges. They are very agile climbers and are as much at home in the trees as on the ground.

Male genets scent-mark by pressing their anal glands onto firm surfaces, and the females can recognise a particular male's scent for up to six weeks. Both sexes defecate in middens near their nest holes, the faeces having the same pleasant, musky smell as their anal gland secretions. Anal gland secretion is also released at times of stress.

A genet is an active hunter of mice and insects; it occasionally takes other live prey, or fruit, but it will not scavenge. Its hunting technique is catlike; a careful stalk followed by a rush and a pounce, but it bites its prey several times wherever it can get at it rather than aiming for a precise killing bite like a cat. A genet eats small birds feathers and all, which distinguishes field signs of its activities from those of a cat, which plucks at least some feathers.

Genets rest up and have their young in rock crevices, holes in the ground, tree holes or the roofs of houses. A radio-tracked genet survived a bush fire by sheltering among boulders.

Tree civet   *Nandinia binotata* No. 265

Tree civets are nocturnal and solitary; males fight fiercely if they meet. They are agile climbers and jumpers and spend most of their time in trees. They eat mostly fruit with some birds, mice and insects.

Tree civets rest and have their young in tree holes or among dense foliage and tangled creepers.

African civet
Civettictis civetta No. 266

Civets are nocturnal and terrestrial, although they will clamber into low trees to reach ripe fruit. Except for small family groups they are solitary, they move around on regular pathways and probably have overlapping home ranges. The presence of a civet in an area is signalled by latrines of faeces near its pathways and by the dark, greasy scent marks it makes by pressing its everted anal gland onto smooth surfaces. Although the secretion of these glands, known itself as civet, is prized as a fixative for high-quality perfumes, its odour in the raw state is rankly animalic.

When foraging a civet moves rather slowly with its head down as it sniffs around for food. If disturbed it crouches and freezes or stands still, and then may either slink away or wait until it is approached more closely before suddenly dashing off.

A foraging African civet.

Civets have catholic tastes in food. They are active hunters of mammals up to the size of hares, ground-living birds and arthropods. In some cases at least they eat large numbers of millipedes, whose defensive secretions most carnivores find distasteful. They also eat carrion, fallen fruit, reptiles and amphibians. Indigestible fruit pips, millipede rings and bone fragments accumulate in their middens. A civet's hunting technique is to stalk, rush and pounce. The prey is bitten haphazardly and then sharply shaken or thrown to one side and grabbed again. These tactics are designed to prevent counterattacks by the prey. Fish and frogs are caught in shallow water. Civets are also reported to eat herbivore dung, probably as a source of vitamins. A civet's general purpose teeth are not very effective at slicing meat, so it holds birds and mammals down with its front feet and tears chunks off for swallowing. It does not pluck the feathers of birds.

95

Suricates are highly social; they live in tight-knit groups of up to 30 animals who forage together during the day and sleep together at night. They dig burrows themselves or take them over from ground squirrels or yellow mongooses.

A suricate group consists of a dominant female and her mate and successive litters of their offspring, occasionally with an immigrant from another group.

Suricate groups are extended families. Even while they are sun-basking to warm up before they go foraging they keep a sharp lookout for danger.

Suricate groups are not completely stable. In large groups the dominating influence of the breeding pair is diluted by numbers and one of the non-breeding females may begin to attract the attention of some of the subordinate males. This female and two or three of her 'boyfriends' may, ultimately, leave the group. These splinter groups rarely survive, as they have too few members for effective guarding and they have to keep on the move through unfamiliar terrain in their search for an unoccupied area in which to set up a territory.

Sometimes an outsider moves into a group. A suricate that has lost its own group may find another one and hang around it despite the likelihood of aggressive rebuffs. By persistent approaches it establishes a familiarity with the group and may ultimately be allowed to join. The price of admission is extra babysitting duties, sometimes for two to three days with no breaks for feeding except the short time between the group's return to the den and sunset. A small group that needs an extra guard or babysitter will probably be more likely to accept an immigrant than a large group with plenty of available labour. Immigrants have been known to eventually become the dominant breeders in their adopted groups.

Group members recognise each other by sight and smell. Because they allogroom, sleep together and scent-mark each other, every member of a group comes to share a common odour. Frequent contact is needed to maintain familiarity; a suricate that returns after only a few hours' separation from its group is treated with suspicion until it gets close enough for its body odour to confirm its identity.

Suricates are strictly diurnal. They emerge from their warrens, still noticeably sleepy and stiff in their movements, at sunrise and warm themselves by basking in the sun with their fur fluffed up to expose its black, heat-absorbing roots. They may allogroom, sniff and scratch around the warren or dig some soil from a tunnel but they are distinctly sluggish first thing in the morning. Once they are warm and fully awake they move off on the day's foraging.

Suricates get nearly all their food from arthropods that they dig out of the ground. They readily tackle large scorpions, which they cripple by snapping bites to the claws and body. They bite off the sting before eating the body. Except when chasing the occasional burrowing lizard they do not hunt co-operatively and the only food sharing that goes on is between juveniles and their caretakers.

Every so often each suricate breaks off from its foraging and props itself up on its hindlegs and tail to scan for approaching danger. Except in groups with less than four or five members, there is nearly always a suricate checking the surroundings and, in addition, a sentinel on guard on a nearby vantage point (see pp 100–2).

During the long days of summer suricates escape the worst of the heat by taking a midday siesta in a warren or in the shade of vegetation. Unless there are young babies at the overnight site the group does not usually go back to it during the day. In winter, with fewer daylight hours for foraging and cooler weather, suricates forage right through the day. In mid-afternoon they begin to work their way towards a warren, the one they left if there are babies there or, often, a different one if the whole group is mobile. By moving from site to site they avoid depleting the food supply in a given area.

They reach the warren before sunset and the period until the sun goes down is given over to intense social interactions such as allogrooming, play – especially among the juveniles and young adults, and sitting snuggling up together. Within a few minutes of sunset the whole group disappears into the burrows.

Suricate groups are fiercely territorial and neighbouring groups fight pitched battles over the position of boundaries. Occupied areas, especially warrens in border areas and the sites of disputes are heavily marked with anal gland secretion by all members of the group. Anal gland marks are made by lifting one hindleg and wiping the gland downwards on a firm surface.

A suricate group's battle tactics involve co-ordinated behaviour by all its members. The first to spot another group gives a long, peeping call that gets the others to look in the same direction. They bunch together, leap up and down and scrabble up clouds of dust to show off their strength and determination, rush at the other group and, if they catch them, take them on in single combat. The large, high-ranking males apparently act as battle leaders. Suricates that become separated from their group during fights provide most of the immigrants to other groups.

The suricates in a group also work as a team against terrestrial predators. Large snakes are surrounded and harried until they flee or are exhausted and can be killed and eaten. Against jackals and foxes suricates bunch tightly together and, with hissing growls, move forward with an exaggerated springing action that gives the impression of a single large, furry creature, in the face of which the predator retreats. Against raptors suricates have no effective counterattack, relying instead on relays of guards that keep watch until the group is safely underground (see pp 100–2).

Only the dominant pair in a suricate group breed, although the whole group is heavily involved in caring for the offspring. The lack of sexual activity among the lower ranks seems to be a result of the physiological effects of attacks by the dominant animals.

While she is pregnant or lactating the mother is excused all other duties so that she can spend as much time as possible feeding. The babies stay at the den for their first month when they are guarded by their grown-up, subordinate siblings. These babysitters take turns to spend a day at the den with no opportunity to forage. It is a clear indication of the strength of the social bonds within a suricate group that they actually compete for a chance to babysit.

After three weeks the babies get their first solid food and a week later they begin to go with the group on foraging trips. Each baby has a caretaker who catches its food, makes sure that it does not wander off, and teaches it how and what to hunt. The youngsters soon begin to catch some of their own food but self-sufficiency comes slowly and even when they are half grown they may scrounge an occasional meal from one of the adults.

Selous' mongoose   *Paracynictis selousi* No. 270

Selous' mongooses are strictly nocturnal, terrestrial and, except for family groups and mating pairs, solitary. They dig their own burrows. They detect arthropod prey by sound and scent and use their long front claws to dig in soil and plant litter.

Bushy-tailed mongoose   *Bdeogale crassicauda* No. 271

About all that is known about the behaviour of bushy-tailed mongooses is that they are nocturnal, terrestrial and solitary and that they eat mainly insects and reptiles.

Yellow mongoose   *Cynictis penicillata* No. 272

Yellow mongooses are mostly diurnal, emerging from their burrows when the first sun reaches the entrances and returning to them before sunset. They tend to become more nocturnal in areas where there is a lot of human activity. They start their days by sunbathing to warm up before foraging. Yellow mongooses sleep in large burrow systems, moving occasionally from one to another for reasons that are not yet clear, but possibly to get away from parasites. They also have smaller boltholes and daytime refuges scattered around their territories. They may share burrow systems with suricates and ground squirrels. All three species contribute to the digging and benefit from one another's vigilance and alarm calls.

Yellow mongooses live singly, in pairs, or in colonies of up to 50 whose members disperse during the day to forage alone. Depending on location they may be solitary and territorial, colonies may have a group territory, or home ranges may overlap. Territorial yellow mongooses defend their areas by fierce and prolonged battles against intruders. Faeces are concentrated in middens, which might serve to mark occupied areas, and the mongooses mark objects with anal gland and cheek gland secretions, sniffing the site thoroughly before and after marking. They also rub and roll against scent marks and old faeces – possibly to anoint themselves with a colony odour. Scent marks are concentrated on territory borders and near the sleeping burrows. Males mark more often than females.

Colony companions groom one another – especially on the back of the head and neck and under the chin where self-grooming cannot reach. A mongoose that wants to be groomed nudges its head under the chin of another.

A colony's males and females have separate dominance hierarchies. When two yellow mongooses meet they approach each other in a crouch, and as they recognise each other the dominant stands while the subordinate remains crouching. They sniff briefly nose to nose and the dominant may push the subordinate down and bite gently at its neck. The subordinate may paw the other's head and, if there is a wide difference in ranks, roll onto its back. While high rank confers preferential access to foraging sites, a subordinate will not give up food it has already secured.

An alerted yellow mongoose waves its head up and down and from side to side as it watches the source of the disturbance; this helps it overcome the handicap of closely spaced eyes in judging distance. If alarmed it gives a short, repeated warning growl that alerts its colony mates without making them flee. A sharp 'tschack' is given if the caller is uncertain about the danger. Sudden, serious danger is signalled by a bark that sends its hearers dashing for cover. A fleeing yellow mongoose holds its white-tipped tail curved upwards – when two make off together they hold their tails higher than do loners. Snakes are harassed by one or more mongooses, who lunge and snap at them.

A yellow mongoose has a varied diet, comprising mostly insects that it detects by sight, sound and smell and takes from the surface or by digging. It also sometimes eats seeds and, to get moisture, succulent plants. It shakes its food to dislodge sand and rubs distasteful prey on the ground to wipe away foul-tasting secretions. Although a yellow mongoose seldom drinks it will do so if it gets the chance, and will also lick the dew from plants.

All the females in a colony breed but because they come on heat at different times a single dominant male is able to monopolise the matings. A yellow mongoose female becomes sexually attractive before she is ready to mate, during which time she screeches at approaching males. When she does become receptive she invites copulation by crouching and holding her tail to one side. Mating takes upwards of five minutes. Juvenile males may also present to adult ones, and be mounted for up to 45 minutes.

All the yellow mongooses in a colony contribute to the babies' upbringing by carrying food to them at the burrows, and accompanying them on their early foraging trips.

KEEPING WATCH: ANTI-PREDATOR VIGILANCE BY SMALL MONGOOSES

There are three species of mongooses in southern Africa that always live in intimately and intricately bonded societies: dwarf mongooses (p 106), suricates (p 96) and banded mongooses (p 105). All three forage by day for arthopods and small vertebrates, most of which they dig out of the ground. If its quarry is well buried a suricate or dwarf mongoose will disappear head first into the hole it is digging, with no chance at all of guarding against a predator's attack from the rear.

While digging for prey a mongoose is very vulnerable to attack from the rear.

Because they are so vulnerable while intent on their foraging two of the social mongoose species – suricates and dwarf mongooses – have an elaborate and highly effective system of co-ordinated guarding. This ensures that at least one sentinel is on duty to watch for predators for the whole of the time that a group is outside the safety of its warrens. A suricate group keeps a guard on duty even during the midday siesta.

Guarding starts when the mongooses emerge first thing in the morning. The first one up stands on its hindlegs with its tail as the 'third leg' of a tripod and looks all around for lurking danger. Hearing the 'all-clear' brings out the rest of the group, and while they warm up and socialise several may be on guard simultaneously. When the group moves out to forage one member stays behind on duty until a new sentinel runs ahead of the group and clambers up to a vantage point on a termite mound, tree or bush.

In a dwarf mongoose group nearly all the guard duty falls to the subordinate, adult males. A dwarf mongoose sentinel spends about 15 to 20 minutes on each duty spell, and, depending on the size of his group, guarding takes up 20 to 30 per cent of his time. Suricates are more egalitarian in their guarding; everybody except a pregnant or lactating mother takes a turn. Duty spells can last up to an hour and the most diligent guarders spend 25 per cent of their time on watch.

If a group has less than four or five adult members it cannot avoid gaps in its guarding schedule, and it is in serious danger of being wiped out by predators unless it can recruit emigrants from other groups.

A sentinel gives a continual all-clear call – a short 'peep' about once every four seconds in dwarf mongooses and a staccato chirp in suricates – that assures the foragers that all is well and saves them even having to look up to check that there is someone on duty. As the foragers get further away from its post, the sentinel calls louder and louder. Even if a predator could eliminate the sentinel before he could give the alarm, the group would be alerted by the sudden silence.

A suricate sentinel.

A dwarf mongoose sentinel directs most of his attention directly away from the direction in which the group is foraging so that he has the best chance of spotting a predator that is sneaking up from behind.

Ground and airborne predators present very different dangers – ground predators can be driven off by co-ordinated counterattacks while raptors can only be avoided or, if the worst comes to the worst and a mongoose is grabbed, a rescue attempt can be mounted. Accordingly the sentinels' alarm calls are predator-specific. Dwarf mongoose sentinels 'tchrr' for ground predators and raptors in trees, and 'tchee' for hunting raptors. A suricate sentinel gives a rasping bark for airborne predators and hoots for danger at ground level. The more immediate the danger, the louder and faster the sentinels call.

As a dwarf mongoose group forages faster and spreads over a larger area more sentinels are sent up, although there are most on duty (perhaps as many as four) when the group is foraging in a bunch at a concentrated food patch.

Dwarf mongoose foragers give short, peeping calls about once every four seconds so that the sentinel can hear where they are. Foraging suricates twitter softly.

A dwarf mongoose sentinel stays at his post until the group is 40 to 60 m away, then looks over his shoulder to check that another sentinel is on duty. If he sees one he jumps down and dashes back to the group to catch up on his foraging. That lone run is perilous – a young adult male is almost twice as likely as one of the rest of the group to fall to a predator.

Baby suricates being escorted across open ground.

As a suricate group forages, babies at the 4 to 6 week 'toddler' stage are escorted between places where safety is a quick scamper away – holes in the ground, fallen trees or dense bushes. When the babies must move across open ground extra sentinels are sent up, the caretakers run back to where the babies are playing and lead and shepherd them in a bunch by the most direct route to the next refuge. The adults on the ground who are escorting the babies frequently stand up to scan the immediate surroundings until the next patch of cover is reached and the group can go back to its foraging.

Large grey mongoose
Herpestes ichneumon No. 273

Large grey mongooses are active mostly during the day and occasionally at night. They are solitary except for male-female pairs and family groups. Both pairs and families have been reported to 'caravan', with the nose of one animal close to the anal gland of the one in front of it.

A frightened large grey mongoose lies flat with its long hair helping to camouflage it. If closely approached or cornered it fluffs up its hair to make itself look bigger and gives a loud, high-pitched, staccato screech.

Their home ranges cover a few square kilometres, whether or not they are territorial is unknown.

Large grey mongooses live in wet areas; they readily hunt in shallow water and are good swimmers.

A large grey mongoose takes a wide range of food, from fruit and insects to hare-sized mammals and guinea fowl-sized birds, including crabs and fish. It cracks birds eggs by throwing them backwards against hard objects. These mongooses are reputed to lure birds within pouncing range by strange antics, such as rearing up and falling sideways, and to approach prey by rolling towards it, but these observations have not been confirmed.

Slender mongoose
Galerella sanguinea No. 274

Slender mongooses are diurnal, they become active about two hours into the morning and return to their dens in holes in the ground, fallen trees or termite mounds before sunset. Their favourite foraging areas are patches of open ground with a fringe of vegetation that they make short forays into. This is why they are so often seen along roads. When alarmed in the open a slender mongoose runs for cover with its body and tail held low. As it reaches relative safety it flicks its black-tipped tail upwards. Why it does this is unknown. Living in the open as they do, slender mongooses are very vulnerable to raptors and they keep a sharp lookout for them. A slender mongoose which sees a bird of prey freezes, then dashes for cover.

Slender mongooses live in overlapping home ranges and an area's males organise themselves into a dominance hierarchy. They are usually solitary but adult males sometimes sleep and forage together. Females are less sociable than males.

In agonistic encounters they spit, snarl, growl and make a buzzing noise. The contact call in male-female pairs is 'huh-nwe'. Both sexes scent-mark by smearing anal gland secretion onto firm surfaces and by cheek rubbing to set the scent of glands just behind the ears. Urine, which is produced a few drops at a time, and faeces which are accumulated in middens, probably also carry odour messages.

A slender mongoose is an active hunter of insects, mice and birds. It is fierce for its size and sometimes tackles snakes up to 1,5 m long, and chicken-sized birds. Nevertheless it will flee from an irate ground squirrel. It also eats fruit and berries, and birds' eggs which it cracks by throwing them backwards against hard surfaces, and it will scavenge from road kills.

A dominant male slender mongoose's home range overlaps those of a few females. He keeps tabs on their sexual condition from their scent marks. He consorts with a female on heat but leaves after mating and has nothing to do with raising the babies.

103

Small grey mongoose *Galerella pulverulenta* No. 275

Small grey mongooses are diurnal with peaks of activity in the morning and afternoon. Except for male-female pairs in the mating season, they are solitary. Youngsters do not leave the den until they are ready to live independently so family groups are not seen.

Small grey mongooses live in overlapping home ranges of 5 to 63 ha. They readily move around in areas of sparse cover, and in places where the vegetation is thick they tend to use paths and open areas and hunt into the fringes of the heavy cover. If disturbed they run for cover but they do not raise their tails as slender mongooses do.

They rest, and probably have their babies, in rock crevices, holes in trees and logs, under debris or in holes dug by other species. Sometimes they move into buildings.

A small grey mongoose has a typical small viverrid diet of invertebrates, mice, small birds and reptiles but there are records of their attacking small antelope lambs. It hunts by sight, sound and scent, poking into vegetation and scratching in leaf litter and other debris. Mice are captured by stalking, rushing and pouncing and are bitten anywhere the mongoose can get hold of. It will scavenge road kills and, presumably, other carrion.

Meller's mongoose *Rhynchogale melleri* No. 276

Meller's mongooses are nocturnal because most of their diet consists of termites, which only come out at night. They are solitary except for mating pairs and families.

Apart from occasional beetles, grasshoppers, other arthropods, reptiles and amphibians Meller's mongooses live entirely on termites which they lick up or scratch out of their mud-covered runs on trees and fallen wood.

White-tailed mongoose *Ichneumia albicaudata* No. 277

White-tailed mongooses are nocturnal and terrestrial. They are usually solitary, although youngsters stay in their family group until they are almost as large as their mother. Where food is very abundant adult females live in groups. They use any convenient hole as a refuge. The males are territorial, whereas females may be territorial or live in overlapping home ranges.

Despite its relatively large size a white-tailed mongoose hunts mainly small rodents, invertebrates, reptiles, amphibians and birds. It also scavenges, but if it should be found eating a lamb, it may well be wrongly blamed for killing it and pointlessly persecuted. Being nocturnal, it finds prey mainly by sound and scent. Scent must be particularly important for finding the underground insects that the mongoose digs up with its long front claws. Herbivore dung provides a favoured place to search for beetles and their grubs.

If disturbed a white-tailed mongoose gives a sharp bark, frizzes up the hair on its back and tail and emits a strong smell that probably comes from its anal glands.

Water mongoose *Atilax paludinosus* No. 278

Water mongooses are crepuscular and solitary. They rest, and probably have their young, among dense vegetation and debris, often in reed beds. Although they are strongly associated with water they sometimes make trips to drier areas. Not surprisingly they swim well.

How they organise their use of space is unknown.

In captivity at least a water mongoose defecates in latrines, which suggests a marking function for its faeces. It also scent-marks with urine and with its cheek glands and anal glands, which open into a closeable pouch around its anus. This is the 'kommetjie' of the Afrikaans name, kommetjiegat muishond. Females anal-mark more than males. A water mongoose can squirt a thin stream of the strong-smelling secretion of its anal glands as a defence against predators.

A water mongoose does most of its hunting on the fringes of water bodies, which can range from strings of pools in riverbeds to swamps, rivers, dams and estuaries. It paddles in shallow water feeling with its dexterous forepaws for food such as crabs and frogs, or sniffs around on land for small rodents, arthropods and so forth. It smashes hard-shelled prey by throwing it against rocks. A water mongoose eats small crabs whole but leaves the carapaces of larger ones. These discarded remnants are a sign that a water mongoose is active in an area.

Banded mongoose   *Mungos mungo* No. 279

Banded mongooses live in groups of up to about 30 animals who sleep together, usually in holes in termite mounds. They come out around sunrise and bask to warm themselves up before the alpha female and her mate lead them off to forage, either as one pack or in smaller groups. Depending on how good the hunting is, a banded mongoose troop may travel from 2 to 10 km in a day.

As they forage the members of a group scatter quite widely but they keep in contact with a continual high-pitched, birdlike twitter. If one banded mongoose spots something dangerous it gives a harsh chittering call to warn the rest of the

A banded mongoose digging for prey.

pack who freeze, stand up on their hindlegs to look around, and then slink silently away into dense vegetation, down holes or to a safe distance away. If surprised at close quarters they scatter at full speed into the nearest available cover, reappearing after a few minutes to look, listen and smell whether the coast is clear. In one case a pack of banded mongooses fled into a tree to get away from a pack of wild dogs.

Banded mongooses do not post guards like suricates and dwarf mongooses, but rely instead only on the extra vigilance provided by more eyes, ears and noses. They do defend each other against predators. When a martial eagle grabbed one member of an East African banded mongoose group and flew to a tree with it, the whole group ran to the bottom of the tree and some of the males began to climb it. The dominant male attacked the eagle which dropped its victim to the ground where it fled with its companions.

Occupied areas are heavily marked with anal gland secretion. Urine is used to mark unfamiliar objects.

Insects make up most of a banded mongoose's diet, with lesser quantities of other arthropods and small vertebrates. They forage by rooting around in leaf litter and amongst vegetation, scratching at likely spots. Prey is detected by sight, smell or sound and buried grubs are quickly unearthed. A banded mongoose's carnassial teeth are not very good for slicing and it has to deal with mice and similar prey by holding them down and tearing chunks off them. It also eats fruit and berries, eggs – which it breaks by throwing them backwards against something hard – and carrion. Piles of dung provide them with rich patches of beetles and their grubs, and a banded mongoose who finds such a pile calls its companions. Prey that produces distasteful secretions, such as a millipede or frog, is rolled around and rubbed in the soil to remove the secretions before it is eaten.

In a banded mongoose pack several females come on heat at the same time. Coutship is rather elaborate; a sexually receptive female rolls on her back in front of a male, rubs against him and anal-marks him. In return he anal-marks her, and since his anal glands are enlarged during the breeding season she becomes heavily daubed with their whitish secretion. The partners also playfully chase, pounce on and nudge one another. During these chases the male holds his tail vertical. Each pair mates repeatedly but the female does not necessarily stick with one partner.

Because mating is synchronised among the females in a pack they all give birth at about the same time. A female suckles any of the babies, apparently without any favouritism towards her own. Until the babies are four or five weeks old one or two of the adults stay with them at the den while the rest of the group goes off to forage. After five weeks the youngsters travel with the pack. The troop's young males catch insects for them. The adults are especially protective of the juveniles, and if danger threatens the whole group bunches together with the young in the middle and moves off in a body.

Dwarf mongoose   *Helogale parvula* No. 280

Dwarf mongooses are highly social, living in colonies of up to about 30 that are strongly territorial. Each territory covers up to a square kilometre and contains several refuges, nearly always in the ventilation shafts of termite mounds, which are used in rotation.

A dwarf mongoose group consists of a dominant, breeding pair, successive litters of their offspring and an occasional immigrant. The dominant female can be recognised by her larger size; she is about 30 per cent bigger than her mate and offspring. Older animals dominate younger ones and within each age group females dominate males, but babies dominate all the adults. In squabbles over food subordinates always defer to dominants. A submissive dwarf mongoose crouches as it approaches the dominant, makes quick, sideways movements of its head, gives a high-pitched twitter and may roll onto its back.

Dwarf mongooses are diurnal, emerging from their resting places after sunrise and returning in the late afternoon or early evening. The alpha female is the first to emerge in the morning. Before they move away to forage they take about a quarter of an hour to sunbathe and socialise by licking and nibbling each other's fur, play-chasing and wrestling. They all defecate in a midden near the termite mound. The alpha female decides when the group sets off, where it forages and which refuge it uses in the evening.

In Kenya dwarf mongooses and hornbills forage together and if the mongooses are late in emerging the hornbills give them a wake-up call and chivvy them so that they start foraging without the usual social session.

Insects are a dwarf mongoose's favourite prey, although it will also eat other arthropods and a variety of small vertebrates. It digs avidly, using the long claws of its forefeet to excavate underground prey, which it detects by scent or sound. It kills both vertebrate and invertebrate prey by bites to the head. Scorpions' stings do not seem to bother dwarf mongooses and they concentrate their attacks on their claws. They eat the stings of small scorpions, but not of large ones. Dwarf mongooses do not co-operate in killing difficult prey. A dwarf mongoose group forages through a different area of its territory each day and sleeps in a different refuge each night. Until they are three or four weeks old babies are carried between refuges by their mother and the babysitters. In this way depletion of the food supply in any one area is avoided and the mongooses can forage effectively on a sustained yield basis. It is highly probable that they use their scent marks as records of their movements to help organise their foraging patterns.

The members of a group cover one to one and a half kilometres a day as they forage together, quite widely scattered but always within earshot of one another. They keep in contact with short, peeping calls. As long as the group is big enough there is always a sentinel on duty to keep watch for predators (see pp 100–2). If there is an alarm the group rushes for cover – they are intimately familiar with the geography of their territory and wherever they happen to be foraging they know where the nearest safe refuge is. After hiding for a few minutes they cautiously re-emerge to check for further danger.

A dwarf mongoose group acts as a unit against snakes and other predators. The oldest, strongest, subordinate animals form the front ranks with the juveniles behind and the alpha male at the back. The alpha female joins in only if there are fewer than three adults in the group. Even fast-striking snakes are no match for a dwarf mongoose's lightning reflexes. There are also eight known cases of successful rescues from raptors.

A sick or injured dwarf mongoose is cared for by its companions, who cuddle, groom and feed it. As long as the invalid is immobile the group forages from the same refuge each day.

Dwarf mongooses mark their territories with anal gland secretion by doing handstands against vertical objects and wiping their anal glands downwards over them. They also mark with glands on their cheeks. Marking is especially heavy around sleeping sites and along territory borders. Piles of scats, which may also be markers, accumulate at overnight refuges. Each dwarf mongoose has an individual anal gland odour that its companions can recognise, but the smell of their cheek gland secretions depends on social status and not on identity. They can smell anal gland secretion even 20 to 25 days after it was deposited. The time it takes for the smell to disappear is probably connected with the mongooses' rotating use of different parts of their territory on an 18- to 26-day cycle.

A dwarf mongoose marks its group's territory with anal gland secretion.

By allomarking each other, allogrooming and sleeping together dwarf mongooses build up a group odour that distinguishes them from members of other groups. Aggression within dwarf mongoose groups is limited to an occasional squabble over food in which the contestants shove with hips and shoulders and scream at each other. Even the competition for the position of breeding female after the death of the previous one involves, not fighting, but a grooming contest between the two highest-ranking contenders. These contests can last for four days, with each animal soaked with the other's saliva. The most persistent groomer takes over as breeding female.

In contrast to the friendly relationships within groups, interactions between groups are usually violently aggressive. Border disputes with territory neighbours are usually over who uses a refuge, and they involve pitched battles in which all group members take part. The mongoose that first sights another group gives a high-pitched 'tsii' call to attract its companions, who bunch together and twitter excitedly. The alpha male leads the attack, followed by the young adults and then the rest of the group. The alpha female brings up the rear with her youngest offspring. The fighting is uninhibited but the losers flee before they are seriously wounded. The winning group marks the battlefield heavily with anal gland secretion. These battles are always won by the biggest group, and a group that loses members to predators or disease will find itself hard pressed to defend its territory against interloping neighbours. Occasionally groups of males stage takeover raids in which they drive out a group's males and settle themselves into their social roles.

It is during border clashes that juveniles most often get separated from their group. If they cannot find their own group again they may join another one, although it make take up to five weeks for them to be accepted.

Only the dominant pair breeds, and full sexual maturation in the others is suppressed by their subordinate social positions. If they show any sexual behaviour they are attacked by the dominants.

Once the babies are born the whole group helps in raising them. The mother stays with them only on the first day, after which she goes out to forage with the group, and up to three babysitters, usually an adult female and two adult males, stay behind. Female babysitters can lactate without ever having been pregnant. There may be a change of babysitters if the group comes back to the refuge for its midday siesta. Although it can mean missing a day's foraging, babysitting is a popular duty, probably because it is a way of rising in the social hierarchy.

From an age of four to six weeks the young dwarf mongooses go out foraging with the group. Each one has a caretaker who guides it, catches food for it and teaches it how, where and for what to forage. A caretaker holds what it has caught in its mouth and growls softly to attract its charge. The baby gives a food-begging squeal as it approaches and takes the food. The alpha male and the high-ranking (but not alpha) females are the most assiduous caretakers. The babies first try hunting when they are four weeks old. They are weaned at six to eight weeks. By the time they are four months old they have learned enough to forage for themselves.

Order PINNIPEDIA
Seals

Family   **OTARIIDAE**
Fur seals

Cape fur seal   *Arctocephalus pusillus* No. 281

A Cape fur seal feeds at sea and hauls out onto land to breed. It does most of its fishing offshore, concentrating on pelagic fish and squid, and sometimes moves closer in for bottom-dwelling species including octopus, crabs and crayfish. It can dive to at least 200 m and can stay under for six to seven and a half minutes, but 70 per cent of its dives are to less than 50 m and last for two to three minutes. In clear water it pursues fish by sight, but in muddy water and at night it picks up vibrations with its long, stiff whiskers. Although several seals may congregate around a shoal of fish there is no co-operation among them.

Cape fur seals come into conflict with human fishermen when they steal fish from nets and lines. While the economic effects of fish thefts on the industry as a whole are negligible, the individual fisherman becomes justifiably infuriated when a seal takes fish from his line and shakes them apart on the surface without eating them. At least part of the problem is probably caused by rogue seals which, like stock raiders among terrestrial predators, are best controlled by individually targeted control measures.

A fur seal swims by rowing with its front flippers, using the back ones only as rudders and for slow manoeuvring. On land it gets around surprisingly well, considering how much its specialisation for swimming makes it unsuited for movement out of the water. It can lift its body clear of the ground on its flippers; at the slowest pace it lifts its four flippers alternately, for faster movement the fore flippers move together and the back ones are dragged along, and and at full speed the front and back pairs are moved alternately and the body is hunched and straightened in a galloping action. A fur seal on land looks as if it is weeping, but only because it has no ducts to drain tears into its nose.

On land Cape fur seals form dense colonies of a few dozen to several thousand animals. Single seals also come ashore in areas where they are not usually seen. Although there are seals at the breeding colonies all year round there is a strict seasonality in the phases of the breeding cycle. Adult males haul out in mid-October and establish small breeding territories only a few metres across by fighting against their neighbours and with later arrivals. Fighting fur seal bulls rear up facing each other, push chest to chest and slash at each other with their teeth. A full-grown bull's teeth and jaws match a large dog's and, although the thick fur, skin and fat on the shoulders limits damage in that area to flesh wounds, bites on the flippers and the back half of the body can commonly produce serious and disabling injuries. The loser of a fight retreats to his own territory if he has one, or to the sea, in either case running the gauntlet of attacks from the holders of the territories through which he flees.

Cape fur seal bulls gather harems of females that they defend from other males.

A submissive male lowers his head, opens his mouth and bellows while backing away. If he turns tail the dominant bites him in the rear.

Once a male has established a territory he guards it continuously for about six weeks, living off his stored blubber. Established territorial neighbours display on their common boundary by rearing up, snapping and snorting for a few seconds. In November the females come ashore to have their pups. Like the males they fight over positions on the beach, preferring to be close to the water, and a territorial bull gains control of whatever females' pupping sites coincide with his territory. He keeps these females within his area by herding them aggressively, at times dragging them bodily back onto his ground, or even picking them up and throwing them. Since the females weigh about 60 kg this gives a good idea of how powerful the bulls are.

A female gives birth in November or early December and stays with her baby for the first week. Near the end of the week she comes into heat and the territorial bull mates her. Once they have mated the bull no longer herds her and she is free to go to sea to feed. When all his females have been mated a bull relinquishes his territory and returns to the sea to replenish his depleted fat reserves. At first a female stays away from her pup for only two or three days at a time, but this period gradually lengthens as the pup matures. A female who has returned from a feeding trip calls her pup by bellowing, and the pup answers with a high-pitched bleat; even in the continual din of the colony mother and pup recognise each other's voices. They rendezvous near where the mother left the pup when she went to sea and move up the beach to their usual resting site. Each female is approached by several hopeful pups, but she makes the final identification of her

111

own by smell and snaps at any of the others who try to suckle. If a pup loses its mother it is doomed to starve because no allomothering occurs.

While its mother is away a young pup joins a nursery group and plays with its peers. From an age of five or six months it begins to practise swimming and fishing in rockpools and shallow, calm water. As its skills improve it moves further offshore and stays away for longer and longer. Although it can feed itself for days at a stretch from an age of about seven months it continues to take milk for another four months or so.

Seals that are not involved in breeding, old and injured males and immature adults of both sexes form separate herds near the breeding colonies.

Order CETACEA
Whales and dolphins

Family **DELPHINIDAE**
Dolphins

A whale or dolphin spends only about 10 per cent of its time at the surface where it can be seen from boats or the shore. With such short glimpses only an expert can say to what species a dolphin belongs and the little that is known about their behaviour does not differ much between species. Therefore the species have been grouped together in the following description of their behaviour.

Dolphins cruising near the surface 'porpoise' by jumping clear of the water in shallow arcs. For fast swimming near the surface porpoising requires less energy than staying submerged. Swimming deeper is even better but dolphins have to come up every few minutes for air.

They ride the pressure waves that a ship's bow pushes out, and do the same with large whales cruising on the surface. Small boats do not displace enough water for dolphins to ride their bow waves but they still swim around small craft; it could be that they are simply curious.

Jumping dolphins may be looking for flocks of feeding birds in order to locate fish shoals.

Dolphins swim in the surf zone to corner fish against the water's edge, to escape large sharks, and to play.

A wide range of sounds such as clicks, pops, whistles and squeaks, which can sometimes be heard above the surface, are used for communication and echolocation.

Dolphins, especially the offshore species, sometimes gather into schools containing thousands, or tens of thousands, of animals. More usual group sizes are less than 100 for some species. Spinner dolphins (*Stenella longirostris* No. 225) group during the day and scatter to feed at night, so schooling might by an antipredator strategy. Dusky dolphins (*Lagenorynchus obscurus* No. 234) and common

Dolphins swimming fast near the surface save energy by 'porpoising'.

dolphins (*Delphinus delphis* No. 224) in a school collaborate to herd fish against the water's surface by circling underneath a shoal and jumping around its fringes.

Dolphins are well known for their bouts of co-ordinated, acrobatic swimming and close socialisation. These could well be practice sessions for the intimate synchronisation needed for collaborative fishing – for dolphins it may be a case of 'no play no prey'.

In various parts of the world wild dolphins have become 'friendly' with people; swimming into shallow water to play and be petted, and sometimes even going so far as to attempt mating with rubber-clad divers. Stories of dolphins 'rescuing' drowning swimmers are difficult to evaluate; dolphins will help each other, and so it is by no means impossible that they would treat a human in the same way. On the other hand there are documented cases of dolphins carrying humans away from land.

Because they are amenable to training, are conspicuously social and have large brains, dolphins have been credited with remarkable intelligence. However, it seems that a large brain is needed just to process echolocation data in a three-dimensional world, and their behaviour is what would be expected for any social predator. There is no evidence that stands up to examination that dolphins are any brighter than elephants or social carnivores.

Family	**BALAENIDAE**
	Right whales

Southern right whale   *Balaena glacialis* No. 237

The only whales that are at all likely to be seen in southern African waters are the southern right whales that breed off the southern Cape coast. Only their most obvious behaviour can be observed because it is against a very necessary and sensible law to approach them with boats or aircraft.

In June females start arriving off the southern Cape coast, moving north from their feeding grounds in the sub-Antarctic. Most calves are born in August. The most important calving grounds are off Cape Infanta and in Mossel Bay. For its first six weeks of life a calf has to swim quickly because it has not yet built up a thick enough coat of blubber to keep it afloat. As it grows and becomes more buoyant it plays more, focusing its activities on its mother. It sucks for about five per cent of the time.

Males, juveniles, and females without young depart southwards earlier than the females with calves, who move back south in December.

Southern right whales bellow while at the surface, a sound that can be heard hundreds of metres away. Lob-tailing (smashing the tail flukes down onto the surface) and flipper splashing may produce sound signals or be defences against killer whales. A breaching right whale heaves as much as two-thirds of its 50-ton bulk above the surface and crashes back in a shower of spray. Youngsters may breach up to 80 times an hour. It may be a way of knocking off parasites, or a signal to other whales.

A sexually active female may be surrounded by a retinue of males who bump and jostle around her.

Why southern right whales breach is unknown.

WHALE STRANDINGS

Most sightings of dolphins and whales are glimpses from the shore or from boats as they appear briefly above the water's surface to breath, jump or breach. Every so often, though, cetaceans come ashore singly or in large groups in ways for which there is as yet no really satisfactory explanation. Considering that our knowledge of how marine mammals behave at sea is miserably inadequate it is hardly surprising that we cannot be certain what happens, and why, when things go wrong.

Strandings are unpredictable, and often in remote places, and nobody has ever recorded what happens from before the first animal runs ashore until the whole group is marooned. In a good number of cases a mass stranding is not even noticed until the only evidence is a row of gull-picked carcasses on the tide line.

Whales and dolphins may simply wash up after they have died. These are just animals that have died at sea and have been brought to land by currents and tides. The real puzzle is posed by whales and dolphins that swim to land and strand themselves.

One thing that we can be certain of is that stranders have not thrown themselves onto the beach as an act of selfless population control. For whales and dolphins to act like this would be as fantastic as lemmings jumping off cliffs and deliberately drowning themselves.

Some stranded cetaceans are obviously diseased – with parasites in their brains or nematode worms in their ear canals for example – and it could be that they are no longer able to navigate or to swim properly. These sick animals usually beach alone and they can turn up anywhere.

The members of six species are more likely than others to strand. Four of these are pelagic, not usually venturing into inshore waters, and social: pilot whales, sperm whales, pygmy sperm whales, and false killer whales. One of them, the killer whale, is a social, inshore animal and one, the Atlantic white-sided dolphin is a solitary inshore swimmer. From this it appears that pelagic animals get into difficulties in shallow waters, and that living in groups leads to stranding and dying in groups.

Most mass strandings are on shallow, gently shelving, sandy beaches with soft muddy bottoms offshore – conditions that are very likely to confuse animals used to echoing sonar off deep, hard bottoms or gauging the shoreline from the noise of the surf.

Some beaches are hotspots of cetacean strandings, and some of these are at places where contours in the earth's magnetic field cut the coast at right angles. There also seems to be a relationship between cetacean strandings and magnetic storms caused by radiation from the sun – there are more strandings in years when the storms are particularly severe. If, as has been suggested, whales and dolphins use the earth's magnetic field to navigate, it might explain why magnetic anomalies make them strand.

Deep water close to the coast seems to contribute to strandings of pelagic cetaceans, because it brings them closer in than they would usually come. In 1936, 58 false killer whales stranded on 1,5 km of beach in St Helena Bay. On 19 August 1981 the same stretch was the centre of a stranding of 65 false killer whales over 93 km of coast. The deep water of the Cape Submarine Canyon shallows out just offshore from this fatal spot.

Some strandings could well be accidents as killer whales and some dolphins sometimes hunt in water too shallow to cover their backs. Killer whales will actually launch themselves onto land to grab seals near the water line and dolphins corner fish in shallow water and stick their heads out to catch those that flap onto the beach. A misjudgement of a jump, the slope of a beach or the surge of a wave could leave the whale or dolphin helpless on land.

What is impossible to explain with any certainty is why, if stranded whales are returned to the water, they often swim back onto the beach. It could be that they are responding to the distress calls of those left behind. Towing or guiding as many as possible of the stranded animals to deep water seems to help them to get their bearings. At least some of the mass strandings appear to be caused by whole groups following a leader into danger and then being unwilling or unable to abandon their grounded companions.

Order TUBILIDENTATA
Aardvark

Family   **EDENTATA**
           Aardvark

Aardvark   *Orycteropus afer* No. 288

Aardvarks are nocturnal and solitary. They travel long distances – up to 15 km a night – in their search for the ants and termites that make up the bulk of their diet. They have anogenital glands which they use for marking, and they bury their faeces, but whether they are territorial is unknown.

An aardvark uses its keen sense of smell to detect underground ants' nests. Its hearing is also acute but its eyesight is poor.

An aardvark is extremely strong and can easily drag a man off his feet. It has an enormous capacity for digging and can tunnel faster than men with spades can dig towards it. As it searches for food it makes shallow, exploratory scrapes in the soil surface. Any ant or termite nests it finds are dug open to expose their tunnels, from which the aardvark licks out the insects with its long, sticky, cylindrical tongue. Excavations into underground nests are usually shallow but an aardvark may make a hole into which its whole body disappears in the cement-hard stucture of a large termite mound. An aardvark will dig itself temporary refuge burrows which it uses for a few days, perhaps returning to them later. It seems to remember the location of these burrows and dashes off towards them if danger threatens. Once inside the aardvark barricades the tunnel with a pile of soil. Much more extensive diggings are used as permanent homes. The tunnels and chambers of these large burrows are added to and modified continually and the efforts of successive occupants produce huge underground systems penetrating as deep as 6 m below the surface. There are stories of human hunters getting lost in such aardvark burrows and having to be dug out by their companions. Aardvark burrows provide refuges and shelters for carnivores from the size of hyaenas and leopards downwards and for herbivores up to the size of steenbok and warthogs.

Young aardvark can be seen moving around with their mothers as early as two weeks after birth, but they do not start digging for their own food until they are about six months old.

116

Order PROBOSCIDEA
Elephants

Family **ELEPHANTIDAE**
Elephants

African elephant   *Loxodonta africana* No. 289

An elephant has to feed for at least 14 hours a day to obtain the 170 kg of fodder it needs to supply its huge body and, in addition, it may have to travel long distances to water. It sleeps standing up for a few minutes at a stretch.

The basic, stable social unit among elephants is a group of closely related adult females with their young of various ages. Adult males join these groups only when one of the females is on heat. A young male leaves his natal group when he reaches adolescence. Males sometimes form small, unstable bachelor groups; an old male may be accompanied by two or three younger ones known as askaris. Family groups and males may aggregate into herds several hundred strong in areas of rich feeding or to escape human disturbance.

Elephants are not territorial but they do occupy home ranges, using various parts of them in seasonal or irregular rotation according to where food and water are to be found. If their usual food and water supplies fail elephants will trek long distances to reach more favourable conditions. In the Kaokoveld their home ranges cover up to 3 000 km² and they make 200 km treks. Bulls in musth (see pp 120–1) also wander much more widely than usual. The movements of a family group are directed by the senior cows who have accumulated the necessary experience over 30 to 40 years of varying climatic conditions. If these old cows are shot their knowledge is lost and the rest of the group wanders aimlessly.

If it is able to, an elephant goes to water once a day to drink, bathe and wallow in mud. On average it will drink 70 to 90 *l* a day but it can down 150 *l* if it is thirsty. The visits become less frequent if the feeding grounds and water supply are very far apart. In the Kaokoveld, where there may be 70 km between food and water, the elephants drink only once every three or four days.

Wallowing in mud cools an elephant off and coats its skin as a protection against parasites. It showers itself with dust and sand for the same reasons, and the sand also acts as an extra abrasive to help dislodge ticks when the elephant rubs itself on rocks and trees. In deep water an elephant will immerse itself completely and will swim across lakes and rivers with only the tip of its trunk showing. Elephants have been seen swimming in the middle of Lake Kariba and have swum for at least 27 hours, with 35 to 40 km between sightings.

An elephant's trunk serves it as an extremely dexterous, and yet enormously powerful, two-fingered hand; with it an elephant can pick up single seedpods or tear down trees. An elephant drinks by sucking water into its trunk and then emptying it down its throat. It also sucks up dust and sand to blow over itself. In addition the trunk is an important means of communication by touch and smell.

The tusks are used for digging, for chiselling the bark off trees, and as weapons of defence against predators and of offence against competitors such as rhino and hippo at water holes and, especially among breeding males, against other elephants. To replace the wear and tear of this diverse usage the tusks grow throughout the elephant's life. Each elephant uses one tusk more than the other, so the favoured one gets worn down more and is more likely to be accidentally broken.

Because it is so big an elephant has relatively little body surface from which to lose the four to five kilowatts of metabolic heat that its huge body generates. As a result it has a continual problem keeping cool. It loses at least 20 per cent of its heat load by fanning its ears back and forward to create a cooling breeze over the complex of large blood vessels that runs through them.

In a serious charge an elephant keeps its trunk tucked under its chin.

Elephants are basically peaceful but they can become extremely aggressive if they are sick, injured or harassed, if they have young calves or if they live in, or have moved away from, an area where elephants are hunted. Whether or not an elephant reacts aggressively is to a certain extent determined by how the rest of its group behaves at the time, and how it has learned to respond to threats as it

The dark streak on this elephant's face is a secretion from its temporal gland.

A young elephant mock-charges a springbok ram.

grew up. An aggressive elephant raises its head and trunk, extends its ears, trumpets and throws up clouds of dust by kicking the ground and shaking its head, then it sways backwards and forwards and charges. Most charges are broken off before the target is reached, and any natural enemy in its right mind will already have fled in any case. If an attack is followed through an elephant is quite capable of killing any other species, including rhino and hippo, and of wrecking vehicles. At top speed an elephant is travelling at 40 km/h – no human can run that fast. A tourist who hid behind a 60 cm mopane trunk was injured when a charging elephant bull smashed it down.

Elephants have been recorded as showing an apparent fascination for elephant

ELEPHANT MUSTH

Musth is an Urdu word for the rutting behaviour of working Asian elephant bulls, when they become unmanageably aggressive and have to be isolated and chained up.

It is now known that African elephant bulls also go through equivalent periods of disturbed behaviour. This was not recognised sooner because there are some differences in detail between the two species. On the sides of an elephant's face, between the eye and ear, are the openings of its temporal glands. In Asian elephants the glands are active only in musth bulls, while in African elephants of both sexes they secrete in response to a wide variety of stressful circumstances, when nothing else the animal does is characteristic of musth. Mating in Asian elephants is very closely tied to musth but African bulls will mate whatever their condition, provided a musth bull does not chase them away first.

Musth is driven by a surge in testosterone, the male hormone.

The signs that an elephant bull is in musth are obvious to both human observers and other elephants. His temporal glands swell up and secrete a sticky fluid that stains the sides of his face. He massages the glands with his trunk and rubs them more frequently on trees. He waves one ear – perhaps to waft the smell of his temporal gland secretion towards other elephants. Instead of urinating backwards between his legs with his penis partly extended he continually dribbles urine with his penis sheathed. The urine stains his penis green and splashes onto his hindlegs, and it has a powerful odour. He walks with his head high and chin tucked in, his ears tensed and spread. As he walks he swings his head in time with his paces in a definite swagger. He kneels to tusk the ground, and throws logs around.

Non-musth males always back down when a musth bull challenges them, but every so often his hand is called in an encounter with another musth male. These tests of real strength and motivation are probably why musth provides such a reliable indicator of an elephant bull's status. Any bull that 'cheated' by going into musth when he was not at the peak of physical condition would risk being beaten and tusked to death by a musth bull who really was in his prime.

A vanquished musth bull returns to ordinary condition very quickly – he may even stop dribbling urine while still being chased by the victor.

A bull does not come into musth until he is at least 25 years old. Between 25 and 35 his musth periods lengthen from a few days a year up to one and a half to three and a half months, until, at 40 to 45 he is coming into musth for four to seven months each year. As age takes its toll he becomes unequal to the demands he faces and his musth periods shorten and come less often and more irregularly. The tragedy is that these days most bulls are shot by poachers before they are old enough to go into musth.

A musth bull covers vast distances in his search for sexually receptive cows. Those he finds he guards from other suitors. He becomes extremely aggressive and will vent his feelings on animals other than elephants, and on man and his works.

His continuous, vigorous activity erodes a musth bull's body condition; it is probably this that limits the amount of time he can spend in each musth season.

bones and ivory, picking them up in their trunks, carrying them around and scattering them over a wide area. Why they behave like this is unknown. That elephants go to special elephant graveyards to die is a myth. The accumulation of bones and tusks in the 'graveyards' build up around water holes where starving elephants have congregated during droughts, going there not to die but to try to stay alive.

The members of an elephant family group take good care of one another. If one of them is sick or injured others will stay with it to defend or support it. The calves get especially close attention; the adults help them climb steep banks, pull them out of sticky mud and protect them from predators. A sick calf's family will try to

A musth elephant bull's head-up, swaggering walk.

Fights between musth bulls are spectacles of uninhibited savagery. The combatants charge head on, slam into one another and wrestle with their trunks and tusks. If he can, the bull who is getting the worse of a contest breaks and runs, but the victor chases him for as much as 3 km, even in the midday heat, and will tusk him in the rump or flank if he catches up. Losers can be killed outright in such battles and at least one case is known of a winner dying later from his wounds.

Elephant cows prefer musth bulls as mates and when she is on heat a cow advertises her condition by the smell of her urine and loud, subsonic calls in order to attract a testosterone-boosted suitor.

get it onto its feet and will stand between it and the sun. Even after a calf has died the group will stay with the body, sometimes for hours.

Elephants communicate by touch, scent, sight and sound. Bellowing, trumpeting and screaming signal alarm and aggression. Groups keep in contact with loud (103 dB), very low frequency (14–35 Hz) calls, which carry for at least 2 km. The sounds of an elephant's 'tummy rumbling' are only the upper harmonics of these contact calls, the rest are below the frequency range of human hearing. Cows in heat and bulls in musth (see pp 120–1) advertise their condition by loud, infrasonic rumbles. The trunk is used for caressing, especially between mother and calf. Elephants can probably recognise each other, assess emotional states and recognise group membership from the smell of their temporal gland secretions. The glands open on the sides of the face between the eye and the ear and their secretion often makes a dark streak down the elephant's face.

Males less than 25 years old are unable to compete for access to females on heat. Between 25 and 35 years they mate, but only early and late in the female's oestrus period when conception is unlikely. Males older than 35 years guard and mate with females at the most favourable time for fathering a calf. A female in early oestrus protests with loud roars against the mating attempts of young males, in mid-oestrus she gives loud, infrasonic calls and solicits guarding and mating by old, musth bulls. Mating takes place at about 8-hour intervals. Excitement spreads through the whole of a receptive female's social group as they keep up a cacophany of rumbling, trumpeting and screaming.

It is a myth that elephants only mate in water. If it were true there would be no elephants in Etosha or Kaokoland, where all the water is in shallow pools.

An elephant female squats to give birth so that her baby falls only a short distance to the ground. She uses her trunk to remove the birth membranes and to help her calf to stand. The calf begins to nurse within a few minutes, using its mouth, not its trunk, to suck from the teats that lie between its mother's front legs. Male calves suck more than females. An elephant calf is suckled for at least two, and sometimes three, years and even after weaning it remains closely bonded to its mother so that a female may be followed by two calves of different ages. A female's successive offspring maintain stronger social ties with each other than with the rest of the group. A calf's attempts to suck from lactating females other than its mother are vigorously repelled, usually with a slap from the cow's trunk. Calves also try to suck from adolescent females who are not lactating. Sometimes these attempts are tolerated; they seem to be a way of comforting a distressed calf. If a calf loses its mother the other females in the group suckle it and care for it.

Young elephants play energetically, splashing and spraying each other with water and mud, trunk wrestling and practising fighting in pushing competitions, they also mock-charge other species such as antelope.

During droughts elephants use their tusks and feet to dig for water in dry riverbeds. Other animals take advantage of these holes, but they have to give way if an elephant wants to use one. An elephant will also make narrow, deep holes by scooping out soil alongside and underneath large grass clumps with its trunk. Only elephants can reach the water that collects at the bottom of these holes.

Elephants eat a very wide variety of plants. A grazing elephant pulls up grass clumps with its trunk and knocks the soil off the roots against a tree or its own front leg. Elephants browse unselectively. They pull off and eat twigs as well as leaves and will tear large branches off trees or demolish the tree itself to get at leaves which are out of reach. They pick up pods and fruits from the ground and may shake a tree to knock down more.

Elephants are wasteful and destructive feeders but under natural conditions the long-term ecological effects of their activities are beneficial. It is only when confined populations of elephants are improperly managed that serious habitat degradation occurs.

Order HYRACOIDEA
Hyraxes

Family   **PROCAVIIDAE**
Hyraxes

Rock dassie   *Procavia capensis* No. 290

Rock dassies live in colonies of which the size depends on how much shelter there is among the rocks in which they live. The social unit is a group of females, and a male monopolises a female group by fighting against other males for the

Rock dassies pack together to keep warm.

territory in which it lives. Rock dassies are mostly active during the day because their slow metabolisms make them dependent on the heat of the sun to keep warm. In cool weather they emerge from their rock crevice shelters only after the sun is well up and immediately find a sunny spot out of the wind in which to bask. In hot weather on moonlit nights they emerge before dawn and stay out after sunset.

Inside their shelters rock dassies pack together in rows or heaps to keep warm, and sometimes they can be seen doing this outside as well.

Despite their unathletic appearance rock dassies are extremely agile rock climbers. The rubbery soles of their feet sweat freely to give them a grip that allows them to run up near-vertical rock faces.

Rock dassies spend nearly all their time basking in the sun with numerous brief periods of grooming and occasional dust bathing.

Rock dassies have a very wide vocal repertoire that includes at least 21 different calls. Not all of these can be associated with particular messages. The alarm call – which alerts its hearers without making them run – is a squeal, but more immediate danger is signalled by a bark that sends the whole colony dashing for cover among the rocks. Teeth-gnashing and growling are threat signals.

In the middle of its back a rock dassie has a glandular patch overlain by long, black hair. The gland is best developed in dominant adult males and the release of its scent by the raising of the hairs is an aggressive threat signal. Submission is signalled by presenting the rump or flank. A rock dassie's weapons are its long, triangular incisor teeth.

Although rock dassies defecate and urinate in large middens it is not known whether these have any significance as scent marks – they may be only incidental to the dassies' continual use of a favourite resting place.

Rock dassies eat grass if it is available, or the roots, leaves, bark and seeds of a wide variety of herbs, shrubs and trees. They readily accept vegetation that is distasteful or poisonous to other herbivores. Dassies are most vulnerable to predation while feeding, especially if a shortage of food near their refuges forces them to forage out onto flatter ground. As a result dassies forage very quickly for only about an hour each day. Where there are no predators, such as in game reserve rest camps and city suburbs, the dassies become bolder and will venture out onto lawns to forage. It is mainly by keeping dassies confined to their rocky habitat that predators such as black eagles and caracals benefit farmers, because they limit the extent to which dassies compete with stock for grazing.

Baby rock dassies are very precocious and start to eat solid food the day after they are born, although they are not weaned for one to five months. They are agile climbers from a few days of age and playfully chase each other over the rocks. They pick up a colony odour from the dorsal glands of the adults when they climb onto their backs.

Tree dassie   *Dendrohyrax arboreus* No. 293

Tree dassies are nocturnal, solitary and, true to their name, arboreal. They may well be territorial because they defecate and urinate in middens under the trees in which they live, and both sexes have a loud, penetrating long-distance call that is answered by their neighbours. The call begins with a few sharp barks and changes to a wavering scream, which is uncannily human.

Tree dassies sleep in holes in trees or in tangled mats of foliage, and feed mostly by browsing. They will come down to the ground to eat grass.

Order PERISSODACTYLA
Odd-toed ungulates

Family   **RHINOCEROTIDAE**
Rhinoceroses

Black or hooked-lip rhino   *Diceros bicornis* No. 296

Black rhino are less active during the hottest part of the day than at other times. They are solitary; a calf stays with its mother until it is about two to four years old, when she has her next calf. A number of males may congregate around a female on heat but such groups are temporary.

Black rhinos live in overlapping home ranges of about 200 ha in rich areas, 400 ha where the vegetation is less dense and 750 km^2 in the Kaokoveld. They scent-mark by defecating in middens and with urine. The males spray backwards between their legs into bushes while standing still and females spray, rarely, while on the move. Their home ranges are not defended and so do not qualify as territories. It may well be that a black rhino's scent marks act mainly as signposts for its own use. After defecating in a midden a black rhino bull scrapes strongly with his back feet, gouging the disturbed soil of the midden to depths of up to 30 cm. In this way he picks up the smell of the midden on his feet and then treads it into the pathways of his home range. Some middens may be shared by a number of rhino, who can probably pick up information about one another from the smells left there.

Black rhinos wallow in water or mud to keep themselves cool and to get rid of parasites.

Hook-lipped rhino bulls scent-mark by spraying urine.

A rhino's eyesight is poor but its hearing is acute and its sense of smell very keen – in fact its nasal passages are bigger than its brain.

Fights between black rhinos are rare because they usually avoid each other. Fights usually occur when two bulls are courting the same female. Some disputes are settled without physical combat; one male leaves in response to a direct stare with the head raised, or a charge from the other bull. If two bulls do come to blows they fence with sideways blows of their heads and horns, trying to force an opening for blows to the body. Fights can become vicious and battle wounds are a major cause of death among eight- to ten- year-old adolescent bulls.

While fighting black rhinos grunt, growl and scream. If startled they give repeated loud snorts. A female black rhino calls her calf with a high-pitched mew and it calls her with a bellowing squeal.

A black rhino is mainly a browser but will occasionally eat some grass and herbs. It pulls shoots, leaves and twigs into its mouth with its dexterous upper lip and cuts them off with its premolar teeth. It prunes bushes neatly rather than pulling them apart as an elephant would. Black rhinos are not particularly selective feeders and they swallow thorns and twigs, of which half-digested remnants in the black rhino's dung distinguish it from that of the square-lipped rhino. They are able to feed on plants such as euphorbias, which to other herbivores are distasteful or poisonous. Black rhinos drink every day if they can but they can survive for four or five days without it by eating succulent plants. When surface supplies dry up they dig for water with their forefeet.

When a female black rhino comes into heat the smell of her urine changes. Males detect this by sniffing and by Flehmen. The bull approaches the cow with a stiff-legged gait, his back legs dragging. She may chase him off at first or they may spar gently with their horns. The bull prods the female's abdomen with his horn. Over a period of several hours the bull will mount the cow repeatedly, following her around between these unsuccessful attempts. When the bull finally

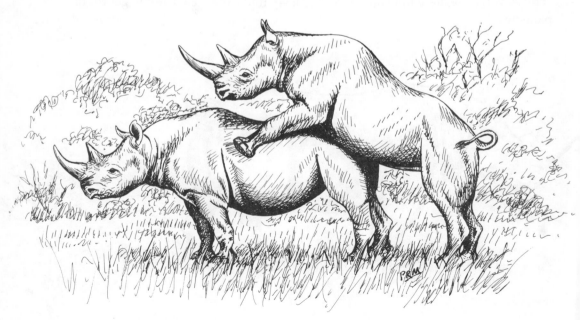

Hook-lipped rhinos mate for 30 minutes at a time.

achieves intromission copulation continues for upwards of 30 minutes while the cow emits low squeals.

A black rhino calf can follow its mother only three hours after birth. The mother always leads the calf and will defend it unhestitatingly against actual and potential danger. A calf starts browsing at about three months but will not be completely weaned for about another nine months. Until it is two to four years old it will stay with its mother, by which time she is pregnant again. A calf that stays around until the birth of its sibling is vigorously repelled by the mother.

Black rhino have a reputation for bad temper. They can charge at 50 km/h, and are most likely to attack if taken by surprise; when walking in areas where black rhinos occur it is a good idea not to move too quietly so that the rhinos have plenty of warning of your approach and have a chance to move away. Cows with calves are especially dangerous and will charge under almost any circumstances.

Square-lipped or white rhino   *Ceratotherium simum* No. 295

Square-lipped rhinos live in small groups, although they can often be seen alone. A group contains a number of females and sometimes some subordinate males. The social bonds within a group are not particularly strong, but if predators attack, a group will often bunch with their rumps together and horns facing outwards.

Dominant bulls are territorial, in Umfolozi and Hluhluwe they defend areas of about 2 km^2. They mark their boundaries by defecating in middens and kicking the dung around with their hindlegs, and by spraying bushes with urine. Neither subordinate males nor females spray-mark or kick dung. Male intruders and subordinate male group members are tolerated as long as they behave submissively by standing with ears back and tail up while roaring and squealing. The dominant bull may approach a subordinate and briefly push horn to horn, or may simply ignore it. In turn a dominant bull may safely move into another territory, to reach water for instance, so long as he defers to the resident. Cows move freely in and out of male territories except that when a cow is on heat a bull may try to herd her within his area.

Square-lipped rhinos have a wide range of vocalisations; they huff when startled, calves squeal when frightened and panting is a contact signal. Shrieking is a sign of submissiveness and snorting or snarling are repellants. Dominant bulls squeal when herding an oestrous female. Tactile communication is used when friendly rhinos rub against each other.

Meetings between territory neighbours are highly ritualised. They approach and repeatedly touch horns, back away and wipe the front horn on the ground, approach and touch horns again. These rituals usually last for a few minutes but can go on for over an hour.

The preliminaries to fighting in square-lipped rhino are deliberate approaches with snarling and charges. Fighting escalates from horn fencing through jabbing with the horn to heavy shoulder ramming and hooking at the opponent's body. Serious injuries and deaths most often occur when an oestrous female is the prize. A defeated territory holder stays on as a subordinate in his old territory.

A square-lipped rhino wallows in water and mud to cool off in hot weather and to remove parasites. After caking itself with mud it rubs against trees, rocks and termite mounds. It rests in thickets to avoid both hot sunshine and cold winds. A territorial bull usually has favourite resting places.

Square-lipped rhinos are grazers who prefer short grass; they move slowly forward a step at a time, swinging the head in an arc to reach whatever grass is available before taking the next step. The grass is cropped between the lips. Square-lipped rhinos drink in the late afternoon or evening every two to four days.

A square-lipped rhino bull can detect when a female is coming into heat from the smell of her urine. Their courtship may involve limited fighting if she is reluctant to be herded within his territory. Herding begins five to 20 days before the female is ready to mate, during which time the bull stays close to her and chases any other bulls away. As the female gets used to the male's approaches she allows him to come closer. The male puts his chin on the female's back and if she is receptive she curls her tail to one side. Mounting lasts for about 30 minutes.

A square-lipped rhino calf can stand within an hour of birth but for the first few days it does not move far and its mother stays in close attendance. The calf walks in front with the cow directing its movements by gently shoving it with her horn. Mother and calf rejoin the mother's herd after three to four weeks. A calf begins grazing when it is two months old and weans at about a year. It stays in close association with its mother until it is two or three years old, when she has her next calf, and maintains close social ties even after that.

Square-lipped rhinos are better tempered than their hook-lipped relatives.

Neighbouring territorial square-lipped rhino bulls rub their horns on the ground in a border ritual.

Family   EQUIDAE
Zebras

Mountain zebra

Equus zebra No. 297

The two subspecies, the Cape mountain zebra and Hartmann's mountain zebra, are very similar in most of their behaviour and can be dealt with together.

Mountain zebras are active during the day; they alternate bouts of grazing with standing, lying or dust-rolling. Cape mountain zebras drink at least once a day and Hartmann's mountain zebras once or more a day if possible, or every two days if grazing and water are far apart. They will dig for water if necessary.

The basic social unit in mountain zebras is a herd of up to half a dozen mares and their foals, which is controlled by a dominant stallion. These herds are formed by the stallions' active shepherding of unattached females, most of which are fillies who have just left their natal group or adult females who have lost their herd stallion. Young stallions may also take over an established herd by defeating its controlling male in a no-holds-barred contest of kicking and biting. Stallions are, apparently, unable to breed until they have gained control of a herd.

There is a dominance hierarchy among a herd's mares, which is established by fighting and maintained by threat gestures. The most common threat is a rapid approach with the head held low, the ears laid back, the teeth bared and the tail lashing. The threatened mare simply moves away, perhaps giving a defensive kick as she does so. High-ranking mares get priority of access to dust baths, shade and other limited resources.

A young male who is confronted by a herd stallion gives a long squeal and lowers his head. Friendly interactions occur in Cape mountain zebras in the form of allogrooming the head, neck and shoulders by gentle nibbling.

Besides their submissive squeal mountain zebras use a harsh snort or a barking 'kwa-ah' as alarm signals, and soft lip-smacking as a contentment or short-range contact call.

When mountain zebra herds meet, at water holes for instance, the herd stallions approach to within a few metres of each other, stand with their heads up and then slowly approach with their heads down and ears cocked. They meet with a nose-to-nose sniff, move to stand head to tail, sniff each other's genitals and rub their heads on the partner's rump. If another male approaches his females a herd stallion stands in a lateral display with his neck arched.

Mountain zebras have large, loosely defined home ranges around which they move on a seasonal basis as the availability of water and grazing changes.

Mountain zebras are unselective grazers because they can efficiently digest coarse fodder. Feeding in a herd is not synchronised, so while some animals have their heads down grazing others are standing up and looking around for predators. They move between grazing areas as the quality of the grass changes with the seasons.

If attacked a herd bunches and flees together; the mare with the youngest foal being most likely to run first. The foals run alongside their mothers and the stallion takes a defensive rearguard position from which he kicks and bites any predator that comes within range. When his herd comes down to water the stallion again takes the most dangerous position; that of leader.

Males that do not hold breeding herds join up into bachelor herds. Most of the animals in these herds are males between two and five years old, with some older males and a few young females that have not yet been picked up by herd stallions. Among the bachelor males there is a dominance hierarchy based on restrained fighting, which involves biting at the opponent's mane and knees and trying to push him off balance. Older and larger animals tend to be dominant. The full-scale fights that herd stallions engage in are not seen among bachelors.

A herd stallion checks the reproductive condition of his mares by sniffing and Flehmen of their urine. The mares urinate more frequently as they come into heat and the male overmarks where they urinate, probably as a deterrent to other suitors. If a stallion makes sexual advances to a mare before she is fully on heat she lashes out at him with her hindlegs. When she is on heat the mare presents to the stallion by standing with her hindlegs splayed and her tail lifted to one side. He rubs his face and muzzle on her genitals and at the height of receptivity she

DONKEYS IN FOOTBALL JERSEYS –
WHY ZEBRAS HAVE STRIPES

General Jan Kemp's 1936 description of mountain zebra was as accurate as it was insensitive – zebra stand out, literally and figuratively, from both their equine relatives and the other large herbivores alongside which they graze, because all three living species are covered with dazzling black and white stripes.

The purpose of the stripes has stimulated a good deal of discussion.

The stripes could be to avoid attracting blood-sucking flies that find their hosts by sight. Zebras do suffer less from tsetse flies than other large grazers, and striped models attract fewer tsetse flies than solid-coloured ones of either black, white or grey. However, tsetse flies live in woodland while zebra are mainly plains dwellers, and zebra populations outside fly areas have the same stripes as those inside them.

Dazzle – no single zebra stands out from this confusion of stripes.

Conceivably the stripes could act as camouflage by breaking up the zebras' outlines but their behaviour does not fit what would be expected from a camouflaged animal. Zebra are noisy and active, they live out in the open and they do not freeze in response to danger.

Another suggestion was that the conglomeration of dazzling stripes in a zebra herd would make it difficult for a predator to concentrate on a particular target or that the narrowing of the stripes towards the head would give a false perspective to a predator's view of its intended zebra prey, and so make it misjudge its pursuit and attack. Nevertheless lions, spotted hyaenas, wild dogs, cheetah and leopard, which have radically different hunting styles, all successfully capture zebra so, if there is a dazzle effect or a distortion of perspective it cannot be very effective.

An important pointer to the function of the zebras' stripes is their effect not on insect pests or predators but on other zebras. Crisp, contrasting stripes are highly visually stimulating and zebras seem to seek out this visual input by approaching each other – they are even attracted by black and white stripes painted onto flat panels. The answer to the question of why zebras like being near stripy animals may lie in their anti-predator tactics. When predators attack, a zebra group bunches and runs in close formation, with the stallion in the rear putting up a

Distortion – a possible predator's eye view disrupted by a zebra's stripe pattern.

defensive screen. Predators make most of their attacks at night and the zebras' manoeuvres have to be carried out in the dark amidst clouds of dust thrown up by their hooves – under these conditions a pattern of sharp black and white stripes provides the best visibility.

Orientation – a zebra's stripes might allow its herd mates to keep close to it in poor visibility.

responds with a little jump of her hindquarters. Mating takes only a few seconds and is repeated hourly for two days.

A mare with a newborn foal is very aggressive, even towards her herd companions. A foal is able to run beside its mother within hours of birth. A mare is extremely possessive and protective towards her own offspring and will spend a lot of time sniffing, licking and nibbling it. Each mare recognises her own foal by smell for the first few days, and then by sight, most likely by its stripe pattern (see pp 130–1), with a confirming sniff. When a foal wants milk it presses against its mother's chest. Foals eat grass after only three days but it is 10 months before they are weaned. Until they are about three and a half months old foals eat small portions of the adults' dung so that they pick up the bacteria they need to digest their food.

The reactions of mountain zebra mares to foals are very variable. One mare adopted a foal whose mother had died and one rejected her own baby in favour of another. On the other hand the dominant mare in a Cape mountain zebra group may harass subordinate mares and their foals so severely that the foals die. She probably does this so that her own foals face less competition as they grow up.

Cape mountain zebra males stay in their natal group until they are about two years old, then leave of their own accord. Male Hartmann's mountain zebras are chased out at 12 to 14 months by the mother when she was her next foal. A young female leaves her natal group when she first comes into oestrus so that she does not mate with her father.

Burchell's zebra   *Equus burchelli* No. 298

Burchell's zebras live in groups of one to twelve mares with their foals and a stallion, who is at least four and usually less than twelve years old. Stallions who have no mares of their own form bachelor groups or live alone. Hundreds of zebras sometimes congregate where there is good grazing. Within these congregations each breeding herd remains as a unit, with the stallion herding his mares and occasionally having to repel other stallions' attempts to steal them. Bachelor males hang around the periphery of the area used by the breeding groups, not to protect them from predators but because both the stallions and the mares attack them. Burchell's zebras are often seen in company with blue wildebeest because both favour short grass.

Burchell's zebras have loosely organised home ranges and they move to wherever food and water are available. In some areas they migrate seasonally.

The members of a group can recognise each other, and probably other zebras, by sight and voice. One greets another by repeatedly opening and shutting its mouth without showing its teeth, while holding its ears forward. Movements as if to bite, with the ears forward or sideways, are playful. The threat gesture is to hold the ears back while pointing the head at the opponent, and a submissive zebra lowers its head, holds its ears forwards, sideways or back and makes chewing movements with its teeth exposed. While herding his females a stallion keeps his head low and his ears back. Group companions groom each other by nibbling with their lips and teeth, and stand leaning against one another.

Vocal communication is also important. Squealing is a threat of attack, a mare whinnies to call her foal and 'nickers' to warn it of danger. A courting stallion also 'nickers'.

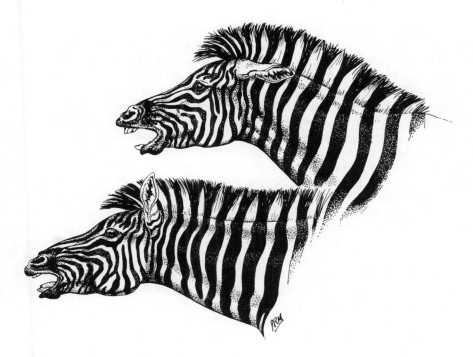

Aggressive (top) and submissive (bottom) Burchell's zebras.

When herd stallions meet, for example at a water hole, they call to each other, approach cautiously, sniff nose to nose and at each others' genitals, and rub against each other. There may be a sudden eruption of biting and kicking; as in the mountain zebra, the favourite target for bites is the opponent's knees.

In full-scale fights between herd stallions the two animals rear and kick at each other with their forelegs and bite at the shoulders, neck and flanks. Their

Full-scale fighting between Burchell's zebra stallions.

favourite targets for bites are the opponent's knees, and the corresponding defensive tactic is to kneel. A kneeling stallion can only attack by biting his opponent's knees, unless he too is kneeling or moving on all four feet to keep out of danger. Thus each fight becomes a tactical interplay of attack and defence in which skill and experience probably count as much as size and strength.

Burchell's zebras are continually alert for predators. The alarm call is a barking 'kwa-ha-ha'. When attacked by predators a breeding herd bunches up. The mares with young foals run in front with the other mares behind them, and the stallion right at the back. They flee from predators at only about half their top speed of 60 to 70 km/h so that the group can keep tightly together and the stallion can manoeuvre in the rear. As long as a zebra stays with its herd it is fairly safe but if it splits away it will be singled out and attacked. Zebra are dangerous prey – as a predator closes in from behind they lash out with a kick that, if it connects, can at least deflect a lion's final spring, may break its jaw, and can kill a spotted hyaena. The number of zebra with scarred rumps from unsuccessful lion attacks testifies to the effectiveness of their defensive kicks.

Burchell's zebras are almost exclusively grazers and they have a strong preference for short, fresh grass. They also like fire-scorched mopane leaves. They drink at least once a day and so are seldom found more than 8 km from water. They dig for water in dry river beds and, if a water source is badly muddied, they scrape a hole near its edge and drink the clean water that seeps into it.

A Burchell's zebra stallion shows the Flehmen expression as he uses his vomeronasal organ to test a mare's urine.

The stallion in a breeding herd checks his females' reproductive condition by smelling and Flehmen of their urine; tipping his head back and curling his upper lip. A sexually receptive young female stands with her back legs astride and her tail raised and to one side. Older females give no postural signals and only the herd stallion is able to detect that they are on heat.

Burchell's zebra mares give birth lying down close to their group. The foal can stand within 10 to 15 minutes, walk after 20 minutes and run within an hour. Mother and foal are closely bonded by sniffing and grooming interactions and while these bonds are cemented during the foal's first few days the mother chases away any other zebras that approach her offspring. Before they start grazing at seven days old the foals eat the fresh dung of adults to obtain the bacteria they need for digestion. They are suckled until they are about 11 months old. Male Burchell's zebra stay in their natal group until they are about four years old. They leave of their own accord, and are not chased away. When she first comes into heat at 13 to 15 months of age a young female Burchell's zebra is cut from her group by stallions but her oestrus is infertile and she usually returns once she is off heat. She leaves her natal group permanently when about two to two and a half years old, after being herded out while she is on heat.

Order ARTIODACTYLA
Even-toed ungulates

Family   **SUIDAE**
             Pigs

Bushpig   *Potamochoerus porcus* No. 299

Bushpigs are mostly nocturnal. They live in groups, called sounders, of up to 12 under the control and protection of a dominant, adult male. Sounders sometimes come together to form temporary groups of up to 30.

Bushpigs are aggressive, especially when there are piglets in the sounder. The dominant boar is usually the one who drives off both predators and other bushpigs. When two sounders meet the males display by raising the bristles on their shoulders, chomping their jaws and wagging their tails. As they approach each other they roll on the ground and throw up dust and clods of earth by pawing with their forefeet. At close quarters they circle and make short charges which may lead to head-to-head pushing until the weaker boar breaks away and leaves with his sounder. In fights between pigs the sharp canine tusks are used only in the most serious encounters, but they are used freely against predators.

While they are foraging bushpigs keep in contact by grunting softly. The dominant male uses a resonant grunt as an alarm call, which sends his sounder scattering into heavy cover.

A bushpig wallows in mud to keep cool and to get rid of parasites. It swims strongly, with its head under water, coming up for breath every 10 to 15 seconds.

Bushpigs have large home ranges, probably so that they have a number of feeding areas to choose from under various conditions. They defecate in latrines.

They mark their ranges with the secretion from glands on their feet, and the boars mark trees by scarring the bark with their tusks and probably by depositing secretions from glands opening near the bases of their tusks. Nevertheless they are not considered to be territorial because the fights between sounders show that dominance is not affected by location.

Bushpigs have a varied diet that includes all sorts of vegetable matter, the eggs and chicks of ground-nesting birds, reptiles, amphibians and carrion, and newborn lambs that the pigs kill themselves. Buried insect larvae and pupae are favoured foods. Their most characteristic style of feeding is to root in soft soil with their tough, muscular snouts, and smell is the most important sense for finding food. They readily wade into water to get at aquatic plants. Bushpigs are serious agricultural pests because they are such wasteful feeders. They destroy as much as they eat, breaking down a mealie plant to eat only one cob or chewing only one mouthful from a stalk of sugar cane.

A sow litters down in a nest, which she builds in a secluded spot by piling long grass together and burrowing into the heap. Her babies later join their mother's sounder and stay in it until they are about six months old, when the adults chase them away.

Warthog   *Phacochoerus aethiopicus* No. 300

Warthogs are diurnal. At night they shelter in large burrows, which they adapt from aardvark holes by digging with their forefeet and shovelling the soil away with the snout. Females make grass nests in their dens. A warthog's hole is protection against cold as much as against predators and in bad weather they stay underground even during the day. A hole does not have a permanent owner, but one warthog may use a particular hole for several consecutive days. A warthog enters its hole backwards so that anything that follows has to face its tusks. This defence is effective against anything except lions, which are able to dig warthogs out of their refuges.

Warthogs live in groups (sounders) of variable composition; usually there is a dominant boar with one or two females and their offspring. The males are attached to the sounders only during the mating season; at other times the females and young of various ages form maternity groups and some of the males form short-lived bachelor groups.

A warthog has a very firmly established home range, which it leaves only temporarily to reach especially rich food sources or water. It scent-marks by lip wiping and urinating, and with the secretions of preorbital glands just in front of its eyes, but it is not territorial; only the area around a nursery den is defended. It begins marking when it is six or seven months old, and males mark more than females. There may be a loose dominance hierarchy among the warthogs living in a particular area; large, old boars can displace other pigs from food, water and mud baths.

Friendly allogrooming occurs within groups. When two warthogs meet they walk slowly towards each other with their ears back and their heads stretched forward until their noses touch for a mutual sniff. Each carefully sniffs the corners of the other's mouth, and its preorbital glands. They may then try head-to-head pushing or simply move apart again.

Predation takes a heavy toll of warthog piglets but adult warthogs are more likely than most herbivores to counterattack against predators. An adult warthog's lower tusks are longer than a lion's canines and considerably sharper on both tip and edge, so that they can inflict both stab and slash wounds. Full-grown warthog boars have little to fear from anything except lions; they have been seen chasing spotted hyaenas, leopards, cheetahs and wild dogs. Female warthogs sometimes successfully defend their piglets from leopards and cheetahs. Although spotted hyaenas eat warthogs the two use the same burrows at different times, or even simultaneously, and have even been seen sleeping in the same patch of shade.

Warthogs grunt and squeal while fighting. To keep in contact with the group adults grunt quietly and piglets give whistling squeals.

During the mating season aggression between boars becomes common. The antagonists approach with bristled manes, arched backs and prancing steps; they mock-charge, paw the ground, bristle up their manes, run sideways and lunge at each other. A head-to-head pushing contest in which both animals go down onto their knees is the next phase and this occasionally escalates to slashing at the opponent's head and shoulders with the tusks. The warts below the eyes are a protection against this.

Warthogs have to kneel to graze comfortably.

A warthog is mainly a grazer but it will also browse and eat fruit, seeds and herbaceous plants. It uses its tough, muscular snout to grub up rhizomes, roots and earthworms, going down on its knees to get better leverage. Because its neck is short and thick it also kneels to graze. It will occasionally take carrion and will even chase wild dogs or cheetahs off their kills. Every so often it kills and eats a snake or rat. Food is detected mainly by smell. Baby warthogs eat their mother's dung to inoculate their guts with the necessary bacteria.

A warthog sow on heat stands and walks with a hunched posture. A boar can detect her condition from the smell of her urine, which he overmarks with his own, probably to deter other males. A courting male warthog approaches a female with a springy walk, rolling his hips and with his tail cocked upright or wrapped along his flank. He chomps his jaws noisily, salivates profusely and grunts rhythmically. He rests his chin on the sow's rump and if she is receptive she backs towards him and mating follows. A boar may check a number of holes to find an oestrous female and the two may sleep together in the same hole. Subadult males do not usually approach females, but if they do the adult male chases them off.

The piglets are born at the back of the mother's burrow in a grass nest on a shelf, which keeps them dry if water runs into the hole during heavy rain. After about a week they emerge and begin grazing. They are suckled for about five months. Warthog families stay close together and when disturbed the piglets follow their mother as she runs off. They all hold their tails up like aerials so that they can see each other better in long grass. The family group breaks up when the mother falls pregnant again but may reform if she loses her new litter. Some social bonds between mother and young persist for more than two years.

Warthogs flee with their tails up so that they can see each other in tall grass.

Family   HIPPOPOTAMIDAE
Hippopotamus

Hippopotamus   *Hippopotamus amphibius* No. 302

Hippos rest during the day in or near water and move away just after sunset to graze.

The basic unit of hippo society is a group of females with their young, which is controlled by a dominant bull who has gained his position in combat against other males. The groups are territorial, each occupying a stretch of river or the inshore waters of a lake and regularly feeding in an area on land that widens away from the water. The herd bull defends the territory against incursions by other hippo groups and also marks it by splattering dung onto rocks and bushes by wagging his short, flat, bristle-fringed tail as he defecates. At frequently marked spots, such as where a path leaves the water, hippo dung can accumulate into heaps half a metre deep. Females and youngsters do not dung-splatter. By defecating in and near the water hippos inject important quantities of energy and nutrients into aquatic food chains.

Hippos leave the water with the herd bull in the lead, and fan out along established pathways in which their feet wear narrow, parallel ruts. The paths are signposted by dung piles. Hippos do not move any further than they need to to reach food, but if the supplies near the water are exhausted they will cover up to 30 km in a night on the round trip between water and grazing. Occasionally a hippo becomes nomadic; one nicknamed Huberta travelled 1 800 km from Lake St Lucia to the Keiskamma River between 1928 and 1930.

Hippos have to spend their days submerged in water because on land they overheat and dehydrate, and suffer from sunburn which cracks their skin. An overheated hippo looks as if it is sweating blood as glands in its skin secrete a sticky, bright red fluid that acts as a natural sunscreen. They prefer water where shoals or gently sloping banks provide the right depth for them to stand or lie on the bottom with only the tops of their heads and backs exposed. In deep water young hippos ride on their mothers' backs. In cool, shady weather some hippos sleep out of the water for part of the day. There has been one intriguing observation of a mother hippo, resting out of the water with her calf, dribbling saliva onto her baby and licking it over its body. Hippos cannot submerge in mud and they wallow in mud holes only when there is no water available. A hippo can stay under water for up to five minutes and can either swim or walk along the bottom if the water is deep enough; it adjusts its buoyancy by inhaling and exhaling. When a hippo is submerged most of its weight is supported by the water and its movements are lightfooted with a strange, slow-motion grace. Their pathways through aquatic vegetation help to keep waterways open.

In droughts hippos pack together in the remaining water. Under these crowded conditions fighting becomes more common. If the losers are not killed they are driven out of the pool and have little chance of survival. Hippos appear to be very reluctant to leave a pool in which even a little water or mud remains, but they have been known to move long distances to find a new pool when their old one has dried up. How they find a new pool is a mystery.

Disputes between adult male hippos over territories and females begin with a yawning display that shows off their formidable teeth. The contestants then scoop water at one another, probably to demonstrate their strength and manoeuvrability. Unless one of them submits by lowering his head, a full-scale fight follows in which the sharp canine tusks are used to slash the opponent's head and shoulders. Despite their thick hides – 5 to 6 cm on the neck of a dominant bull – hippos suffer serious and sometimes fatal wounds in these battles.

Hippos also use their teeth against other species. In the water their main natural enemies are crocodiles, which stand no chance against an adult hippo. Hippos also attack boats that get too close, especially if a female has a calf. On land a hippo can charge at 40 km/h and is surprisingly agile. To get between a hippo and water is to risk being trampled as it tries to get to safety, and more people are killed by hippos than by any other wild African mammal. They have the curious reputation of stamping out camp fires built close to rivers; most likely this arose from hippos charging through camp sites to get back to the water.

Hippos let out a blast of air as they surface after a dive, they grunt and roar during a fight and give a deep roaring grunt, followed by a series of short grunts, probably to advertise that a particular area is occupied.

A hippo will eat grass down to a smooth lawn by plucking it with the hard edges of its lips. As a rule it will not eat water plants. Hippos show great interest in carcasses but it is not certain that they actually eat any meat (see p 140).

A hippo's threat yawn shows off his dental weaponry.

STRANGE BEHAVIOUR BY HIPPO

Hippopotamuses' legendary habit of stamping out camp fires is not the only odd aspect of their behaviour.

Although they are grazers they have been seen several times nibbling at carcasses floating in the water. Presumably these are favoured delicacies, because in one instance the carcass was appropriated by a dominant herd bull. On the bank of the Crocodile River at Malelane a crocodile feeding on a kudu cow it had caught was repeatedly driven away from its victim by a hippo, who proceeded to chew at the carcass itself. A hippo in the Shitlave dam in the Kruger National Park actually caught and killed an eland calf that got stuck in the mud when its herd came to drink. The hippo dragged the carcass into the water and chewed and tossed it about. Hippos may have inherited a taste for meat from an omnivorous, pig-like ancestor.

More puzzling than these instances of possible carnivory are observations of hippos apparently trying to rescue other animals. When a kudu cow fled into a water hole to escape from a spotted hyaena, two hippos herded her towards the bank and lifted her up with their snouts. Despite their efforts the kudu kept returning to deep water, and she eventually drowned. The hippos carried on shoving her body towards the bank for another hour and a half.

The most astonishing and intriguing behaviour by a hippo would be impossible to believe if it had not been recorded on film by Dick Reucassel. At a water hole in the Kruger National Park an impala ewe was dragged into the water by a lurking crocodile. As the impala weakened after a 15-minute struggle to keep its head above water, the crocodile was beaten off by a charge from an adult hippo. The impala managed to reach dry land but it dropped from exhaustion and loss of blood at the water's edge. After watching it for a moment the hippo moved towards the impala and used its lower tusks to gently lift it to its feet then, as the ewe staggered off, the hippo bellowed. Once more the impala fell and the hippo examined the wounds from the crocodile with its lips, and then supported the impala's head, once on top of its snout and once with its open mouth. The hippo stayed with the antelope then moved about 10 m away and lay down watching as it died. Fifteen minutes later the hippo returned to the water.

Only the dominant male hippo of a herd mates with the females; he checks their reproductive condition by smelling, and perhaps tasting, their urine. Mating takes place in the water with the female completely submerged, coming up occasionally for breath. Apart from whales and dolphins, hippos are the only African mammals that mate in the water. Females give birth in very shallow water or on land in secluded places with dense cover. Births in water deep enough for the baby to have to swim up for its first breath are very rare. The baby can walk and swim within a few minutes of birth and can nurse under water. It stays in the water for the first few days, after which it goes with its mother when she feeds, walking in front of her or alongside her head. In water that is too deep for it to stand, a baby hippo uses its mother as a raft. A mother hippo does not introduce her calf to the herd until it is 10 to 14 days old, once she does the rest of the females act as babysitters. In crowded hippo populations dominant males kill youngsters and newborn babies – whether they single out the offspring of other males is unknown. The females sometimes successfully repulse these attempts at infanticide. Calves begin grazing at five months of age and they are weaned at 12 months. The herd bull drives out adolescent males when they are seven to eight years old. Young females usually stay with the herd.

Family   **GIRAFFIDAE**
            Giraffe

Giraffe   *Giraffa camelopardalis* No. 303

A giraffe usually feeds and moves around during the cooler parts of the day. At night and in the midday heat it rests, either standing up or lying down. It sleeps for only a few minutes at a time, with its head pillowed on its body.

Because its legs are so long a walking giraffe moves both legs on a side at almost the same time. It can gallop at up to 56 km/h but can hardly jump at all, the highest fence a giraffe has been recorded clearing was only 1 m high. They are able to step over 1,4 m barriers.

A giraffe's build makes it difficult for it to groom itself and it is usually peppered with ticks. It scratches against trees to try to rid itself of these parasites.

Giraffes live in loose, unstable herds containing both males and females of various ages. Mature bulls roam alone but will associate with a herd that has an oestrous female in it. Giraffes are not territorial; each herd has a home range with a very indefinite border whose location changes through time. Occasionally they make excursions into new areas and then return to their old haunts. Some cows leave their home ranges to give birth in a familiar calving ground.

Among an area's giraffes there are separate dominance hierarchies among males and females. A dominant giraffe stands with its head high and in line with its neck, a submissive one holds its head low and at an angle to its neck and drops its ears.

The social interaction in which giraffes are most likely to be seen is necking. This occurs during courtship, when it has a gentle, stroking action, and between young adult males when it is a test of strength, each trying to wrestle the other slightly off balance. The winner emphasizes his dominance by briefly mounting the loser. In real fights old bulls swing their heads like medieval maces, landing thudding blows on the opponent's body. A giraffe's neck is so long that the swing looks slower than it is and the blows less hard, but the sounds of their impacts

Necking giraffes; two young males try to wrestle each other off balance.

can be heard from 100 m away and a blow from a captive giraffe was enough to knock a bull eland off its feet and kill it. Each bull rides its opponent's blows by jumping slightly at the moment of impact. Since they cannot jump and swing at the same time the two opponents give the impression that they are taking turns to give and receive blows. Fights like this can go on for more than half an hour but they are rare because of the dominance hierarchy.

Giraffe defend themselves against predators by kicking with either the fore or hind feet. Their large and heavy hooves can break a lion's back and at least one human has been kicked to death by a giraffe.

Giraffe are browsers. Their height enables them to reach food which no antelope can get at. Males tend to feed at full stretch, reaching up to 5, 8 m from the ground. Females feed lower with their heads down, even bending their necks to reach the tops of low bushes. The sex of a feeding giraffe can be seen from a distance from this difference in feeding styles. A giraffe is a very selective feeder. It pulls leaves and small twigs into its mouth with its tongue and nips off the edible parts between its lower incisors and its upper gums. It spits out thorns and tough twigs. The presence of thorns protects a tree by slowing a giraffe's browsing; at least 11, and up to 20, hours a day will be spent feeding.

In areas where the soil is poor in phosphorus or calcium giraffes get these minerals by chewing bones.

A giraffe will sometimes eat newly sprouted grass; to reach it, it has to splay its front legs and bend its knees in the same way as when drinking, before bending its neck to get its head down to ground level. A giraffe in this position is very vulnerable and it always looks around carefully and makes sure it has a firm footing before bending. Its brain is protected by a special system of blood vessels from the sudden changes in blood pressure that come from raising and lowering the head.

A wandering bull tests the reproductive condition of females he encounters by smelling and using his vomeronasal organ in Flehmen. A female is attractive at least 24 hours before she becomes receptive and she will be consorted by a series of increasingly high-ranking bulls as each suitor is displaced, usually with no more than a standing-tall display, by one further up the hierarchy. By the time the female is receptive she is being courted by the area's top bull, and these dominant animals achieve nearly all the matings.

In the Serengeti nearly all giraffe calves are born in traditional calving grounds to which a female will return even if she has to leave her home range. Apparently,

Fighting giraffe bulls batter each other with their heads.

Giraffe bulls feed at full stretch while cows bend down.

there is nothing special about the topography or vegetation of the calving grounds and how they came to be chosen is a mystery. Whether southern African giraffes do the same is unknown. A female gives birth standing up, or even while walking, with her hindlegs bent to lessen the calf's fall. At first the mother chases other giraffe away so that her calf bonds only to her. The calf can stand within five minutes and suck within an hour. While it is still wobbly on its legs its mother guides it with nudges of her head and forelegs. For the first three weeks the calf lies out. The mother grazes up to 3 km away from it and returns to suckle it and spend the night near it. Calves in the same herd establish social bonds by playing and nose-to-nose sniffing. They first eat solid food at two weeks, are weaned at 12 to 14 months and leave the mother at 15 to 17 months.

Family   **BOVIDAE**
Antelope and buffalo

Black wildebeest   *Connochaetes gnou* No. 305

There are three types of social unit in a black wildebeest population. Bulls in their prime are territorial; yearling, subadult and non-territorial males form bachelor herds, and females of all ages herd together.

A territorial male marks his ground with urine, faeces and the secretions from interdigital and preorbital glands, and by pawing up the soil. He advertises his status with loud, high-pitched 'ge-nu' calls, stiff-legged cantering with his head high, bucking, tail swishing and head pitching while galloping. In confrontations with his neighbours he rolls over, kneels and digs up clods of earth with his horns; a territorial bull can be recognised by the mud and broken vegetation sticking to his horns. Real fights are rare but when they do occur they involve horn-clashing and head-to-head pushing.

A submissive black wildebeest holds its head low and may even graze to demonstrate its lack of hostility. Territory neighbours generally behave submissively towards one another once they have established their common border. Other intruding males are promptly chased off.

Female herds contain up to 60 black wildebeest and these wander through the bulls' territories. During the mating season each bull tries to herd as many females as he can within his territory so that he can mate with them as they come on heat. Females moving between territories cause conflict between the bulls and displays and fights are more frequent, and more intense, during the rut than for the rest of the year.

A territorial black wildebeest bull's horns are adorned with mud and broken vegetation.   145

When a single male black wildebeest and a herd of females have been reintroduced to an area the male has attacked the cows and calves, presumably because there was no other outlet for his territorial aggression.

Black wildebeest are grazers but if there is no grass they switch to the leaves of small bushes. They drink daily.

Loud snorts and foot-stamping are used as alarm signals, which bring a whole herd to attention. They may all run off and then swing to look back at the source of the danger.

Female black wildebeest stay in the herd to have their calves and these can run with the adults within hours of birth. The mother-calf bond is very strong. A calf stays with its mother until she chases it off when she has her next one. Yearling males then leave to join a bachelor herd.

Blue wildebeest   *Connochaetes taurinus* No. 306

Blue wildebeest have the same social units as the black, territorial males, female herds and bachelor groups. The bachelor groups are unstable and have hardly any social structure, although in one instance two bachelors supported a third after he had been darted. In areas of favourable grazing or with a good water supply hundreds or thousands of blue wildebeest may congregate, but these huge aggregations have no social structure above the female and bachelor herds. If chased by a predator a blue wildebeest tries to run into the densest part of its herd.

A territorial bull advertises his status and position by a rocking-horse canter with head held high, and low-pitched 'ugh' calls. When a herd has gathered in his territory the resident bull can be recognised as he carries his head higher than the others.

146   *A ritualised border clash between two blue wildebeest bulls.*

A blue wildebeest bull courting and herding females.

A territorial male scent-marks by rubbing his preorbital glands on the ground or low vegetation, by depositing interdigital gland secretions as he patrols or paws the ground and by defecating on dung piles. The interdigital gland secretion has a sharp, tarry odour that even humans can smell in areas where blue wildebeest have been. A territorial bull who is approached by another male displays with an exaggerated 'rocking-horse' canter with his head held high and horizontal. An intruder who does not heed this warning will be engaged in horn-clashing and head-butting. Both contestants kneel during these ritualised fights, which very seldom lead to injury. In strongly migratory populations breeding bulls move with the herds and stake out temporary territories wherever there is a pause in the migration.

Blue wildebeest snort to signal alarm or as a territorial challenge. Calves bleat when separated from their mothers, who answer by lowing. Bulls bellow and grunt when herding females.

Blue wildebeest are grazers who prefer short grass. Where water and grazing are available all year round the populations are sedentary and the males are permanently territorial. In seasonally variable habitats they migrate in their thousands. They also make shorter journeys in response to localised rainfall; probably responding to the sight and sound of lightning and thunder. They need to drink every day and so seldom feed more than 15 km from water. They readily drink badly muddied water.

In the mating season a territorial bull herds females into his territory by circling them with his head down and his tail lashing, or by chasing them with his body low and tail streaming behind. While herding he bawls and grunts. He courts females by stretching his head and neck forward and by rearing onto his hindlegs in a heraldic rampant pose. Courtship and territory defence leave a breeding bull hardly any time for feeding and there is a turn-over of breeders between territories and bachelor herds as exhausted territory holders are replaced by fresher animals.

A female may mate with a succession of territorial bulls within a short period. She leaves her herd to give birth but returns to it as soon as she can in an attempt to avoid predators, for whom the calves are a favourite target. The calves can run after only five minutes and can keep pace with the adults after only a day. A female blue wildebeest will suckle only her own calf, which she recognises by sound and smell. She aggressively spurns approaches by others. She will fiercely defend her baby against predators. Attacks by lone hyaenas are beaten off, but her defence is useless if she must face two or more attackers because she can only tackle one at a time.

Blue wildebeest calves start eating grass in their second week but they are suckled for at least another eight months. A calf twice this age can be seen suckling if its mother has lost her next calf. Young females usually stay in their natal herds, whereas males leave for a bachelor group after about two years.

Lichtenstein's hartebeest   *Sigmoceros lichtensteinii* No. 307

Lichtenstein's hartebeests live in groups of up to about 10 females with their young, attended by an adult bull in whose territory they live. A bull whose territory contains a rich food supply can control more cows than one on poorer ground. Territories are marked with dung middens and patches of soil that the bull digs up with his hooves and horns and marks with his preorbital glands. He also marks his own flanks with the preorbital gland secretion, which leaves a distinct, dark smear.

Males who cannot secure a territory live alone or, rarely, join bachelor herds in unfavourable habitat on the periphery of the territory areas.

A territorial bull acts as a sentinel and guard for his cows; he stands on elevated ground to get a better view and if the herd flees he takes up the rearguard, sometimes stopping to check for pursuit.

Lichtenstein's hartebeests are grazers who occasionally browse. They prefer freshly sprouting grass.

In the mating season territorial males may try to steal each other's females. This leads to contests of horn-clashing and pushing with the horns interlocked.

A bull courts an oestrous female by approaching her with his head, neck and tail stretched horizontally. He sniffs her anogenital area and may mark her rump with his preorbital gland before mounting a few times in quick succession. A receptive female faces away from the male with her hindlegs astride and her tail to one side.

A Lichtenstein's hartebeest calf is able to follow its mother soon after birth but she usually leaves it lying down, not necessarily hidden, while she feeds. Young males leave the herd at 10 to 12 months; if young females leave it is at an age of 15 to 18 months.

Red hartebeest   *Alcelaphus buselaphus* No. 308

Red hartebeest live in herds of up to about 30 which sometimes join up in aggregations of a few hundred to a few thousand where the grazing is good. Each herd contains females, their offspring, a few subordinate males and a dominant bull.

There is a dominance hierarchy among the females which is maintained by horn sparring, butting and chasing. The bull is territorial and he herds his females. Territories are established and maintained by fighting, which involves charges and horn-lunges by one contestant which the other parries with his horns. The ridges on their horns interlock and the two try to throw each other off balance by twisting and shoving. The horn-clashing during such a fight can be heard from hundreds of metres away. Fights are especially fierce and frequent during the rut. Territories are marked by dung patches, most of which are on borders and are used by both neighbours.

A territorial bull stands on a patch of raised ground or a termite mound to display his status and to get a good view of the surrounding area. As well as watching for intruders he is vigilant for predators. He signals alarm by snorting and stamping a forefoot, which alerts the females and young. Red hartebeest herds tend to flee in single file.

Bachelor herds contain males who have not established territories. They are found in poor habitat.

Red hartebeest graze and browse. They are fond of freshly sprouted grass and will temporarily leave their herd territories to reach areas where rain or fire has flushed new growth.

Territorial bulls do all the mating. A bull checks the condition of his females by vulval sniffing – he does not show Flehmen. If he finds one on heat he courts her by approaching with his head low and his ears down and nudging her with his nose. Successful matings occur after several failed attempts.

Females have their calves in dense cover away from the herd. For the first few days the calf lies out. When its mother returns to suckle it she consumes its urine and faeces so that predators cannot sniff it out. When the calf is introduced to the herd its mother keeps other adults away from it. Mother and calf can recognise each other by sight over as much as 300 m. If a herd is alarmed the calves join their mothers and run alongside them. A calf that cannot keep up drops flat and freezes in an attempt to avoid being noticed by a predator with its attention on the fleeing herd.

A calf starts grazing at about two weeks old and is weaned at about eight months. As it gets older it spends more time with other calves and less with its mother.

Bontebok   *Damaliscus dorcas dorcas* No. 309

Bontebok are most active first thing in the morning and late in the afternoon. They avoid both heat and rain by sheltering among bushes, or standing in the open with their heads down.

Adult males establish stable territories through which groups of up to eight females roam. Non-territorial males form bachelor groups, which also contain a few yearling females, and they wander through the territories despite the residents' efforts to keep them out. In each female herd a dominance hierarchy is established and maintained by threats and horn-clashing. In bachelor groups there is almost no social structure, and few interactions apart from practice horn-fencing by yearlings.

A territorial male goes through a wide range of postural and movement signals to advertise his status. The most important seems to be the 'proud' posture in which he stands with his head high and his ears flared, often on a patch of higher

149

ground to make himself more visible. If a strange male approaches, the territory holder shows off his size by a lateral display, nods his head, snorts, prances, bucks and stands as if urinating or defecating. If the intruder persists in his approach he and the territory holder stand head to tail, sniffing each other. In rare cases both animals kneel and feint with their horns. Encounters hardly ever escalate beyond this stage but if one does the contestants lock horns and push against each other.

A territorial male wipes secretions from his preorbital glands onto grass stalks and urinates and defecates in middens. The scent marks and latrines by themselves do not keep intruders out, but by wiping his horns on fresh scent marks, and by lying in his middens and digging in them with his horns, the territory holder picks up a smell that indisputably labels him as the territory's long-term resident, who will be more prepared to escalate a conflict than will an intruder.

Bontebok are grazers who prefer short grass. They drink at least once a day.

During the rut a territorial ram herds females into his territory. He checks his females' condition by vulval sniffing without showing Flehmen. He courts them by stretching his head and neck forwards and his tail backwards. If she is not receptive a female circles him with her head down, and kicks backwards to keep him away. If she is on heat she stands with her legs apart and her tail to one side.

Young males leave their natal herd and join a bachelor group when they are about a year old. Females tend to stay in the herd where they were born.

Blesbok   *Damaliscus dorcas phillipsi* No. 309

Except for a few particulars a blesbok's behaviour is very similar to that of a bontebok.

A territorial blesbok ram wipes preorbital gland secretions onto grass stalks and then rubs his horns against the mark. The grooves on his horns accumulate a mixture of preorbital gland secretion, soil from horning the ground and crushed vegetation from thrashing bushes.

Territories are marked by dung middens; the resident ram lies and rubs his neck and face in them so that the odour he picks up labels him as the territory holder.

Territorial rams stand sideways-on to each other, approach and mutually anal sniff, perhaps spar with their horns or simply graze close together.

The peculiar stance taken by blesbok during very hot weather.

Fighting between males is vigorous and males have been found dead from horn wounds, although outside the rutting season the males are tolerant of trespassers. From May to December the territorial system tends to break down and the female herds amalgamate into groups of a few hundred.

A blesbok's alarm call is a snort through the nose.

During very hot weather blesbok stand in small groups with their necks drooping and their faces close to the ground. Every so often one of them snorts, stamps or shakes its head, or runs in a tight circle back to its place.

During the rut, which extends from February to April, the rams become more fiercely territorial. Each one herds groups of up to 25 females by running in front of them with his head low and stretched forward, his tail curled up and his ears held out sideways and downwards. Receptive females are courted with the same action. Mating takes only two to three seconds.

Blesbok ewes stay in their herd to give birth. The calves can stand after a few minutes and run after 20 minutes. Each mother keeps other females away from her calf and will suckle only her own offspring, driving others away. A calf that is separated from its mother gives loud 'bé-bé' bleats, which she answers by grunting. The calves are weaned at four months.

A rutting blesbok ram courting females.

Tsessebe
Damaliscus lunatus No. 310

Tsessebe form female breeding herds of up to 20 animals that are controlled by territorial bulls. Bachelor groups contain up to 30 non-territorial males.

A territorial bull patrols his area at a steady walk, and displays on patches of raised ground by standing tall with his head tipped backwards. He scent-marks with faeces and by inserting grass stems into his preorbital glands to leave a smear of secretion. If he marks a stem repeatedly the secretion builds up into a transparent mass. He will also wipe his face on the ground or against termite mounds, deposit interdigital gland secretion by pawing the ground, dig up soil

151

with his horns and cake himself with mud by rolling in it. Females also dig with their horns.

The territory bull challenges intruders by approaching them while tossing his head and rearing up. If the intruder responds with the same display the two circle each other, drop to their knees and clash horns. In the rare serious fights the combatants lock horns and push. The male herds his females by walking with a slow, exaggerated high-stepping gait with his head held high and his ears pressed downwards.

A territorial dispute between two tsessebe bulls.

Tsessebe are grazers who prefer fresh sprouted grass.

Tsessebes' great speed and endurance allow them to outrun predators and when frightened they run for only a short distance, then stop and turn to check for pursuit. This makes them very vulnerable to shooting.

A tsessebe calf can run with its mother soon after birth. While its mother is feeding it joins other calves in a small nursery group that is usually watched over by a nearby female. If there is an alarm the herd runs to collect the calves before fleeing.

Young males join bachelor herds when they are about a year old. Females tend to stay in their natal herds.

Blue duiker   *Philantomba monticola* No. 311

Blue duiker are extremely wary and secretive. They live solitarily or in pairs which are faithful for life, in dense forest from which they emerge at first light to graze and browse in open glades. They also eat fallen fruit and leaves, picking up what gets knocked down by monkeys and birds.

A male courting a female nibbles her neck and shoulders and wipes his preorbital glands on her face.

Red duiker

Cephalophus natalensis No. 312

Red duiker live solitarily in dense forest and thickets. They defecate in communal middens and are probably territorial. They make a loud sneezing noise that might be an alarm signal. They eat fresh leaves, forbs and fallen fruit.

Common duiker

Sylvicapra grimmia No. 313

A common duiker is active in the early morning, and from the late afternoon until very late into the evening. The rest of the time it lies up in the shade of dense vegetation. It is solitary and probably territorial except when mating or if it is a female with a lamb. It scent-marks with preorbital gland secretions.

When disturbed it initially freezes, then dashes away on a zigzag course into heavy cover.

A common duiker will eat a large range of vegetable food including leaves, bark, flowers, fruit, gum and roots, but rarely grass. It will sometimes take nesting birds, lizards, caterpillars and even small mammals. It rarely drinks, but will eat wild melons as a source of moisture.

A female common duiker drops her lamb in heavy cover and leaves it there, returning two or three times a day to suckle and clean it. If the baby is approached it freezes with its head flat on the ground and its ears back in an attempt to avoid being seen. If it is threatened it gives an alarm bleat, which brings its parents rushing to protect it. This defence is probably quite effective against small and medium-sized predators.

Springbok

Antidorcas marsupialis No. 314

Springbok form herds of a few dozen animals but congregate in much larger groups in areas of good feeding. Mass migrations of whole springbok populations, involving hundreds of thousands of animals, are things of the past.

There are three types of social unit within a springbok population; mixed herds of adults and juveniles of both sexes, bachelor herds and territorial males.

It takes a male three to three and a half years to attain territorial status, and usually his tenure will be between six and twenty months. Males are not permanently attached to their territories but they will stay on them even when the scarcity of springbok in the area suggests that conditions have become unfavourable. A territory holder advertises his status by standing and walking around conspicuously. He urinates with his hindlegs stretched backwards and apart and his body low to the ground, then he brings his legs forward into a hunched posture and defecates on top of the urine. By repeatedly urinating and defecating in the same places he builds up middens in which he scratches with his forefeet before adding to them. He also thrashes at low bushes with his horns, picking up green stains on his horns and face in the process. Apparently springbok do not use their preorbital glands for marking.

Fights between adult males over territories are tests of strength and agility as they lock horns and try to push and wrestle each other off balance. Fatal gorings, broken necks and the two combatants dying with their horns locked together have all been recorded. Short bouts of horn-sparring occur between young males. Adult females repulse approaches from other springbok with a dip and swing of their horns.

Because the females and non-territorial males occur together in the mixed-sex herds the territorial rams have to tolerate the presence of males in their territories.

A springbok grazes, browses, digs up roots, and eats pods, seeds and fruit according to what is available. It can survive without water by eating succulent vegetation and wild melons, and by grazing at night when the water content of the grass rises from 8 per cent to 26 per cent. While feeding it faces away from the sun so that its white rump reflects the heat and less water has to be used to keep cool.

While feeding springbok give quiet muttering grunts that probably help to keep the herd together and serve as fail-safe signals that nothing untoward is going on. Females 'grunt-bellow' to call their calves, which reply by bleating. Territorial males bellow while herding females. The alarm call is a whistly snort.

Springbok rely mainly on their keen eyesight and sprinting abilities to avoid predators. Within a herd there are always some individuals on the lookout as they take a break from feeding. One of the disadvantages faced by a lone, territorial male is that he has to feed without companions keeping watch. In the Kalahari springbok move down at night onto riverbeds and dry pans where the harder surface gives them a better chance of outrunning predators. If a herd is startled its members dash away in all directions with spectacular leaps that can take them 2 m off the ground and cover 6 m. This sudden explosion of movement makes it difficult for a predator to concentrate on a particular target. Once the springbok have located the cause of the alarm they sprint away at up to 88 km/h. The springbok's spectacular pronking display (see p 156) may be another anti-predator tactic.

The mating season for springbok depends on when rainfall brings on a flush of new plant growth. This varies regionally but within a given area most of the springbok females come on heat at about the same time. A territorial ram then starts to herd them onto his ground by running in front of them with his head,

A springbok ram's exaggerated urination and defecation postures advertise his occupation of a territory.

Courtship in springbok.

neck and tail held horizontal or, at high intensities, with his tail curled upwards. Sometimes females pronk while being herded. He checks their condition by urine-sniffing and Flehmen; the females usually avoid his attempts at vulval sniffing. During the rut, courtship, mating and territory defence take up 20 per cent of a breeding ram's time.

When he finds a female on heat the ram walks or trots towards her with springy steps, his head high and his ears vertical. He follows one or two metres behind in a normal posture and when he comes up behind her he puts one foreleg between her hindlegs and moves it from side to side without touching her. This is a ritualised version of a courtship behaviour seen in other species of antelope. If she is willing to mate, the female parts her hindlegs and holds her tail to one side. The male stands on his hindlegs behind her; his chest does not rest on her rump and he does not clasp her with his forelegs. On average each territorial male serves 15 ewes.

When the females drop their lambs the males in the mixed-sex herds move off to join the bachelor groups. The smell of the birth fluids is apparently stimulating to adult males and they can be seen sniffing and unsuccessfully courting females who have just given birth.

For the first two days the lambs stay hidden in long grass or under bushes. They cannot run and dodge well enough to get away from predators so they freeze to avoid detection instead. Before the end of the first week they sprint away if disturbed but it takes them a month to match full springbok speeds. Often the lambs form nursery groups. They begin eating plants at two weeks and are weaned at two months. Young females stay in their natal herds, but some of the young males move off to bachelor herds when they are about six months old.

WHAT PUTS THE SPRING IN SPRINGBOK?
THE PUZZLE OF THE PRONK

When fleeing from predators, antelope of some species put on a display of exaggerated, bouncy running called stotting. The stotting action differs between species; Damara dik-dik bounce rhythmically along, grey rhebok run with a rocking-horse action, and reedbuck kick their hindlegs backwards at the crest of each leap.

The most spectacular of these displays is a springbok's pronk; it launches itself into the air with legs stiff, feet close together, head down and back arched. Very often it flares the fan of brilliant white hair on its back. These leaps can clear 3 m but the springbok covers hardly any ground between takeoff and landing.

Springbok pronk in a variety of circumstances; while a herd is trekking to food or water, when there is a mild disturbance, even just before a break in the weather, and sometimes for no apparent reason at all. The most puzzling thing about pronking is that it is also a reaction to pursuit by predators, when it would seem that the sensible thing would be to do some proper running as soon and as swiftly as possible.

Stotting has been studied most carefully in the springbok's East African relative and ecological equivalent, the Thompson's gazelle, and it is clear that when predators are involved a stotting antelope is actually signalling to them to reduce its own chances of being chased and captured. When a stalking cheetah sees a buck stotting it knows that it has been seen itself and that it has lost the advantage of a surprise attack, and with it its chances of making a kill, so it abandons the stalk, which is obviously to the prey's advantage. Predators such as hunting dogs and spotted hyaenas, which wear down their prey in a long chase, do better if they select weaker animals as their targets. Stotting seems to tell these animals 'Don't bother chasing me, I'm fast and agile so you might not catch me', and a stotter is less likely to be targetted by hunting dogs than a buck that simply runs away.

A baby Thompson's gazelle will stot to attract its mother to come and defend it.

Springbok seem to pronk 'just in case' a predator might be around. If one pronks as a herd files past a patch of dense cover, where danger might be lurking, those coming behind will pronk as well as they reach the same spot.

A springbok's white, dorsal crest grows out of a strip of glandular skin that produces a waxy secretion with a rich, sweet smell. The secretion's odour is released as the crest is flared and the smell, coupled to the sudden flash of white, might be an alarm signal or even a signal to the predator.

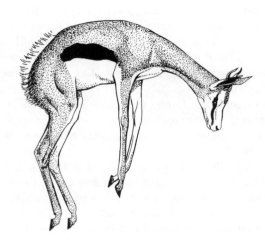

A springbok's spectacular pronk.

A newborn springbok lamb flattens itself to the ground to avoid detection.

Klipspringer   *Oreotragus oreotragus* No. 315

Klipspringers live singly, in pairs or in family groups of three. Larger groups may be seen at favourable feeding sites or when several males are attracted to an oestrous female, but these are only temporary and have no social structure. A male and female pair for life, they rest next to one another and very rarely move more than 15 m apart. They take turns feeding and watching for danger, but the male does most of the guard duty so that the female can stay in good condition for breeding.

Klipspringers are mostly diurnal but they sometimes feed by moonlight. They rest in the shade of rocks and bushes during the hottest part of the day.

A klipspringer is incredibly agile; leaping with ease from boulder to boulder and using small cracks and ledges to climb cliffs. It stands on the tips of its hooves, which are ovals with soft pads in the middle and hard rims to provide grip. On rocky ground a klipspringer can outrun and outmanoeuvre any predator and if it is disturbed while feeding on flat ground it immediately makes for the sanctuary of the rocks. A predator can catch a klipspringer only if it surprises it at close range, which is why a klipspringer that spots a predator some distance away does not immediately run but just stands watching it. If the predator approaches, the klipspringer jumps onto a rock and repeatedly stamps its foot and gives a penetrating alarm whistle. This alerts the klipspringer's mate, who also stands on a rock and whistles, but most importantly it tells the predator that it has

157

A klipspringer stands on the tips of its specialised hooves.

been seen and that its chances of making a kill have vanished, and so it may as well try somewhere else.

Klipspringer pairs are territorial and are as faithful to their area as they are to each other; one male was resighted in his original territory after eight years. Either member of a klipspringer pair will fight to defend their territory. These fights are serious and sometimes fatal, so intruders usually withdraw as soon as a resident approaches. The resident klipspringers' habit of standing prominently on rocks helps to advertise their possession of a territory. Territories are demarcated by preorbital gland marks and dung middens which may be a metre across and 10 cm deep. Both partners scent-mark by manoeuvring the tip of a thin, bare twig on a low bush into the opening of the preorbital gland. This leaves a sticky, sickly-sweet smelling black smear about 5 mm long, which builds up to a black blob from repeated markings on the same twig. The male usually quickly over-marks his mate's marks. Klipspringers release the odour from scent marks by licking them.

Klipspringers browse on a wide variety of newly sprouted leaves, flowers and fruit, but hardly ever eat grass. They can survive without water but they drink if it is available.

A baby klipspringer is born in the shelter of rocks or vegetation and for the first month it stays hidden, relying on its cryptic colour to avoid being noticed. Its mother visits to suckle it three or four times a day. It forages with its mother from the age of three months and is weaned at four to five months. The parents chase it out of their territory when it is about a year old.

A klipspringer demarcates its territory with scent marks from its preorbital gland.

Damara dik-dik   *Madoqua kirkii* No. 316

Damara dik-diks live singly, in pairs, in families of three or in temporary groups. They occupy definite home ranges that are crisscrossed by regularly used pathways. Measurements of home range areas vary from 0,3 ha to 10 ha. Both sexes urinate and then defecate in middens, but only the males dig with their forefeet first. After adding to a midden both sexes deposit secretion from their preorbital glands on nearby vegetation. The secretion is black and tarry and it builds up into blobs when a marking site is used repeatedly. Middens tend to be made near path junctions, and those on home range borders are used by both sets of neighbours. Strangely, the middens are also used by small carnivores. It seems likely from their scent-marking behaviour that Damara dik-diks are territorial but this is not known for certain. A male Damara dik-dik makes a rasping sound by grating his ridged horns on woody stems. In the process the ridges get packed with dirt and crushed bark.

Damara dik-diks are most active in the early morning and late afternoon and evening although they may be seen moving around and feeding in short bouts at any time of the day.

Their contact call is probably the high, quavering whistle they give. When alarmed they give either a sharp single whistle as they dash for cover, or repeated whistles in time with the jumps of an exaggerated stotting action.

Damara dik-diks have a varied diet of browse, grass, flowers, fruit and freshly fallen leaves. They prefer fresh, growing tips and they seem to select what to eat by smell. They do not need to drink but will do so.

A courting Damara dik-dik male makes a stiff-legged approach to the ewe with his head low and stretched forward and the crest of hair on his forehead erected. A receptive female crouches and sometimes displays rosettes of white hair on her haunches, which are shown off as she twitches her tail rhythmically from side to side.

The lambs are born in heavy cover, they lie out and are visited for suckling four times in 24 hours. They are weaned at six weeks and stay with their mother until her next lamb is born. The male grooms the baby. Whether youngsters leave of their own accord or get chased away is unknown.

Oribi   *Ourebia ourebi* No. 317

Oribi are active during both day and night. They rest lying down with their heads up, often on a patch of raised ground so that they have a clear view all round.

The basic social unit is a male with one or two females and their lambs. Single animals and aggregations of up to about a dozen can also be seen.

Oribi have more scent glands than other southern African antelope: a preorbital pair, interdigital glands on all four feet, inguinal glands, sub-aural glands, which show as black patches just below the ears, carpal glands on the forelegs just below the knees and metatarsal glands on the hindlegs.

Male oribi are territorial. They stand prominently inside their area and mark it with preorbital gland secretion. The black secretion is dabbed onto the top of tall grass stems, but if the grass is too tall the oribi bites it off at head height for convenient marking and to ensure that the mark is at nose level. The glands on the feet simply mark as the oribi walks around. Oribi will defecate in a communal midden if they happen to be near one; if not they drop their dung anywhere.

A ram's female companions are not territorial but as long as they have enough food they stay inside his borders. After a female has defecated and urinated the territorial male marks nearby with his preorbital glands, scratches at her faeces with his forefeet to mark them with his interdigital glands, and defecates and urinates where she did.

Oribis are continually alert. Their alarm call is a whistly snort which sends other oribis off with a rocking-horse action. They like to keep the danger in sight and when they flee through long grass they jump every now and then to look around. Unless they are chased they stop within 200 m and may inquisitively walk back towards the cause of the disturbance.

An oribi grazes and browses very selectively, carefully picking the most nutritious parts of a variety of grasses and forbs. Even if water is available it does not drink.

Oribi courtship involves gentle butting and nuzzling and the ram kicks the female's hindlegs with his foreleg. For their first month baby oribi lie out, securely hidden in long, dense grass or thick bush. If they are approached they flatten themselves to the ground.

Steenbok

Steenbok are solitary and territorial except for mating pairs and females with young. They are mainly diurnal and are most active in the cool of the early morning, late afternoon and evening.

Steenbok have preorbital, interdigital and throat glands, which are probably used to mark their territories. Near their territory boundaries they defecate and urinate in middens but elsewhere they have the unusual habit of digging a hole with their forefeet and burying their excrement. Actual fights over territories are rare; intruders readily move off once they realise that an area is occupied. Intruders may be allowed into a territory as long as they behave submissively towards the resident.

To gain access to the water hole an intruding steenbok has to defer to the local resident.

When alarmed a steenbok usually dashes away for a short distance and, if not pursued, stops to look back at the cause of the disturbance. Otherwise it hides by lying in thick vegetation and only flees at the last moment. Steenbok have been known to take refuge in aardvark burrows.

Steenbok have a varied diet. They are mainly browsers and they prefer forbs to woody plants. They can live without water by eating melons and digging up juicy roots. If these fail they use water holes and have to defer to the holders of the territories in which these lie.

A ram who is courting a female nibbles at her face and kicks her from behind with his foreleg. Steenbok lambs are born in dense vegetation and they stay hidden there while the mother feeds. When danger threatens the young lie with their heads flat on the ground and their ears back. They eat their first grass at two weeks and are weaned at three months.

161

Grysbok
Raphicerus melanotis No. 319

Grysbok begin their nocturnal activity at dusk. Most of the time they live alone; the females in overlapping home ranges and the males in territories. Male-female pairs can be seen during the mating season from March to June. Both sexes urinate and defecate in middens up to 1 m across. Adult males also scent-mark with their preorbital glands.

They are mainly grazers but they take fruit and can be a problem in vineyards where they eat the vine tips and developing grapes.

If alarmed they dash away and suddenly drop and freeze.

A female on heat is followed closely by a ram who licks and nuzzles her genitals. Mating occurs on the move and it is hardly surprising that most mountings are unsuccessful.

Sharpe's grysbok
Raphicerus sharpei No. 320

These shy antelope are nocturnal and, except for male-female pairs and females with young, solitary and territorial. They avoid danger by hiding in thick vegetation and fleeing at the last moment with a slinking run, which contrasts with a duiker's bounds.

They browse on both leaves and fruit and eat a little grass.

Suni
Neotragus moschatus No. 321

Suni live in small social groups of a male with one or more females and their young. Each group lives in a territory that is marked by dung middens and preorbital gland secretion. Subordinate males may be tolerated inside a territory.

The dominant male in a group does nearly all the preorbital gland marking. He places most of the marks on stalks and twigs up to about 6 cm high in areas where an intruder would be likely to feed with its nose near the ground. Through repeated markings of a single twig, hard pea-sized lumps of black secretion build up. To the human nose the secretion has a very faint, oily smell. Dung middens are nearly always next to the worn pathways that the sunis use to get about in their dense habitat.

When alarmed a suni first freezes in an attempt to avoid being seen. If this fails and the danger approaches, it runs for the nearest heavy cover, giving a high 'chee-chee', which is probably an alarm call.

Most of a suni's diet consists of freshly fallen leaves but its favourite food is fruit. It also browses on green leaves and eats mushrooms. They are very selective feeders, picking the choicest leaves one at a time. They get all the water they need from their diet and so do not have to drink.

Impala and black-faced impala
Aepyceros melampus No. 322

For most of the year impala live in two sorts of herds; bachelor groups that contain males of all ages and breeding herds that contain adult females, young males and females, and one or two adult males. In the autumn breeding season some of the males become territorial and the herds then contain either only males or only females, because the breeding rams chase all other males out of the breeding herds. The most common herd sizes are from six to 20. In the winter aggregations of up to 100 can be seen.

Impala are adaptable feeders and will browse or graze according to what is available. They readily eat fruit, flowers and acacia pods. They are dependent on water and will go down to drink every day if they can.

Except for rutting males impala are alert and wary. They benefit from the extra eyes, ears and noses that being in a herd provides. If one detects something suspicious it gives a loud snort, which alerts its companions. They look up from resting or feeding and locate the danger by looking in the same direction as the caller. As long as they have a predator in sight they will usually move away slowly, or even approach to get a better view. If attacked they sprint away, weaving expertly among bushes and trees. If a herd is suddenly alarmed at close range, it explodes in all directions. Impala are known to leap up to 3 m high and to cover 11 m in a single leap. The sudden turmoil makes it difficult for a predator to pick out and concentrate on a target.

The explosive leaps of a startled impala herd make it difficult for a predator to concentrate on one target.

The tuft of black hair on an impala's hindleg surrounds a gland which produces a secretion with a pleasant cheesy smell but uncertain function; it has been suggested that the gland is fluffed open during alarm leaps to leave an airborne scent trail for the rest of the herd to follow.

In January as the days get shorter the adult males in the bachelor herds become aggressive. They give roaring calls which start with a rasping sound and run into a series of harsh grunts, and begin to fight by horn-clashing and pushing. This breaks up the bachelor herds and the males that are big enough, skilled enough and in sufficiently good physical condition establish territories of at least one to two ha, and usually about 10 ha, by fighting off intruders. Most of the successful territory holders are between three and a half and eight and a half years old. The unsuccessful males reform bachelor groups, which keep away from the places where territories have been set up.

An impala ram roaring to advertise his status as a territory holder.

A territorial ram advertises his status by patrolling his ground, roaring and scent-marking by rubbing the glandular skin of his forehead and face on vegetation. While roaring he stands with his head, neck and tail held out horizontally. He threatens intruders by snorting, sticking out his tongue, lowering his horns and dipping his head with his ears held back. He may chase intruders who retreat and will fight those that stand their ground. Impala fights are short, but savage and sometimes fatal. The winner roars as the loser retreats. An intruder may be allowed to pass through a territory as long as he behaves submissively by walking in a slouched posture and holding his ears forward. The intruder may approach the resident ram, sniff the glandular areas of his face and forehead and nibble his neck to compare the ram's body odour with the scent marks he has left in his territory.

164

In March a territorial ram starts herding females and chasing young males out of the breeding herds by low-intensity roaring and head-nodding threats. He tests his females' reproductive condition by sniffing, Flehmen and licking their urine and genitals. If one of them is on heat he courts her with his head low and his nose stretched forward, grunting and bleating. If she is receptive he mounts her repeatedly for about 10 seconds at a time. After successful copulation he roars and snorts.

At the peak of the mating season in May a territorial ram has very little time to feed between chasing out interlopers, herding females and mating. With strenuous activity round the clock his body condition deteriorates and he may be displaced by a fresher challenger. At the season's peak the average territorial ram's tenure is only eight days.

An impala lamb is very wobbly on its legs for the first two days and it stays hidden in dense cover. Once it can follow its mother it joins the breeding herd. At first mother and lamb stay close together but when the lamb is fully mobile it mixes freely with the herd and only goes back to its mother to be suckled. Females grow up in their natal breeding herd, but young males are chased out by territorial rams when the next breeding season comes around.

Grey rhebok   *Pelea capreolus* No. 324

The grey rhebok social unit is an adult male with up to half a dozen females and their offspring. Each group has a home range and the male defends part of this against other males. A young male cannot collect a group of females until he has secured a territory by occupying a vacant area or driving out a resident.

Territorial rams are exceptionally aggressive and their straight horns are deadly weapons. They can become a problem on farms because they attack sheep and goats and gore them to death.

Occupied areas are marked with secretions from the pedal glands as the resident walks around.

A territory resident also uses visual and audible signals to repel intruders. If a strange male approaches, the resident walks towards it with exaggeratedly slow steps. He turns sideways to make himself look bigger, and snorts and stamps.

The grey rhebok alarm signal is a snort.

Unless it is closely pursued a grey rhebok runs with a rocking-horse action while flashing the white of the underside of its tail and its rump. If hard pressed they switch to ordinary running.

Grey rhebok are browsers who can survive without drinking.

During the April rut a grey rhebok ram defends his territory more vigorously. He tests his females' reproductive condition by sniffing their genitals. If one is on heat he courts her by tapping the inside of her hindlegs with his forelegs.

Roan   *Hippotragus equinus* No. 325

Roan are most active in the early morning, late afternoon and evening. They rest in the shade of trees and move out into long grass to feed.

The social units in a roan population are breeding herds, bachelor herds and solitary, breeding bulls. The herds usually contain one or two dozen animals but, obviously, they will be smaller in reserves where only a few roan have been introduced. The nursery herds occupy home ranges that are stable for as long as 30 years. The home ranges of neighbouring herds do not overlap but they are not defended and are therefore not true territories. A dominant male associates with a nursery herd whenever it is within his home range. He chases other males out of a zone around the herd which is between 300 and 500 m wide. This zone moves with the herd so that it, too, is not a territory. If another male approaches his herd the dominant bull stands with his neck arched, his head high, and his ears out sideways. Unless the intruder displays submission by lowering his head, keeping his ears straight up and waving his tail or tucking it between his legs, horn-clashing and head-pushing will occur. This is usually enough for the resident to demonstrate his strength, and his ability and willingness to fight, and the intruder breaks away and is chased to the border of the herd's exclusion zone. If the intruder is intent on a takeover, prolonged bouts of horn-clashing, lunging and head-pushing occur, in which both males drop to their knees. They suffer horn cuts on their faces and necks but one of them usually breaks and runs before he is seriously injured. A herd bull who has been defeated lives alone rather than joining a bachelor group.

A territorial roan bull displaying his status.

A roan herd's home range is marked by small trees and bushes from which the leaves, bark and branches have been stripped by the roan slashing at them with their horns. They also dig up the soil with their horns and they mark everywhere they go with their interdigital glands.

Among the females in a breeding herd there is a dominance hierarchy that is based mainly on age. The females' dominance pose is the same as the males' and old, high-ranking females occasionally horn-spar even with the herd bull. The herd is led by the highest-ranking old female and during feeding the old females station themselves as sentinels on the fringes of the herd. A herd usually scatters when attacked but its members may act together to drive off even lions. Human hunters have been charged by wounded bulls. As a last resort roan use their teeth as defensive weapons.

Roan get most of their food by grazing. They prefer long grass and, unlike most grazers, are not attracted by freshly sprouted grass. They will completely submerge their heads to feed on underwater plants. They chew bones for their calcium and phosphorus content.

A resident roan bull regularly checks the reproductive condition of his herd's females. He approaches one with his head high, nose and ears forward and his tail slightly lifted. He sniffs her genitals and puts his nose in the stream of urine that she produces in response. He tests the urine by Flehmen – lifting his head and curling his upper lip to bring his vomeronasal organ into use. If the female is in oestrus he courts her by gently tapping the inside of her hindlegs with one foreleg. If the female is receptive copulation follows, if not she circles around the bull until he gives up.

A roan cow leaves her herd a few days before she gives birth to find a secure place for her calf to hide. She stays near her calf to guard it for the first few days then returns to the herd and visits the calf morning and evening to suckle and clean it. After feeding the calf goes alone to a new hiding place so that predators cannot find it by following its mother's scent trail. The calf lies out like this for about six weeks before it joins the herd. Initially it stays close to its mother but soon spends less time with her than with other calves. Weaning is complete by six months. Females stay in the herd where they were born but young males are chased out by territorial bulls when they are about two years old. They live in small bachelor groups for about the next four years and then begin their attempts to take over breeding herds.

Gemsbok   *Oryx gazella* No. 327

Gemsbok live in small herds of up to a dozen animals; larger numbers can be seen together where the grazing is good. Mature males are territorial but will temporarily join mixed herds containing adult females, their calves and non-territorial males up to five years old. There are also bachelor herds made up of young males, and nursery herds that contain only females and calves. Apart from the territorial males who stay within areas of about 5 to 10 km^2, gemsbok wander very widely to take advantage of the grazing that follows the unpredictable rains of their arid habitat.

Territorial male gemsbok mark their areas by thrashing bushes with their horns, pawing the ground and defecating in small piles from a low squatting position. Gemsbok have interdigital glands that mark the ground wherever they walk.

Because their territories are so large solitary bulls cannot intercept all intruders. Most intruders leave as soon as a sight of the resident shows that an area is occupied. The young males in mixed herds are usually tolerated by the territorial bulls.

A dominant bull holds his head high with his neck arched and his horns angled

The gemsbok bull on the right is displaying his dominance over the submissive one on the left.

towards his rival, and takes slow, high steps. A submissive gemsbok has a hunched posture and keeps its head low. Serious opponents circle tensely and slowly, paw or horn the ground or kneel to thrash bushes fiercely with their horns. Although a gemsbok's horns look like rapiers they are used for stabbing only in the most serious encounters; the skirmishing blow is a downwards or sideways slash that lays the length of the horn across the opponent's hide. Be-

Skirmishing gemsbok bulls.

cause of the length and angle of his horns a gemsbok bull does not fight by low-ering his head and stabbing forwards; instead he hooks backwards and sideways over his shoulders. The skin on a bull's neck and shoulders is 6 mm thick to protect against these blows.

A gemsbok's horns are very effective against predators but if attacked by a group the gemsbok depends on finding a thorn bush into which it can back to protect its rear while it slashes at attackers approaching from the front.

Gemsbok are mainly grazers but they will browse on bushes and forbs if there is no grass to be had. They dig up succulent roots and eat wild melons for the water they contain, and graze at night when the lower temperatures lead to an increase in the water content of the vegetation. Even dead grass that has been baked by the sun all day can take up 40 per cent of its weight in airborne moisture during the night. By using these sources of moisture, producing concentrated urine and allowing its body temperature to rise rather than sweating, a gemsbok is able to survive without drinking.

Gemsbok mate at any time of the year. A territorial bull herds any females that are on his territory and tests their reproductive condition by sniffing their geni-tals, and smelling and Flehmen of their urine. Other males, adult females and juveniles also use Flehmen to investigate urine. If he finds a female in heat the bull approaches with his head high or stretched forward and taps her hindlegs with his foreleg. If she is ready to mate she stands still and he mounts her up to six times in quick succession; if not she simply moves away.

For its first three to six weeks a gemsbok calf usually hides itself in dense grass or under bushes while its mother grazes up to 2 km away. A young calf is suckled three times a day, reduced to once a day by the time it is five months old. When a cow comes for suckling she calls her calf out with a nasal whirr rather than going to find it. A calf frequently spends the night with its mother and finds itself a new hiding place in the morning as much as 3 km from the old one. The mother may have to threaten or strike her calf with her horns to make it go and hide. Once the lying out phase is over the calf follows its mother with the rest of the herd, and joins creches with its peers. Calves are weaned when about six months old.

Sable   *Hippotragus niger* No. 326

Sable are active in the early morning, late afternoon and evening. They go down to drink in the late morning or early afternoon.

Sable breeding herds contain adult females and juveniles of both sexes while bachelor herds contain young and old males. Most of the herds are 20 to 30 strong but these sometimes amalgamate for short periods to form aggregations of up to 200. The nursery herds are led by dominant, old females who act as sentinels and appear to know the best feeding and watering places at different seasons.

Adult bulls are territorial, especially during the mating season. The rank body odour of a territorial bull is noticeable even to a human. Casual intruders are in-timidated and ejected by the resident's standing with his tail out, his neck arched and his chin tucked in so that his horns are shown off. A persistent intruder will adopt the same pose and the two will warily approach one another. They stand head-to-head with their tails twitching and held stiffly horizontal, then drop to their knees, clash horns and try to push each other off balance. These fights last as much as an hour and can become vicious; the combatants roar and bellow as they lunge with their horns, fencing for an opening for a sideways slash. Sable are ag-

Sable bulls fighting for territory.

gressive and their horns are deadly weapons so it is not surprising that territorial battles are sometimes fatal.

A territorial bull advertises his status and occupation of an area by slashing bushes and small trees to pieces with his horns.

Sable prefer to graze but they will browse when grass is unavailable or of poor quality. They have to drink every day.

Sable of both sexes use their horns against predators. If it can the sable will

A sable bull courting one of his cows.

back into a thorn bush to protect its rear and hook at anything that attacks from the front, or go down onto its knees to use a deadly sideways sweep of its horns.

Sable sometimes threaten other herbivores.

In the breeding season a territorial bull aggressively herds the females in his territory by running around them with his neck and head horizontal, snorting and sweeping his horns at females who try to move away. He tests the reproductive condition of his females by sniffing their genitals and performing Flehmen on their urine. He courts females on heat by tapping between their hindlegs with a foreleg.

A sable cow leaves her herd to give birth in dense cover where the calf remains hidden for its first two weeks. The mother visits once or twice a day to suckle and clean it. The calf moves to a new hideaway each day to avoid building up an odour that a predator could detect. If it is attacked the calf gives a loud call, which brings its mother and her companions to the rescue. They are certainly able to drive off leopards and would probably deter even lions and spotted hyaenas. Sable calves eat their first solid food when they are about one month old and are weaned at eight months.

Females stay in their natal herds, but young males are chased out by the territorial bulls when they are about three years old. They live in bachelor herds for another three years, then start trying to establish territories.

Buffalo   *Syncerus caffer* No. 328

Buffalo live in large herds containing up to a few thousand animals of both sexes and all ages. Old males tend to wander solitarily or to form small groups of up to about half a dozen. Some of the young bulls form bachelor groups. The largest herds are seen during the dry season; after the rains when food is plentiful herds more than 500 strong split into smaller units. Within each herd there are social subunits containing upwards of 15 to 20 animals who stay closer to each other than to the rest, and within a subunit family groups of related buffalo also tend to bunch together.

There are separate dominance hierarchies among the males and the females in a herd, and bulls dominate cows. Status is determined by fighting ability, which in turn depends on size and age, except that females move up in rank when they have a calf at foot. High rank brings the privilege of travelling and feeding in the front and centre of the herd, and thus obtaining good grazing and maximum protection from predators. The low-ranking animals at the back have to graze what the herd leaves, and they suffer most heavily from predation.

As the herds get larger the hierarchies become less distinct, probably because particular pairs of animals meet less often. Dominance is signalled by a buffalo's holding its head high with its nose pointing downwards and its shoulders hunched; to emphasize its size it may stand sideways-on to its opponent. A submissive buffalo will hold its head low and horizontal so that its horns are back; if the two animals are close together it will put its nose under the belly of its superior. More intense threat displays involve head-tossing, short chases, horn-hooking and digging up the soil with the horns. In full-scale fights the combatants charge each other with their heads up. At the last moment they lower their heads, clash horn bosses and follow through by pushing. The weaker bull is pushed sideways and he immediately breaks and runs to avoid a horn in the flank. When two 800-kg bulls charging at 20 km/h collide head-on the impact is equivalent to a car hitting a wall at 50 km/h. It is not surprising that nearly all disputes are settled after the first full-scale charge. If the bulls attack from close quarters the impact is less damaging and they carry on the fight by clashing heads and hooking and wrestling with their horns. Fights between cows are always less intense than those between bulls.

Buffalo herds have home ranges that do not overlap with those of neighbouring herds but are not defended as territories. The home ranges of old bulls are smaller than those of herds; maybe as little as three to four square kilometres. Herds use known routes between water and grazing; they are led by bulls or cows in the upper half of the dominance hierarchy.

The group of buffalo in the foreground are a family group within the herd.

Adult male buffalo wallow in mud as a protection against biting flies and to keep cool. Females and youngsters rarely wallow, suggesting that it also has a social significance.

Buffalo in herds are placid, although some old bulls are irascible and prone to charge when disturbed. The animals on the fringe of a herd are more watchful than those in the middle. If buffalo are alerted they sometimes approach the source of the disturbance with noses high to catch a scent or get a better view. When alarmed a whole herd will stampede, to the peril of any predator in its path. A herd protects its members, especially calves whose distress bleats bring the whole herd to the rescue; even lions have been chased up trees by buffaloes. Sometimes the mere sight of a predator, even one that is not hunting or, apparently, just the suspicion of one's presence will provoke a 'pre-emptive strike', especially from old herd bulls. When hunted by humans, buffalo have a reputation for circling back on their pursuers and counterattacking, but whether they do the same to natural predators is apparently unrecorded.

172   Buffalo are predominantly grazers but they will browse shrubs and forbs if

grass is unavailable or of poor quality. They show no particular preference for freshly sprouted shoots over tall grass but they do prefer leaves to stems because the leaves are more nutritious. They do most of their grazing at night, in the early morning and in the evening so that they can escape the heat of the day by standing or lying in shade while they ruminate. They drink up to 30 to 40 *l* twice a day; after the morning feed and before the evening one. To obtain minerals and trace elements they use salt licks, and lick termite mounds and the mud stuck to their companions.

The nose-up posture of an alerted buffalo.

Buffalo bulls detect when a cow is on heat by regular sniffing and Flehmen of her genitals and urine. During the three days that she is on heat a female is tended by bulls who court her by laying their chins on her rump, and she may form a focus for fights between bulls. It takes a buffalo bull at least eight years to fight his way high enough up the dominance hierarchy to be able to secure opportunities to mate. Old males occasionally return to the mixed herds to mate, beating off other males by virtue of their greater size and long combat experience.

The top-ranking bulls mate nearest the time of ovulation when the chances of conception are highest.

A female buffalo remains with the herd when she gives birth but she and her calf may be left behind temporarily if the herd moves off in the few hours before the calf is strong enough to walk. In the meantime the cow may hide the calf in thick cover while she feeds nearby. The calves are not very fast runners and they get left behind with their mothers if the herd bolts – this is why the herd's co-ordinated anti-predator defence is so important. The calf suckles for about 15 months. Social ties remain strong between female calves and their mothers but males disperse into the body of the herd.

Kudu   *Tragelaphus strepsiceros* No. 329

Kudu are normally active in the early morning and evening but in developed areas they become nocturnal to escape hunting and other disturbance. They live in small herds of up to about a dozen but large numbers can sometimes be seen at water holes in arid areas. The composition of the herds changes during the year. In the mating season, from May to August depending on locality, males and females occur together. The rest of the time the sexes are separate; the females stay in their herds and the males live singly or in bachelor groups. A kudu cow can come into oestrus outside the usual breeding season and a bull will then join the herd she is in.

Kudu are very secretive and they spend nearly all their time hidden in thick bush. If they have to come out into the open they appear nervous and ready to run for cover. Their secretive behaviour has allowed them to survive in farming areas where other large herbivores have been wiped out.

When disturbed in its bush habitat a kudu will usually watch and listen to assess the situation and then move away quietly or dash off after giving a loud, sharp alarm bark. Although they run rather heavily kudu move surprisingly quietly through dense bush. As they run the males lay their horns back so that they do not hit overhanging branches. The tail is curled up over the back so that

174   *A kudu bull displays mild aggression by horning bushes.*

its white underside provides a visual alarm signal and a marker for the rest of the herd to follow.

Kudu are famous for their fence-jumping abilities. A 2 m fence seems to be an inconvenience rather than a barrier and they have been known to jump 3 m spontaneously and 3,5 m under stress. Kudu bulls can jump across the 3,7 m wide Eastern National Water Carrier Canal in Namibia but the cows cannot, and they get trapped after trying.

Kudu are mainly browsers on a wide variety of forbs, bushes and trees. They sometimes do serious damage to crops.

A kudu bull courting a female on heat.

Depending on locality, kudu usually mate between May and August. Bulls compete for access to female herds by lateral displays with their horns vertical and manes erect. They thrash vegetation and dig up soil with their horns, lock horns with each other and push and twist, but there is no charging. Fights last for up to 15 minutes. The winner is the one that manages to push his opponent backwards or twist him off balance. The loser breaks and is seen off for up to 500 m before the winner returns to the females. Breeding bulls may tolerate young males or may merely lunge at them or chase them for a few metres. The young males move away, groom themselves or stand with their heads up looking away from the old bull.

A bull who has access to females checks their reproductive condition by sniffing and Flehmen of the small amounts of urine they produce when he nuzzles their genitals. As each female comes into heat the bull follows closely alongside her with his head stretched forward and his horns back. He stands behind her with his neck high or alongside her with his neck across her back. They mate only once, for five to ten seconds; the bull chooses the best time for conception from the smell of the cow's urine.

A kudu calf is born in tall grass or other close cover. Its mother stays with it for the first day then returns to her herd and visits to suckle it three to five times a day while the calf lies out for its first one to two months.

Sitatunga

Sitatunga are active in the reed beds of their swamp habitat at all times of the day, with more intense activity at dawn and dusk. At night they move out into the surrounding drier woodland. They make platforms of flattened reeds to rest on. They live alone, in pairs, in small herds of a male with half a dozen females, or in juvenile herds.

When walking in shallow water sitatunga move in a careful, silent tiptoe by dipping each foot point-first into the water. They are excellent swimmers and when closely pursued or wounded they will submerge themselves completely except for their nostrils.

Sitatunga move silently through swamps by carefully dipping each hoof point-first into the water.

They feed mainly on papyrus, either the freshly sprouted leaves or the flowering heads, which they reach by breaking down the stems.

A sitatunga bull's dominance display is to stand sideways-on with his neck extended and chin raised. The subordinate animal sniffs beneath the dominant's chin. In more aggressive interactions the contestants horn the soil and vegetation and clash horns.

A sitatunga bull courts a female by approaching with his horns tipped right back against his neck, and rubs his face on her rump and flanks. Sitatunga calves are born on secluded reed platforms prepared by the mother who visits for suckling two to four times a day. They can swim before they can walk properly.

Nyala

Although nyala can occasionally be seen in herds of up to about 30, and frequently in groups of two to four, the only stable social bond is between a mother and her offspring. The other groups are temporary; animals join and leave over periods of a few hours. Males become more solitary with age. Nyala live in overlapping home ranges.

There is a dominance hierarchy among an area's male nyala, who have a complex repertoire of status displays. Even when no other nyala are around a male digs up soft soil with his horns and strokes his face and horns on bushes with a nodding action of his head. Although this looks like scent-marking, no visible secretion is deposited and it could be that he is picking up the odour of the soil or the plants. He may thrash bushes with his horns just before or after an encounter with another male, either as a way of demonstrating his strength and speed or of redirecting his aggression. Occasionally he will paw the ground during a thrashing bout.

The full aggressive display by a nyala bull.

A male nyala's striking colours are used in a visual dominance display. At low intensity he slightly raises the crest of white hair along his neck and back, which contrasts with his slate-grey flanks. At high intensity he exaggerates his size by fully erecting his crest, and he holds his head high and parades slowly with high steps of his yellow legs. In the full display he curls his tail up over his back and fans out the white hairs on its underside, and lowers his head so that his horns point forwards. A submissive male lowers his crest, waves his head sideways and slowly wags his tail. He will break off the encounter by grooming or feeding.

Males who are not intimidated by each other's displays will clash horns and push against each other. These fights can become savage, and fatal gorings occur. 177

Most fights are over females. Female nyala are much less aggressive than the males, although sometimes they butt each other.

Nyala give a deep bark as an alarm call, and the calves bleat when separated from their mothers, who answer with the throaty clicking noise that they also give when on heat.

Nyala get most of their food by browsing but they relish newly sprouted grass. They strip the bark from trees and eat flowers and fallen fruit. They will follow troops of monkeys and baboons to take advantage of what gets knocked down from the treetops.

A nyala bull checks the reproductive condition of any female he meets by sniffing and Flehmen at her genitals. If she is on heat he courts her by following with his head stretched forward, and pushes his nose between her hindlegs forcibly enough to lift her hindquarters off the ground. When she becomes receptive he pushes her head down with his own, moves around behind her and mounts.

A nyala calf is born in thick cover where it lies out for two to three weeks. If danger threatens it flattens itself to the ground.

Bushbuck   *Tragelaphus scriptus* No. 332

Bushbuck usually feed at night and in the early mornings and late evenings. If they are active during the day it is usually in cool weather.

Bushbuck are mostly solitary but male-female pairs, small groups of two or three females or two to three males, and small aggregations at rich feeding sites also occur. They live in overlapping home ranges and within an area the animals know each other and have a dominance hierarchy. Their home ranges are no larger than they have to be to provide food and water, and in rich habitats they cover as little as half a hectare.

A bushbuck's alarm call is a sharp bark which has a curious ventriloquial quality so that predators cannot locate the bushbuck from its call. Bushbuck are rather slow runners and rather than fleeing they try to avoid detection by freezing and lying flat.

Bushbuck are exceptionally aggressive, both in intra-specific fights and in defence against predators. Males will fight to the death over females and there is at least one case on record of a bushbuck ram fatally goring a human. The aggressive display is a slow circling with exaggerated high steps and the mane erected. Combatants charge each other, clash horns and twist for an opening to stab.

Bushbuck are mainly browsers but they supplement their diet of leaves with a little grass. They eat buds, flowers and fruit as these become seasonally available. They readily paddle in shallow water when feeding and they are strong swimmers.

A female bushbuck on heat is consorted by a male who has detected her condition from the smell of her urine, and who drives other males away. The consort gives a twittering contact call. Bushbuck babies are born in dense undergrowth and they lie out for the first four months. They do not change sites from day to day. Mutual grooming between mother and lamb helps to cement the bond between them.

Eland are most active during the day but sometimes carry on feeding after dark.

Eland calves are strongly gregarious, while old bulls are increasingly solitary. Huge aggregations of several hundred eland sometimes form but their basic social units are small herds whose composition changes seasonally. Breeding herds contain animals of both sexes and all ages. They split into mixed-sex adult herds and herds of juveniles and subadults as the calves become independent. During the winter cows and bulls herd separately and in spring the calving females join the younger animals to form a nursery herd. This is in turn joined by adult males to make a breeding herd and complete the cycle.

In areas where food is available all year eland are sedentary. Elsewhere they make local movements, for example in the Drakensberg where they move to high ground in the summer and down on to farmland in the winter, or undertake large-scale migrations that follow the rain-stimulated growth of new grass. Eland are not territorial.

In an eland herd there is a dominance hierarchy in which larger, older animals are usually high ranking and bulls outrank cows. Head shaking with the head up is a threat display, and if the other eland does not move away quickly enough the shaking may be followed by an upward jab with the horns. Head shaking with the head down signals submission. Dominants keep their ears up, subordinates lower theirs. Blows with the sides of the horns are used by dominants to move subordinate animals away from some favoured spot and, forcefully, by females against strange calves who try to steal their milk. The most serious threat is a head-down charge with the ears held horizontal.

A bull eland has a patch of curly hair overlaying a gland on his forehead. The hair is often caked with mud from scent-rubbing.

THE INTERPLAY BETWEEN BEHAVIOUR AND ECOLOGY IN AFRICAN ANTELOPE

The ecologist P.J. Jarman classified the African bovids into five groups according to their body sizes, social organisations, habitats, diets and feeding behaviour. The classification, like the list of colours in a rainbow, splits up what is really a continuous spectrum but it still helps to clarify how environment and behaviour interact to shape an animal's lifestyle.

Group A contains the smallest antelope such as sunis, Damara dik-diks, klipspringers, duikers and grysbok. Because they are small their energy needs are low and they eat small quantities of protein-rich, freshly sprouted leaves, flowers, fruits and even some animals. Foods like this occur in small, scattered clumps that can support only one or a few animals, so social groups are very small, and each defends a territory to keep others away from its food patches. Small body size and the need for protein-rich foods allows and obliges them to live in dense, bushy habitats where they can rely on hiding first and fleeing as a last resort to keep away from predators.

Antelope in group B, such as oribi, reedbuck and grey rhebok, are less restricted feeders but they still select the most nutritious plants and parts of plants from both grass and browse. Their slightly broader diet frees them from food patches and so they can form small groups, which helps with predator detection in their mixed woodland and grassland habitats. Their main way of avoiding predators is still to hide. Only the males are territorial, and then only when food is sufficiently abundant and reliable.

Group C includes kudu, waterbuck, puku, lechwe, springbok and impala; medium to large antelope that graze or browse according to the season. Their food is widely distributed so that they can form herds of a few or a few hundred individuals without depleting their resources. Breeding males of some species are territorial seasonally e.g. springbok, impala or permanently e.g. waterbuck. To avoid predators they hide (kudu) or scatter explosively in all directions (springbok and impala).

Group D are the selective grazers such as black and blue wildebeest, hartbeest, blesbok and bontebok, who favour short, nutritious grass and will migrate long distances to reach new feeding grounds. During their sedentary periods they live like the group C antelope. Because they are small to medium-sized they can feed delicately on the best, leafy parts of the grass, and they need this quality of food because it has to pass more quickly through their bodies than it does through bigger animals. Vast herds can form where suitable grass covers large areas. Females and bachelor males live in home ranges shared by groups of several dozen animals, breeding bulls are territorial. In the open grassy habitat predators are detected by group vigilance and herds stick together as they flee.

Group E includes heavyweight grazers – roan, eland and buffalo for example – that take in large quantities of low-quality forage as they feed over wide areas in mixed-sex herds up to a few thousand strong. Their large size prevents them from delicately selecting nutritious plant parts; they have to feed by the bunch, but in turn it allows them to digest coarse fodder efficiently by passing it slowly through their digestive systems. Within the herds there are dominance hierarchies but home ranges are not defended as territories. They are big and formidable enough to gang up and counterattack against predators.

Eland bulls fight over females in heat by clashing and locking horns and then pushing and twisting against each other. The loser breaks contact and runs but fatal horn wounds are sometimes inflicted. Cows also fight but never as seriously as the males.

There are friendly interactions among herd members, usually in the form of allogrooming in which one animal licks the head, neck and rump of the other.

A dominant bull bellows to advertise his status and grunts when displacing a subordinate. A cow barks when disturbed and moos, clicks and grunts to attract her calf, who answers by bleating. A calf whimpers if it is lost or is approached by a stranger. Eland make a distinct clicking noise as they walk; its origin is unknown but it is thought to come from their knees.

The chestnut-to-black, curly hair on a bull eland's forehead covers a patch of glandular skin whose secretion has a sweet smell. The bull rubs his horns and forehead on the spot where he, or an oestrous female, has just urinated. His horns and forehead get caked with smelly mud that is rubbed off when he horns bushes.

Eland are mainly browsers but they also eat some grass. If the foliage of a tree is out of reach an eland will wedge a branch between its horns and twist if off, or hook its horns over the branch and drag it down. When the eland are feeding in a group the branch-breaking efforts of one may be taken advantage of by the others unless it is dominant to them and chases them off. Eland are not very selective feeders and will eat twigs up to the thickness of a pencil. They can survive without drinking.

Despite its bulk an eland can clear a two-metre fence, although it will usually jump only when pursued. Its large size gives an eland a fighting chance against predators and it will defend itself with both horns and hooves. If a group is attacked they may bunch with their heads together to present a ring of kicking back legs to the predators.

All the eland in a herd, females as well as males, regularly test each other's urine by smelling, tasting and Flehmen. When he detects a female on heat the dominant bull stays close to her and drives away any other males. He courts the female by rubbing his head against her flanks, licking her, resting his chin on her back, sniffing and licking her genitals, and pawing and horning the ground.

An eland calf can stand almost immediately and can follow its mother after three to four hours. It lies out for the first two weeks, and mother and calf join the herd after four to six weeks. A calf will follow any adult eland and will try to feed from other females besides its mother. A female may be followed by several calves but she will allow only her own to suck. A herd's females will act together to drive off large predators while the calves bunch and run.

Reedbuck   *Redunca arundinum* No. 334

Reedbuck are basically nocturnal but in the winter when the forage is poor and they have to spend more time feeding, they are also active during the day. They make themselves comfortable resting places by trampling down patches of grass.

They live in pairs or family groups on territories that are defended by the male. Where the food supply is seasonal, such as the Underberg and Highlands regions in Natal, the males hold territories only in the April to August mating season. In the rich feeding areas around St Lucia, territoriality is uneconomical and dominance hierarchies are set up instead. In the Kruger National Park where the food supply is reliable but less rich than at St Lucia, the males hold permanent territories. A territorial ram horns vegetation while he is setting up his territory and, once it is established, he advertises his presence and his status by cantering with a rocking-horse action and standing with his legs stiff and his neck erect so that his white throat band and horn bases stand out. He may emphasise the threat by urinating and defecating in the display posture or make sure that he is noticed by whistling and stotting (stiff-legged jumping on the spot). If two males meet they dip their horns towards each other and display by defecating with exaggerated slowness. If neither withdraws they progress to horn-clashing and pushing. In serious fights the contestants lunge and parry with their horns. These fights are very ritualised and may go on intermittently all day with the contestants taking frequent breaks to rest or feed. One contestant always retires before he suffers serious injury. A submissive reedbuck stands with its head low and its horns tipped backwards. In amicable greetings the reedbuck touch noses with their heads lowered, or sniff under one another's tails.

A reedbuck whistles through its nose when alarmed or excited, to keep in contact with its mate and to advertise its presence to its neighbours. A fleeing reedbuck flicks its tail to expose the white patches on its thighs, pronks and, in time with each jump, snorts and makes a popping noise that is said to come from the rapid opening of its inguinal glands as it kicks its hindlegs backwards. They are not very fast runners and rely on the cover of their dense habitat to evade pursuers.

Reedbuck are grazers but will browse if grass is unavailable or of low quality.

A reedbuck ram's 'proud' posture advertises his territorial status.

They drink frequently, especially in hot weather and during the winter when their food is dry.

A courting male reedbuck stretches his head forward horizontally. He approaches a female and nudges her genitals, whereupon she urinates, and he sniffs and Flehmens. If she is receptive she stands with her head down in the submissive posture and mounting follows up to 53 times at intervals of eight to 15 seconds before the male succeeds in entering the female. The female goes off alone to give birth and the lamb stays hidden for the first two to four months. The mother visits it once or twice a day to clean and suckle it but she will not go near its hiding place if she suspects danger. The lamb finds itself a new refuge after each visit.

Mountain reedbuck   *Redunca fulvorufula* No. 335

Mountain reedbuck are active mainly in the early morning, the evenings and at night when they move out to feed on flat ground near the rocky slopes where they rest during the day.

Female mountain reedbuck live in small herds of three to six or, occasionally, up to 30. The membership of each herd is continually changing as females move from one to another. The home ranges of the female herds, and of individual females, overlap the territories of several solitary males. Males who do not hold territories live alone or join bachelor groups on the fringes of the territories.

A ram displays his territorial status by standing in an alert posture, stotting and whistling. As he moves around his area he leaves scent from glands on his feet and below his ears. In disputes the fighting stroke is a forward and downward tip of the head, which suits the forward curve of the sharp horns. A territorial male mountain reedbuck is strongly attached to his patch of ground and will stay on it unless a shortage of food forces him off. If he is chased out of his area he soon returns to it.

A mountain reedbuck signals alarm by whistling through its nose. This alerts the rest of its group and they run off with a bouncy, rocking-horse gait with their tails up. Usually, but not always, they run along the slope or obliquely downhill.

Mountain reedbuck are grazers, and they browse only occasionally. They select grass blades and leave the stems. They have to drink daily and so they are never found far from water.

Male mountain reedbuck do not breed unless they hold a territory. A territorial male herds females and tests their reproductive condition by smell. If one of them is on heat he courts her by approaching with his head stretched forward, and taps between her hindlegs with a foreleg. If she is ready to mate the female stands with her head down in the submissive posture.

A female mountain reedbuck leaves her herd to give birth and the lamb lies out for the first two or three months. Its mother visits warily once or twice a day to suckle and clean it, and it moves to a new hiding place after each visit. If, despite these precautions, the lamb is in danger from a predator it gives an alarm whistle which brings its mother to its aid. Young males are chased out of the female herds by territorial rams when they are about nine to 15 months old.

Waterbuck   *Kobus ellipsiprymnus* No. 336

Female waterbuck and non-breeding males live in herds which usually contain eight to 12 animals and, exceptionally, up to 30. The breeding males establish territories in areas where a rich food supply allows them to be very sedentary. Female and bachelor herds have home ranges that overlap several male territories. Bachelors are kept away from the best feeding areas by the territorial bulls. Occasionally a territorial bull will tolerate the presence of a younger male who helps with territorial defence and stands a good chance of falling heir to the territory.

A waterbuck bull's territorial display.

A territorial male waterbuck advertises his status by standing rigidly erect with his head high and tail out. If he faces his opponent the white patches on his throat and face emphasise the signal. If he stands sideways-on he shows off his size and the thickness of his neck. Lowering his head and shaking it is also a threat. Most intruders move off as soon as a sighting of the resident shows them that an area is occupied. A bachelor male may be tolerated as he moves through a territory if he displays submissively by holding his head low and walking with a cringing posture. If an intruder is intent on displacing a bull from his territory, serious fighting will occur and deaths from horn wounds are quite common among waterbuck. Combat between neighbours or between a territorial bull and a challenging bachelor involves pushing with locked horns and attempts, sometimes fatally successful, to gore the opponent in the flank.

184   When territory neighbours who know each other meet, one stands broadside

to the other with his chin tucked in, his head high and his horns tilted towards the other, then with his head high and horizontal. The other makes the same movements and the two repeat the performance as they move closer together and come to stand head to tail. They then swing round until they are facing each other, swish their tails and make attacking feints and blocks. The end of the encounter usually comes when the bulls take turns to advance a short distance while the other retreats, shaking his head from side to side. They then move apart to graze without any physical contact having occurred.

A territorial bull also displays his status by horning grass and bushes and pitching their fragments into the air.

When a bachelor herd enters his territory the resident bull stands in the head high 'proud' posture. The bachelors flick their tails, nod their heads in a way that flashes the white patch under their chins, and bleat. One bachelor then approaches the bull very cautiously with his head stretched forward and his tail wagging until the bull makes a threatening forward lunge with his horns and the bachelor turns and runs off.

Within the bachelor groups there are dominance hierarchies that are established by pushing contests. Older, larger animals tend to be higher in rank.

Waterbuck readily take to water to avoid predators. The white target ring on a waterbuck's rump may be to help the herd keep together as it flees through dense bush.

Waterbuck have a strong, goaty odour; in a light breeze even a human can smell a territorial bull 500 m away.

A waterbuck bull courting one of his females.

Waterbuck are predominantly grazers but they browse occasionally on herbaceous plants, shrubs or trees, and they will take fallen fruit. They drink several times a day.

A territorial waterbuck bull herds females onto his ground and regularly tests their reproductive condition by sniffing and Flehmen of their urine and genitals. If a female is on heat the bull courts her by rubbing his face and the base of his horns on her back, and tapping between her hindlegs with his forelegs. If she is receptive the female stands in a hunched-up position with her tail to one side. There will be up to 10 copulations, usually all with the same male.

A female waterbuck leaves her herd to give birth and the calf lies out in thick cover for about a month. The mother visits one to four times a day for suckling and calls her offspring by bleating or snorting. The calf finds itself a new place to hide after each visit. Calves are weaned at six to eight months. Young females tend to stay in their mother's herd while young males are chased out by territorial bulls just after weaning.

Red lechwe have a distinctive high-stepping gait when they run through shallow water.

Red lechwe

Kobus leche No. 337

Red lechwe are active in the mornings and evenings. During the day they rest on drier ground but at night they stay near water to avoid predators. Red lechwe are gregarious but the herds, which can be a few thousand strong, are unstable and there are no lasting social bonds between their members.

Breeding red lechwe rams defend small mating territories that are 50 to 200 m across. They are often strung out along a stretch of open water or bunched together in a mating ground 300 to 400 m across. The territorial display consists of standing with the head high, the legs slightly apart and, sometimes, the penis erect. Territorial neighbours parade along their common boundary. Sweeping the horns through the grass is a more serious threat and it may lead to horn-clashing and vigorous head-pushing. These fights end when both contestants break away and stand a few metres apart shaking their heads or, presumably when the contest was very one-sided, when one contestant breaks away suddenly to avoid being gored and is chased for up to a kilometre. The net result of these territorial clashes is that the best fighters come to occupy the central territories. Groups of females move around on the mating ground and each of the territorial males herds as many of them as he can. This type of mating system – males defending small, grouped territories onto which females move for mating – is known as lekking, and the mating ground as a lek.

A red lechwe's commonest response to danger is to flee into the water, where it runs with a distinctive bounding action, lifting its hindlegs high to clear the surface as it brings them forward. If the water is too deep for running it swims strongly instead.

Lechwe eat grass and reeds almost exclusively. They drink frequently in hot, dry weather.

A territorial ram who has females in his area tests their reproductive condition by sniffing their urine and genitals. If he finds one on heat he walks alongside her, grunting and lifting one foreleg in a ritualised version of the leg-tapping of other antelope. If the female is receptive she stands still but several mountings are usually necessary before mating is successful.

Females move away from the herds to give birth in tall grass in drier areas. The calves lie out for two to three weeks with their mothers visiting them morning and evening for suckling. Once the calves join the herds their social bonds with their mothers rapidly weaken and they associate only for suckling.

Puku   *Kobus vardonii* No. 338

Puku are crepuscular and are always found near water. They live in herds of up to 50, the usual size being about half a dozen. Adult bulls are territorial. Other males live in bachelor herds.

Puku are predominantly grazers.

Territorial bulls herd females and test their reproductive condition by sniffing their urine and genitals. They court them by tapping them on the belly between their hindlegs with one foreleg. A receptive female stands with her back hunched and her hindlegs astride.

Puku calves lie out, and they do not have close social ties with the mother.

GLOSSARY

AGGREGATION   A group of animals with no social structure, or the process of such a group's formation.

AGGRESSION   Threat, chasing and attacks.

AGONISTIC   Behaviour associated with conflict, including threats, chasing, attacks, defence and appeasement.

ALLO-   A prefix denoting that a behaviour the animal usually directs at itself is being directed at another animal. For example, ALLOGROOMING is grooming some other animal, and ALLOMOTHERING is looking after another one's off-spring.

ALPHA-   A prefix denoting that an animal is the highest-ranking in a group.

ALTRUISM   Behaviour that inflicts a cost on the animal that does it (the ALTRUIST) while benefiting another animal.

ARBOREAL   Spends most of its time in trees.

BEHAVIORISM   An animal psychology movement that takes the extreme position that all mammal behaviour is learned responses to simple stimuli.

CREPUSCULAR   Active at dusk and dawn.

CULTURE   Behaviour transmitted from one animal to another by (usually imitative) learning. If young animals learn from older ones the cultural transmission can continue indefinitely through the generations.

DISPERSAL   An animal's movements, nearly always permanent, away from its birth-place to another area where it breeds.

DIURNAL   Active during the day.

DOMINANCE   A social status that allows privileged access to resources because subor-dinate animals defer to dominant ones.

DRIVE   An obsolete abstraction used to explain changes in motivation.

ECHOLOCATION   A means of locating objects from the way they reflect sounds pro-duced by the animal.

ETHOGRAM   A list of everything that animals of a particular species do.

FITNESS   An animal's success in bequeathing its genes to subsequent generations.

FIXED ACTION PATTERN   A behaviour pattern that, once triggered, follows a fixed, internally determined sequence independent of stimuli from the outside. Fixed action patterns are extremely rare in mammalian behaviour.

FLEHMEN   A German word, with no English equivalent, for the curling and wrinkling of the lips and nostrils which bring the Jacobsen's organ into play, often for testing chemical signals produced by sexually receptive females.

FORM   A shallow, unlined depression in the ground used as a nest by rabbits and hares.

FUNCTION   What a behaviour is for. 'Function' should strictly be used only when the behaviour has been shaped by natural selection for its present purpose.

HAREM   A group of females guarded by a male who maintains mating rights over them by driving off other males.

HIERARCHY   A type of social structure in which the animals in a group can be arranged on the steps of a ladder (linear hierarchy), or of a pyramid (branching hierarchy). Domi-nance hierarchies are common in mammalian societies; an animal is dominated by those above it in the hierarchy and in turn is dominant to those below it.

HOME RANGE   The area in which an animal goes about its daily business.

INFRASOUND   Sound with a frequency below the lower limit of human hearing.

INNATE   Inborn features that an animal shows at birth or develops later independently of environmental influences. Innate features are likely to be genetically programmed but 'innate' and 'genetic' are not synonymous. No mammal behaviour is fully innate.

INSTINCT   A classical ethological concept; instinctive behaviours are those that are driven from within the animal. Often used as a synonym for innate.

JACOBSEN'S ORGAN   A sense organ lying between the roof of the mouth and the nasal passages and connected to one or both of them. It is specialized for the detection of chemical signals connected with reproduction and is brought into use during Flehmen.

LEARNING   The modification of behaviour by experience.

LEK   A mating system in which males stake out adjacent small territories onto which the females move for mating. Often the males who are in best condition hold the central territories.

MOTIVATION   Changes within an animal associated with differences in its response to the same stimuli under different circumstances. For example, a hungry animal will eat while a thirsty one will drink when given both food and water.

MUTUAL   Animals doing the same thing to each other at the same time, for example; two animals licking each other are engaged in mutual grooming.

NATURAL SELECTION   A process of weeding out; animals that are less able to face the challenges presented by their environment leave less offspring than those better endowed.

NOCTURNAL   Active at night.

PHEROMONE   A chemical signal in which a single substance triggers a definite behaviour or developmental process. Very few mammalian chemical signals are pheromones.

PREORBITAL   Just in front of the eye.

RELEASER   A feature of an animal which is used for communication and which triggers a definite response. Less applicable to mammals than to other classes.

RUT   Breeding season, especially applied to large herbivores.

SCAT   A carnivore's faeces.

SCENT-MARKING   The use of urine, faeces or glandular secretions to anoint an object or, sometimes, a social partner with a chemical signal.

SEMIOCHEMICAL   Chemical signal.

STRATEGY   A course of behaviour that can be seen as a way of achieving a long-term goal.

TACTICS   Behaviour that can be seen as a way of achieving a short-term goal by rapid adjustments to changes in circumstances.

TERRITORY   An area where the resident animal can dominate others who might dominate it elsewhere.

THREAT   Behaviour that shows that an attack is imminent.

ULTRASOUND   Sound with a frequency above the upper limit of human hearing.

VOMERONASAL ORGAN   See Jacobsen's organ.

FURTHER READING

Kalahari Hyaenas by M.G.L. Mills (1990). Unwin Hyman, London, distributed in South Africa by Book Promotions, Cape Town. A very detailed account of the behaviour and ecology of spotted and brown hyaenas in the Kalahari National Park and the Kalahari Gemsbok National Park.

The Encyclopaedia of Mammals, volumes I and II edited by D.W. Macdonald (1984). George Allen and Unwin, London. Ecology, behaviour, classification and evolution of everything from aardvarks to zorros.

The Collins Encyclopedia of Animal Behaviour edited by P.J.B. Slater (1986). Collins, London. The principles of ethology, illustrated with examples from throughout the animal kingdom.

Mongoose Watch: A Family Observed by A. Rasa (1986). John Murray, London. The definitive popular book on dwarf mongooses.

Unravelling Animal Behaviour by M. Stamp Dawkins (1986). Longman, Harlow. A pocket-sized outline of modern ethology.

The Study of Animal Behaviour by F. Huntingford (1984). Chapman and Hall, London. Comprehensive coverage of modern ethology, academic but accessible.

Running with the Fox by D.W. Macdonald (1987). Unwin Hyman, London. What it takes to be an ethologist.

An Introduction to Ethology by P.J.B. Slater (1985). Cambridge University Press, Cambridge.

The Understanding of Animals edited by G. Ferry (1984). Blackwell, Oxford. A fascinating collection of articles and news items about animal behaviour from *New Scientist*.

The Oxford Companion to Animal Behaviour edited by D. Macfarland (1981). Oxford University Press, Oxford. An encyclopaedia of animal behaviour.

The Evolution of Primate Behaviour by A. Jolly (1972). Macmillan, New York. A detailed, but eminently readable, survey of the behaviour of primates – including man.

FIELD GUIDES

Since the publication of Reay Smithers' *Mammals of the Southern African Subregion* in 1983, bookshop shelves have blossomed with a crop of field guides. Most of them are very good indeed.

Land Mammals of Southern Africa. A Field Guide by R.H.N. Smithers. Updated edition (1992). Southern Book Publishers, Halfway House.

An Introduction to the Larger Mammals of Southern Africa by J. Dalton (1987). Natal Branch of the Wildlife Society.

Signs of the Wild by C. Walker (1988). Struik, Cape Town.

Maberly's Mammals of Southern Africa. A Popular Field Guide by R. Goss (1986). Delta Books, Craighall. An updated version of Maberly's *The Game Animals of Southern Africa*.

Field Guide to the Mammals of Southern Africa by C. Stuart and T. Stuart (1988). Struik, Cape Town.

A Field Guide. Mammals of Southern Africa by B. Cillié (1987). Frandsen Publishers, Sandton.

INDEX